KASHMIR ACROSS LOC

KASHMIR ACROSS LOC

DEBIDATTA AUROBINDA MAHAPATRA
SEEMA SHEKHAWAT

GYAN PUBLISHING HOUSE
NEW DELHI-110002

Kashmir Across LOC

Rs. 630

ISBN: 81-212-0968-4

Published in 2008 in India by
Gyan Publishing House
5, Ansari Road, Darya Ganj,
New Delhi-110002
Phones : 23282060, 23261060
Fax : 011-23285914
E-mail: books@gyanbooks.com
Website: www.gyanbooks.com

Laser Type Setting by: Rudra Computer Graphics, Delhi
Printed at : Singhal Print Media, Delhi

Contents

	Preface	7
	Abbreviations	11
1.	The History	13
2.	Legal and Constitutional Setup	39
3.	Politics and Governance	79
4.	Sectarian Turbulence	115
5.	Movement for Independence	143
6.	Water Issues	161
7.	Earthquake and its Implications	197
8.	Intra-Kashmir Dialogue: Problems and Prospects	219
	Conclusion	243
	Appendix	251
	Bibliography	309
	Index	319

Preface

Kashmir across the 778 km LOC has become increasingly a matter of focus in recent years. Especially after the opening of trans-LOC routes in 2005 and 2006, the earthquake, and the involvement of the people in the peace process, it has come into focus in its multiple dimensions. While the earlier discourse was mostly confined to the happenings in J&K, the recent discourse has taken into account the happenings across the LOC, both in 'AJK' and 'NA.' The book makes an attempt to widen the discourse on Kashmir by studying the developments across the LOC, as it argues any resolution of the Kashmir issue must take into cognizance not only the realities in J&K, but also the lesser known realities in the areas under the control of Pakistan.

Among numerous themes which the book endeavours to concentrate upon, two issues seem most crucial. First, Pakistan's perception, attitude and policy towards Kashmir under its control are characterized by not only ambiguity and contradiction but also subjugation and exploitation. Second, Pakistan's propagation in international forums that it supports politically, morally and diplomatically Kashmir's right to self-determination has been equally contrasted by the ideology of Kashmir's accession to Pakistan incorporated in the constitution of 'AJK' and which also applies to 'NA.'

The first chapter in the book attempts to trace the history of the region since its creation in 1947. The second chapter analyses the legal and constitutional status of both the entities.

The third chapter focuses on the system of governance in both the regions. While the fourth chapter deals with sectarian turbulence, the issue of movement for independence is focussed in the fifth chapter. The sixth chapter focuses on water issues and related controversies. The seventh chapter has been devoted to the October 2005 earthquake and its implications. The ongoing intra-Kashmir dialogue has been the focus of the last chapter. The authors express guarded optimism regarding the success of the peace process in the complex scenario.

Though literature on Kashmir abound, that on 'AJK' and 'NA' is scarce. Hence, reliance on primary sources while writing this book. Authors' stint at the University of Jammu from January 2005 to May 2007 provided opportunity to monitor the happenings in the region from a close quarter. Field surveys in the Kashmir valley in March 2005, Kargil district in July 2006 and May 2007, Poonch and Rajouri districts in April 2007, Leh district in May 2007 provided valuable insights. The opportunity to interact with cross-section of people from both sides of the LOC provided first hand information.

In the book, Kashmir or undivided J&K denotes the erstwhile princely state of Jammu and Kashmir; J&K denotes the parts of Kashmir in Indian side; 'AJK' and 'NA' refer to the areas under Pak control.

Thanks are due to persons who have proved helpful in writing the book. Special thanks to Prof. Amitabh Mattoo for continuous encouragement and Garib Dass, SSP, Kargil for issuing special permit to facilitate research in the sensitive areas. Thanks to Ghulam Rasul Dar and Mohammad Afzal, who accompanied the authors throughout the surveys in the mountainous terrains and also worked as interpreters to translate Balti and Shina languages spoken by the people in Kargil. We owe thanks to Shafiq Mughal, his wife Tabassum and the whole family for making our survey in Poonch and Rajouri comfortable. Above all, we would like to express our thanks to persons like Justice Abdul Majeed Mallick, Sheikh Mohammad Ahmadi, Mirza Zahid Baig, K. D. Sethi, Balraj Puri,

Bashir Ahmed Khan and many others interactions with whom were very useful and provided insights into the issue.

We thank our family members and friends for their encouragement and moral support.

We are thankful to Gyan Publications for publishing the book. Special thanks to Amit Garg for bringing the book within the stipulated time. However, all the errors, if any, in the book are ours.

July 15, 2007
Debidatta Aurobinda Mahapatra
Seema Shekhawat
Mumbai

Abbreviations

'AJK'	—	'Azad Jammu and Kashmir'
APHC	—	All Party Hurriyat Conference
APNA	—	All Party National Alliance
BNF	—	Balawaristan National Front
CBM	—	Confidence Building Measure
ERRA	—	Earthquake Regulation and Rehabilitation Authority
EU	—	European Union
FCR	—	Federal Crime Regulations
HM	—	Hizbul Mujahideen
HRCP	—	Human Rights Commission of Pakistan
HRW	—	Human Rights Watch
ICG	—	International Crisis Group
IKA	—	International Kashmir Alliance
ISI	—	Inter Services Intelligence
JeM	—	Jaish-e-Mohammad
JI	—	Jamaat-i-Islami
JKLF	—	Jammu Kashmir Liberation Front
JuD	—	Jamaat-ul-Dawa
JUI	—	Jamiat Ulema-e-Islam
KANA	—	Kashmir Affairs and Northern Areas
LeT	—	Lashkar-e-Toiba
LFO	—	Legal Framework Order
LOC	—	Line of Control
MAF	—	Million Acre Feet
MC	—	Muslim Conference

MMA	—	Muttahidda Majlis-e-Ammal
MQM	—	Muttahidda Qaumi Movement
'NA'	—	Northern Areas
NALC	—	Northern Areas Legislative Council
NAM	—	Non Aligned Movement
NATO	—	North Atlantic Treaty Organization
NC	—	National Conference
NWFP	—	North West Frontier Province
PDP	—	Peoples' Democratic Party
PML	—	Pakistan Muslim League
PPP	—	Pakistan People's Party
UJC	—	United Jehad Council
UNCIP	—	United Nations Commission for India and Pakistan
UNICEF	—	United Nations International Children's Emergency Fund
UNSC	—	United Nations Security Council
UN	—	United Nations
WAPDA	—	Water and Power Development Authority
WHO	—	World Health Organization

1

The History

The history of 'AJK' and Gilgit-Baltistan can not be separated from the history of the princely state of J&K. The transfer of power from the Sikhs to the Dogras, the further extension of the Dogra rule to the north, the subsequent British interest in the region due its strategic location and the fear of the Soviet intrusion, the freedom struggle in the Indian subcontinent and its impact on princely states including Kashmir, the partition of the British India, the attitude of the ruler to the question of accession, subsequent war between two emergent nations in Kashmir, the involvement of the UN - have all shaped the history of both the entities. This chapter makes an attempt to focus on these above elements to develop an understanding of these two entities since their emergence.

The Treaty of Amritsar

Until 1846, Kashmir was part of the Sikh empire. In that year, the British defeated the Sikhs and sold Kashmir to Gulab Singh for Rs. 7.5 million under the Treaty of Amritsar. Article 1 of the treaty read, "The British Government transfers and makes over for ever in independent possession to Maharajah Gulab Singh and the heirs male of his body all the hilly or mountainous country with its dependencies situated to the eastward of the River Indus and the westward of the River

Ravi including Chamba and excluding Lahul, being part of the territories ceded to the British Government by the Lahore State according to the provisions of Article IV of the Treaty of Lahore, dated 9th March, 1846." In return, the Maharaja, as mentioned in the Article 3 of the treaty, promised to pay the British Government the sum of seventy-five lakhs of rupees, fifty lakhs to be paid on or before the October 1, 1846. The British promised to provide aid to Maharaja Gulab Singh in protecting his territories from external enemies. Article 10 of the treaty read, "Maharajah Gulab Singh acknowledges the supremacy of the British Government and will in token of such supremacy present annually to the British Government one horse, twelve shawl goats of approved breed (six male and six female) and three pairs of Cashmere shawls." Gulab Singh died in 1857 and was succeeded by Ranbir Singh (1857-1885). Two other Maharajas, Partap Singh and Hari Singh ruled the state in succession.

The Accession Controversies

The princely state of J&K was one of the more than five hundred princely states of India on which the British domination lapsed on August 15, 1947. As per the terms of the British withdrawal and partition of India, the rulers of all the princely states were given the option of joining either of the dominions- India or Pakistan, basing their decisions on considerations of geographic contiguity and the wishes of their population. The vast majority of the rulers accordingly opted for either of the two dominions. However, despite seeming simplicity of these principles, they were not easily applicable to Kashmir. The state had a predominantly Muslim population and a Hindu ruler. Though Junagarh and Hyderabad too posed the same problem of ruler and majority of subjects pursuing different religions, yet their issue was resolved in the due course of time. In case of J&K, which abutted both neighbouring states of India and Pakistan and was claimed by both, the problem was complicated. Apart from territorial claims the possession of Kashmir, a Muslim-majority state, had significance for both India and Pakistan for different reasons. The profoundly divergent conceptions of nation-building underlay the Indian and Pakistani nationalist movements wherein the former was committed to the notion of creating a secular and democratic state and the latter sought to create a Islamic state.[1]

The provision for accession made in the Government of India Act of 1935, as adopted under the Independence Act of 1947, read: "An Indian State shall be deemed to have acceded to the Dominion if the Governor General has signified the acceptance of an Instrument of Accession executed by the Ruler thereof." There was no provision in the Act of 1947 that the accession would be conditional. Hence, as per the act, once the accession is made the concerned princely state becomes an integral part of one or the other of the two dominions. Neither the law had any provision for consulting the people of the princely states nor was there any provision that the accession had to be ratified by the people. It made the ruler's decision final. Lord Birdwood mentioned in his book *Two Nations and Kashmir*, "...with Mr. Jinnah, the approach (of accession of princely states to India or Pakistan) was governed by the strictly constitutional attitude, that it was for the ruler, and the ruler alone, to decide." Pakistan wanted Junagarh and Hyderabad, ruled by Muslim rulers with a Hindu majority population, to accede to it. Hence, treating Kashmir as an exception to the rule led to subsequent conflict.

The issue of accession of Kashmir acquired further complexity due to the ongoing political situation within the state. The reigning Maharaja, Hari Singh, was facing a strong opposition from his own subjects, primarily from the majority Muslim population. The simmering discontent against the Dogra rule had been politically organized with the establishment of the All Jammu and Kashmir Muslim Conference in October 1932. This movement, though representing the Muslim elite interest, to begin with, gradually got secularized. Its leader, Sheikh Mohammad Abdullah, came under the influence of Mahatma Gandhi and Pandit Jawaharlal Nehru who were leading the freedom struggle at the national level and changed the name of the party in 1939 to the All Jammu and Kashmir National Conference to make it secular. Thereafter, it became a mass movement with the goal of freedom from autocracy and the establishment of a popular rule. However, the conversion of the name and character of the party led to split of the movement with the traditional elite resisting the secularization of the organization and later reviving the Muslim Conference. This split also took place on regional and ideological lines. The National Conference leadership was predominantly Kashmir valley-based and was close to the Indian National Congress. The revived Muslim Conference, with its support among the Muslims of Jammu region, had close ties with Jinnah's All India Muslim League that advocated the creation of Pakistan. Following the national Quit India Movement in 1942, Sheikh Abdullah launched Quit Kashmir Movement to overthrow the Dogra monarchy.[2] The movement got the support of the Congress leadership. Leaders like Gandhi and Nehru espoused the cause of the people of Kashmir seeking political freedom from autocratic rule. However, to curb the movement Hari Singh detained the leaders of both the parties.

Facing a formidable challenge from the people and at the same time wooed by India as well as Pakistan, Maharaja evaded the question of political future of Kashmir. Months after partition, he did not accede to either of the states. His indecisiveness, however, further exacerbated the conflict. In an attempt to remain independent, Hari Singh requested standstill agreement to both newly independent states. While the government of India asked for further negotiations on this request of the Dogra ruler, the government of Pakistan agreed to the agreement. Under this agreement, Pakistan assumed charge of the post and telegraph system of the state. It also undertook the supply of foodstuffs and other essential commodities. But, the non-acceptance of the standstill agreement by India immediately aroused suspicion amongst Pakistanis. The release of Sheikh Abdullah from detention on September 29, 1947 too was noted with disapproval by Pakistan due to proximity of the Sheikh and his party with India. Suspecting that Hari Singh was inclined to accede to India and knowing that Sheikh Abdullah was opposed to accession of state to Pakistan, Karachi decided to put pressure on the Maharaja.[3] It many times stopped the regular supply of the material to the state.[4]

The uprising in Poonch in western reaches of Kashmir against the ruler and subsequent infiltration of armed groups from Pakistan complicated the problem further. India claimed that Pakistan, intending to 'grab J&K by force,'[5] sent its troops disguised as local tribesmen.[6] To quote V. P. Menon, "When Lt. Colonel Rai (Commander of the Sikh Battalion which was sent first to Srinagar) contacted the so-called 'raiders' he found them to be an organized body of men armed with light and medium machine-guns and mortars, and led by commanders who knew modern tactics and the use of ground."[7] Pakistan, however, argued that the atrocities perpetrated by Maharajas' forces against the Muslim population of Poonch provoked spontaneous reactions both within the state and from ethnic as well as religious kin across the border.[8] Amidst these competing claims, the invaders occupied Muzaffarabad on October 22, 1947 and then advanced towards Srinagar.

This development forced Hari Singh to send his troops that, however, proved incapable to check the advance of the invaders. After even the troops borrowed from the Maharaja of Patiala failed to halt the column, he appealed to the Lord Mountbatten (Governor General of India, 1947-48), for help. India decided that troops could be committed only if Hari Singh acceded to the Indian Union. Mountbatten also introduced one key caveat that the people of the state would have to ratify the accession as soon as law and order have been restored. Agreeing to the condition, Maharaja sent a letter to Governor General on October 26, 1947 in which he agreed to accede to India. The full text of the letter has been given below:

I have to inform your Excellency that a grave emergency has arisen in my State and request immediate assistance of your Government.

As your Excellency is aware the State of Jammu and Kashmir has not acceded to the Dominion of India or to Pakistan. Geographically my State is contiguous to both the Dominions. It has vital economical and cultural links with both of them. Besides my State has a common boundary with the Soviet Republic and China. In their external relations the Dominions of India and Pakistan cannot ignore this fact.

I wanted to take time to decide to which Dominion I should accede, or whether it is not in the best interests of both the Dominions and my State to stand independent, of course with friendly and cordial relations with both.

I accordingly approached the Dominions of India and Pakistan to enter into Standstill Agreement with my State. The Pakistan Government accepted this Agreement. The Dominion of India desired further discussions with representatives of my Government. I could not arrange this in view of the developments indicated below. In fact the Pakistan Government are operating Post and Telegraph system inside the State.

Though we have got a Standstill Agreement with the Pakistan Government that Government permitted steady and increasing strangulation of supplies like food, salt and petrol to my State.

Afridis, soldiers in plain clothes, and desperadoes with modern weapons have been allowed to infiltrate into the State at first in Poonch and then in Sialkot and finally in mass area adjoining Hazara District on the Ramkot side. The result has been that the limited number of troops at the disposal of the State had to be dispersed and thus had to face the enemy at the several points simultaneously, that it has become difficult to stop the wanton destruction of life and property and looting. The Mahora powerhouse which supplies the electric current to the whole of Srinagar has been burnt. The number of women who have been kidnapped and raped makes my heart bleed. The wild forces thus let loose on the State are marching on with the aim of capturing Srinagar, the summer Capital of my Government, as first step to over-running the whole State.

The mass infiltration of tribesmen drawn from distant areas of the North-West Frontier coming regularly in motor trucks using Mansehra-Muzaffarabad Road and fully armed with up-to-date weapons cannot possibly be done without the knowledge of the Provisional Government of the North-West Frontier Province and the Government of Pakistan. In spite of repeated requests made by my Government no attempt has been made to check these raiders or stop them from coming into my State. The Pakistan Radio even put out a story that a Provisional Government had been set up in Kashmir. The people of my State both the Muslims and non-Muslims generally have taken no part at all.

With the conditions obtaining at present in my State and the great emergency of the situation as it exists, I have no option but to ask for help from the Indian Dominion. Naturally they cannot send the help asked for by me without my State acceding to the Dominion of India. I have accordingly decided to do so and I attach the Instrument of Accession for acceptance by your Government. The other alternative is to leave my State and my people to free-booters. On this basis no civilized

Government can exist or be maintained. This alternative I will never allow to happen as long as I am Ruler of the State and I have life to defend my country.

I am also to inform your Excellency's Government that it is my intention at once to set up an interim Government and ask Sheikh Abdullah to carry the responsibilities in this emergency with my Prime Minister.

If my State has to be saved immediate assistance must be available at Srinagar. Mr. Menon is fully aware of the situation and he will explain to you, if further explanation is needed.

Following is the text of the Instrument of Accession executed by Maharajah Hari Singh on October 26, 1947:

Whereas the Indian Independence Act, 1947, provides that as from the fifteenth day of August, 1947, there shall be set up an independent Dominion known as INDIA, and that the Government of India Act 1935, shall with such omissions, additions, adaptations and modifications as the Governor General may by order specify, be applicable to the Dominion of India.

And whereas the Government of India Act, 1935, as so adapted by the Governor General, provides that an Indian State may accede to the Dominion of India by an Instrument of Accession executed by the Ruler thereof.

Now, therefore, I Shriman Inder Mahinder Rajrajeswar Maharajadhiraj Shri Hari Singhji, Jammu & Kashmir Naresh Tatha Tibbet adi Deshadhipati, Ruler of Jammu & Kashmir State, in the exercise of my Sovereignty in and over my said State do hereby execute this my Instrument of Accession and

1. I hereby declare that I accede to the Dominion of India with the intent that the Governor General of India, the

Dominion Legislature, the Federal Court and any other Dominion authority established for the purposes of the Dominion shall by virtue of this my Instrument of Accession but subject always to the terms thereof, and for the purposes only of the Dominion, exercise in relation to the State of Jammu & Kashmir (hereinafter referred to as "this State") such functions as may be vested in them by or under the Government of India Act, 1935, as in force in the Dominion of India, on the 15th day of August 1947, (which Act as so in force is hereafter referred to as 'the Act').

2. I hereby assume the obligation of ensuring that due effect is given to provisions of the Act within this State so far as they are applicable therein by virtue of this my Instrument of Accession.

3. I accept the matters specified in the schedule hereto as the matters with respect to which the Dominion Legislature may make law for this State.

4. I hereby declare that I accede to the Dominion of India on the assurance that if an agreement is made between the Governor General and the Ruler of this State whereby any functions in relation to the administration in this State of any law of the Dominion Legislature shall be exercised by the Ruler of the State, then any such agreement shall be construed and have effect accordingly.

5. The terms of this my Instrument of Accession shall not be varied by any amendment of the Act or the Indian Independence Act, 1947, unless such amendment is accepted by me by Instrument supplementary to this Instrument.

6. Nothing in this Instrument shall empower the Dominion Legislature to make any law for this State authorizing

the compulsory acquisition of land for any purpose, but I hereby undertake that should the Dominion for the purpose of a Dominion law which applies in this State deem it necessary to acquire any land, I will at their request acquire the land at their expense, or, if the land belongs to me transfer it to them on such terms as may be agreed or, in default of agreement, determined by an arbitrator to be appointed by the Chief Justice of India.

7. Nothing in this Instrument shall be deemed to commit in any way to acceptance of any future constitution of India or to fetter my discretion to enter into agreement with the Government of India under any such future constitution.

8. Nothing in this Instrument affects the continuance of my Sovereignty in and over this State, or, save as provided by or under this Instrument, the exercise of any powers, authority and rights now enjoyed by me as Ruler of this State or the validity of any law at present in force in this State.

9. I hereby declare that I execute this Instrument on behalf of this State and that any reference in this Instrument to me or to the Ruler of the State is to be construed as including a reference to my heirs and successors.

Under the instrument of accession the Indian union was arrogated powers to make laws in respect to Kashmir in broad areas of defence, external affairs, communications and ancillary. Under the heading of defence following areas came under the control of India: 1. The naval, military and air forces of the Dominion and any other armed forces raised or maintained by the Dominion; any armed forces, including forces raised or maintained by an acceding State, which are attached to, or operating with, any of the armed forces of the Dominion. 2. Naval, military and air force works, administration of cantonment areas. 3. Arms, fire-arms, ammunition. 4. Explosives. Under the heading of external affairs following areas came under the control of India: 1. External affairs; the implementing of treaties and agreements with other countries; extradition, including the surrender of criminals and accused persons to parts of His Majesty's Dominions outside India. 2. Admission into, and emigration and expulsion from, India, including in relation thereto the regulation of the movements in India of persons who are not British subjects domiciled in India or subjects of any acceding State; pilgrimages to places beyond India. 3. Naturalization. Under the heading of communications following areas came under the control of India: 1. Posts and telegraphs, including telephones, wireless, broadcasting, and other like forms of communication. 2. Federal railways; the regulation of all railways other than minor railways in respect of safety, maximum and minimum rates and fares, station and services terminal charges, interchange of traffic and the responsibility of railway administrations as carriers of goods and passengers; the regulation of minor railways in respect of safety and the responsibility of the administrations of such railways as carriers of goods and passengers. 3. Maritime shipping and navigation, including shipping and navigation on tidal waters; Admiralty jurisdiction. 4. Port quarantine. 5. Major ports, that is to say, the declaration and delimitation of such ports, and the constitution and powers of Port Authorities therein. 6. Aircraft and air navigation; the provision of aerodromes; regulation and organisation of air traffic and of aerodromes. 7. Lighthouses, including lightships, beacons and other provisions for the safety of shipping and aircraft. 8. Carriage of passengers and goods by sea or by air. 9. Extension of the powers and jurisdiction of members of the police force belonging to any unit to railway area outside that unit. Under the heading of ancillary following areas came under the control of India: 1. Election to the Dominion Legislature, subject to the provisions of the Act and of any Order made there under. 2. Offences against laws with respect to any of the aforesaid matters. 3. Inquiries and statistics for the purposes of any of the aforesaid matters. 4. Jurisdiction and powers of all courts with respect to any of the aforesaid matters but, except with the consent of the Ruler of the acceding State, not so as to confer any jurisdiction or powers upon any courts other than courts ordinarily exercising jurisdiction in or in relation to that State.

The UN Resolutions

Kashmir acceded to India on October 26, 1947. However, the legality of accession of Kashmir to India under the circumstances became a permanent source of difference between both the newly independent countries. India contended that it has legal right to all of pre-1947 Kashmir because of Hari Singh's October 1947 Instrument of Accession. It further argued that the military aggression by Pakistan and allied tribal forces were provocations designed to overthrow a legally binding agreement by force. Pakistan, on the other hand, took the stand that Kashmir's accession to India was illegal since it was in violation of the standstill agreement. It argued the accession was illegitimate since Maharaja had abandoned his throne prior to signing the Instrument of Accession by leaving the Kashmir valley. Nevertheless, on October 27, 1947, Indian troops were sent to Kashmir, leading to a full-scale war between India and Pakistan. The principal Indian military unit sent to the state, 161st Infantry Brigade, succeeded in arresting the advance of the raiders. On October 30, 1947, emergency government was formed in the state with Sheikh Mohammad Abdullah as its head. This government supported the decision of Maharaja to join India and helped combat advancing Pakistani forces. It needs to be mentioned here that until the troops arrived, it were mainly the Muslim volunteers under the command of Sheikh Mohammad Abdullah who resisted invaders. Indeed, Balraj Puri, a veteran political commentator on J&K has observed that many Kashmiris were 'outraged' by the Pakistani attempt to secure accession firstly by wooing the Maharaja, and after that failed, "to decide the issue by force."[9]

On the advice of Mountbatten, India filed a complaint against Pakistan under Article 35 of the UN Charter in the UNSC on January 1, 1948. India approached the Security Council with the missive that "such a situation now exists between India and Pakistan owing to the aid which invaders, consisting of nationals of Pakistan and of tribesmen from the territory immediately adjoining Pakistan on the North West, are drawing from Pakistan for operations against Jammu and Kashmir, a State which has acceded to the Dominion of India and is part of India...The Government of India request the UNSC to call upon Pakistan to put an end immediately to the giving of such assistance which is an act of aggression against India." Precisely, government of India requested the Security Council to ask the government of Pakistan:

(1) To prevent Pakistan Government personnel, military and civil, from participating or assisting in the invasion of the Jammu and Kashmir State;

(2) To call upon other Pakistani nationals to desist from taking any part in the fighting in the Jammu and Kashmir State;

(3) To deny to the invaders: (a) access to any use of its territory for operations against Kashmir, (b) military and other supplies, (c) all other kinds of aid that might tend to prolong the present struggle.

The UN resolution on January 20, 1948 created the UNCIP to investigate facts pertaining to the dispute and to mediate the conflict. Subsequently on April 21, 1948, the Security Council passed resolution 47 noting that both states had agreed to determine the question of Kashmir's accession through the democratic method of a free and impartial plebiscite. The UN resolution of August 13, 1948 can be considered one of the most significant resolutions passed by the UN on the Kashmir issue. It clearly stated that Pakistan was to vacate its troops from the whole of the state. The subsequent truce agreement made the following rules to be accepted by both India and Pakistan:

A.

1. As the presence of troops of Pakistan in the territory of the State of Jammu and Kashmir constitutes a material change in the situation since it was represented by the Government of Pakistan before the Security Council, the Government of Pakistan agrees to withdraw its troops from that State.

2. The Government of Pakistan will use its best endeavour to secure the withdrawal from the State of Jammu and Kashmir of tribesmen and Pakistani nationals not normally resident therein who have entered the State for the purpose of fighting.

3. Pending a final solution, the territory evacuated by the Pakistani troops will be administered by the local authorities under the surveillance of the commission.

B.

1. When the commission shall have notified the Government of India that the tribesmen and Pakistani nationals referred to in Part II, A, 2, hereof have withdrawn, thereby terminating the situation which was represented by the Government of India to the Security Council as having occasioned the presence of Indian forces in the State of Jammu and Kashmir, and further, that the Pakistani forces are being withdrawn from the State of Jammu and Kashmir, the Government of India agrees to begin to withdraw the bulk of its forces from that State in stages to be agreed upon with the Commission.

> 2. Pending the acceptance of the conditions for a final settlement of the situation in the State of Jammu and Kashmir, the Indian Government will maintain within the lines existing at the moment of the cease-fire the minimum strength of its forces which in agreement with the commission are considered necessary to assist local authorities in the observance of law and order. The Commission will have observers stationed where it deems necessary.

Interestingly, a resolution on assurances to India was adopted by UNCIP before the August 13, 1948 resolution to be agreed by Pakistan. It stipulated that the responsibility for the security of Kashmir would rest with India and the sovereignty of the J&K government over the entire territory of the state would not be brought under question. Similarly, it made clear that there shall be no recognition of the so-called *azad* (free) Kashmir government and the territory occupied by Pakistan shall not be consolidated to the disadvantage of the state of J&K. Further, it stipulated that the administration of the evacuated areas in the North shall revert to the government of J&K and its defence to the government of India, who will, if necessary, maintain garrison for preventing the incursion of tribesmen and for guarding main trade routes. It excluded Pakistan from all affairs of Kashmir in particular in the proposed plebiscite and in case plebiscite is found to be impossible for technical or practical reasons, the Commission will consider other methods of determining fair and equitable conditions for ensuring a free expression of people's will. It made clear that plebiscite proposal shall not be binding upon India if Pakistan does not implement Part I and II of the resolution of August 13, 1948. However, the UNCIP could not make Pakistan accept these assurances. Consequently, the very basis of the UN resolution was jeopardized. Pakistan violated the UN resolutions especially that of August 1948 that stipulated the withdrawal of Pakistan forces from the Kashmir territory under its control. On the contrast, the ensuing months witnessed Pakistan advancing deep into Gilgit-Baltistan and 'AJK.' Nevertheless, the ceasefire was announced and a line was drawn in Kashmir with substantial parts remaining under the occupation of Pakistan. Later in 1972 the ceasefire line was rechristened LOC.

The Provisional Government

The 'AJK' entity came into existence on October 24, 1947 at the Plandhari town of Poonch of the then princely state of J&K, with the establishment of a provisional government. The declaration issued by the provisional government on its emergence is worth reproduction here:

"The Provisional Azad Government, which the people of Jammu and Kashmir have set up a few weeks ago with the object of ending intolerable Dogra tyrannies and securing to the people of the State, including Muslims, Hindus and Sikhs, the right of free self-Government has now established its rule over a major portion of the State territory and hopes to liberate the remaining pockets of Dogra rule very soon. In view of these circumstances it has been reconstituted with Mr. Ibrahim, Bar-at-Law of Poonch as its provisional head, and its headquarters have been moved to Plandhari in Poonch.

The new Government represents the united will of the Jammu and Kashmir State to be free from the rule of the Dogra dynasty which has long suppressed and oppressed the people.

The movement of liberty which has culminated in the formation of the present provisional Government has a long history dating from 1929. Thousands of Jammu and Kashmir people, including members of all communities, have suffered death and imprisonment in the cause of this movement. One of its forms was the Quit Kashmir launched in the Kashmir valley last year.

It will be recalled that Pandit Jawaharlal Nehru as a friend of the suffering people of Indian States went to help this movement at the time but was not allowed to enter the State territory under the orders of the ex-Ruler Hari Singh. The tyrannies perpetrated by the Raja and his officials and his troops on the people increased with the increase in the desire of the people for freedom and self-Government.

Recently a prominent Hindu patriot, who wanted to proceed to Karachi and New Delhi to represent the intolerable conditions in the State to our neighbouring Dominions of Pakistan and India was arrested by the ex-Ruler's officials.

The united will of the people has, however, overcome the organized violence of the Ruler's armies. He and his so called Prime Minister have fled from Kashmir and will perhaps soon flee from Jammu as well.

The Provisional Government, which is assuming the administration of the State is most emphatically not a communal Government. It will include Muslims as well as non-Muslims in the provisional Cabinet which will serve the people, the temporary purpose of restoring law and order in the State and enable the people to elect by their free vote a popular legislature and a popular government.

The Provisional Government entertain sentiments of the utmost friendliness and goodwill towards the neighbouring Dominions of India and Pakistan and hopes that both the Dominions will sympathize with the people of Jammu and Kashmir in their efforts to exercise their birthright of political freedom. The Provisional Government is further anxious to safeguard the identity of Jammu and Kashmir as political entity.

The question of accession of Jammu and Kashmir to either Dominion can only be decided by the free vote of the people in the form of a referendum. The Provisional Government will make prompt arrangements for this and hopes to invite independent observers to see that the question is decided by the free will of the people".

It would be matter of interest to note that how the declaration by the provisional government was later diluted substantially. For instance, its proclamation of itself "not a communal government" and it would "enable the people to elect by their free vote a popular legislature and a popular government" witnessed drastic corrosion in subsequent enactments. This aspect would be dealt with in detail in a later chapter. Most strangely the provisional government declared itself to be representative of the whole of undivided Kashmir though the area under its control included only a small portion of Kashmir.

The Karachi Agreement

The ceasefire line, later rechristened LOC, divided Kashmir into three parts: 'AJK' and the Gilgit-Baltistan on Pakistan side and J&K on Indian side. The territory of 'AJK' comprised an area of 13,297 sq. kms. and the territory of Gilgit-Baltistan comprised of an area of 72,495 sq. kms. With the signing of the Karachi Agreement between the Muslim Conference (MC), represented by its head, Chaudhary Ghulam Abbas, Pakistan, represented by Minister without Portfolio Mushtaque Ahmed Gurmani, and the President of 'AJK,' Sardar Mohammed Ibrahim Khan, Islamabad established its tight grip over the areas that came under its control. The agreement divided powers between the three signatories. Under the agreement, the following matters came under the purview of Pakistan: defence; foreign policy; negotiations with the UNCIP; publicity in foreign countries and in Pakistan; co-ordination and arrangement of relief and rehabilitation of refugees; co-ordination of publicity in connection with plebiscite; all activities within Pakistan regarding 'AJK' such as procurement of food, civil supplies running of refugee camps and medical aid; and all affairs of Gilgit-Baltistan under the control of Political Agent appointed by Pakistan.

The following matters came under the purview of 'AJK' government: policy with regard to administration of 'AJK' territory; general supervision of administration in 'AJK' territory; publicity with regard to the activities of the 'AJK' government and administration; advice to the Minister without Portfolio with regard to negotiations with UNCIP; and development of economic resources of 'AJK' territory. The MC was vested with the following powers: publicity with regard to plebiscite in the 'AJK' territory; field work and publicity in J&K; organization of political activities in the 'AJK' territory and in J&K; preliminary arrangements in connection with the plebiscite; organization for contesting the plebiscite; political work and publicity among the Kashmiri refugees in Pakistan; and advise the minister without portfolio with regard to the negotiations with the UNCIP. The agreement clearly reflected the total control of Pakistan over the affairs of 'AJK.' There was no representative from Gilgit-Baltistan in the agreement.

Gilgit-Baltistan

The Gilgit-Baltistan border the Wakhan corridor of Afghanistan to the northwest, the Xinjiang territory of China to the northeast, J&K to the southeast, the region of 'AJK' to the southwest and the North West Frontier Province (NWFP) of Pakistan to the west. The region is home to some of the world's highest mountain ranges such as the Karakoram. It remained independent for nearly 900 years from the middle of the 10th century. The region was one of the most popular trade routes linking Indian subcontinent, Central Asia, China and West Asia. Its high passes and valleys made it possible for the exchange goods such as textiles, spices, raw silks, carpets, etc. Buddhism came to the region around the period of 1080 AD, when Sri Badat of the Shah Rais dynasty ruled it. After Sri

Badat, who was the last Buddhist ruler of Gilgit, the Hunza ruler Shamsher founded the Tarakhan dynasty in Gilgit. Shamsher patronized Islam in the region. The reign of the Tarakhan dynasty was succeeded by Taj Mughal of Badakhshan in 1335. The region continued to witness invasions by Afghan rulers. Following the end of the Mughal rule in Kashmir during the mid-eighteenth century, the region came under the rule of Sikh King, Maharajah Ranjit Singh in 1819. The Sikh rule in the region came to an end when the British East India Company defeated the army of King Daleep Singh and signed the Treaty of Amritsar on March 9, 1846. From the Sikhs, the region came under the control of Gulab Singh, the Dogra ruler of Jammu in 1846. Gulab Singh gradually expanded his dominion to more remote Himalayan regions of Ladakh and Baltistan. The Dogras subdivided the region into two wazarats, placing Hunza, Nagar, Ashkoman and some tribal areas under the Gilgit wazarat, while Ladakh and Baltistan came under the Ladakh wazarat.

The emergence of the Soviet Union, after the Socialist Revolution of 1917, had caused concerns in the mind of the British. Besides, the cool climate of Kashmir as also its strategic position also attracted the attention of the British government. To quote E. F. Knight, "The climate of this paradise of Asia appears to be well adapted to the European constitution.... Had we not sold the sale of this beautiful valley to the Maharaja, a great military cantonment would no doubt have long since established here. This would not only have been most advantageous from a strategic point of view but would have avoided much of the sickness and mortality which thin the ranks of our white army in India."[10] Similarly, Lord Curzon argued, "It is one of the northern gates of India, through which a would-be invader must advance, if he advances at all. Gilgit occupies a strategic place and the India Government, harassed by Russia's growing restlessness in Central Asia, knew it for the key of great northern gateway into India, a key worth holding even at some cost in toil, money and valuable though less-human lives."[11]

The British set up the Gilgit Agency in 1877 with the appointment of Sir John Biddulph as the Political Agent. Hunza and Nagar were subjugated under the British Agency in 1891. In 1901, the Gilgit and Ladakh wazarats were recognized and put under the control of the state government, while the remaining districts of the Gilgit Agency were put under the control of the Political Agent. In 1935 the British signed a 60-year lease with Maharaja Hari Singh under the Treaty of Jammu for what are now called the Northern Areas by Pakistan. The treaty stipulated that the state flag would continue to fly over the leased territory and Baltistan and Astor would remain under the Maharaja's control. The British recognized Maharaja's sovereignty over the whole region and as an acknowledgement of this factor the British garrison in Gilgit presented arms to Maharaja on his birthday and other state occasions.

The following are the main provisions of the lease treaty:

Article I – The Viceroy and Governor-General of India may at any time after the ratification of this agreement assume the civil and military administration of so much of the w*azarat* of Gilgit Province (herein after referred to as the 'said territory') of the State of Jammu and Kashmir as lies beyond the right bank of the river Indus, but notwithstanding anything in this agreement the said territory shall continue to be included within the dominions of His Highness the Maharaja of Jammu and Kashmir.

Article II – In recognition of the fact that the said territory continues to be included within the dominion of His Highness the Maharaja of Jammu and Kashmir salutes and customary honours shall be paid in the said territory of the administration on the occasion of the birthday of His Highness, Baisakhi,

Dussehra, Basant-Panchmi and on such other occasions as may be agreed upon by His Excellency the Viceroy and Governor-General of India. The flag of His Highness will be flown at the official headquarters of the agency throughout the year.

Article III – In normal circumstances no British Indian troops shall be dispatched through that portion of the *wazarat* of Gilgit Province which lies beyond the left bank of the river Indus.

Article IV – All rights pertaining to mining are reserved to His Highness the Maharaja of Jammu and Kashmir. The grant of prospecting licenses and mining leases will be made during the period of agreement mentioned below.

Article V – This agreement shall remain in force for sixty years from the date of its ratification and the leases will terminate at the end of that period.

The Gilgit Agency was handed over to the Dogra regime on August 1, 1947. Brigadier Ghansara Singh along with Chief of the General staff of the state army, General Scott and Captain Saeed Durrani arrived in Gilgit on July 30, 1947 and took over charge from Lt. Col. Beacon, the English political agent. The Maharaja then appointed Brigadier Ghansara Singh as his governor to the region. Hence, in this context Gilgit-Baltistan were already an integral part of the J&K princely state before India and Pakistan came into being in August 1947. Census reports from 1911, 1921, 1931 and 1941 confirm this point of view.

As the historians commonly agree that Major Brown of Gilgit Scouts, awarded later *Sitara-e-Pakistan* (star of Pakistan), played the pivotal role in Pakistan's occupation of Gilgit-Baltistan. It is argued that the British continued to interfere in Kashmir even after the lease treaty terminated. It is argued that some of the British officers had a tilt towards

Pakistan which was clearly evident from dramatic events that took place in Gilgit-Baltistan after August 1947. Major Brown was responsible for ensuring smooth transfer of power from British to Dogra regime. His service was retained in the Gilgit Scouts on his own consent. Hence, as per the rules he was responsible to Governor Ghansara Singh. Yet, defying his duties, under the well-known Operation Datta Khel conceived by him, the Gilgit Scouts arrested Governor Ghansara Singh on October 31, 1947.[12] Before that Major Brown had made a suggestion to the Governor that is worth mentioning. In his words, "I suggest you hold an immediate referendum in the Province. It goes without saying that the result will be in favour of accession to Pakistan but that is beside the point. You can then announce that the will of the people has been ascertained, though confirmation must be kept pending until a plebiscite is completed in the rest of Kashmir. The Governor General of India has made it clear that such a plebiscite will be held as soon as order is restored. With the will of the people here a fait accompli, you can continue to govern the Province in a temporary capacity, though I would suggest that you feign a nervous breakdown and hand over charge to Colonel Majid who is a Muslim."[13]

The occupation of Gilgit led by Major Brown was followed by that of Baltistan that had come under Maharaja much before Gilgit. The next seventeen days Gilgit-Baltistan virtually remained 'independent.' The 'independent' People's Republic of Gilgit and Baltistan witnessed establishment of a provisional government headed by Rais Khan. Following the hoisting of Pakistani flag on November 1947 by Major Brown Pakistan was invited to 'help administer' the region. Grabbing the opportunity Pakistan immediately appointed Sardar Mohammad Alam as the political agent.

It is argued that inviting Pakistan in the area was a tactical move by Major Brown to counter the attempt of Mirza

Hassan to establish an independent state of Gilgit-Baltistan that the former was deadly against. To quote Brown, "At every move, I was thwarting Mirza Hassan and his satellites from their dream of a United States of Gilgit. If I could be disposed of, however, they would be free to pursue their nefarious plans.... After hoisting of Pakistan flag in a ceremony, I breathed a sigh of relief. A very definite step had now been taken against Mirza Hassan and the gang. Let him dare to remove the Pakistan flag and replace it with that of his United States." Thus, a British officer, who should have served the Maharaja under the rules, jeopardized the fate of Gilgit-Baltistan - from being a part of undivided Kashmir to short span of 'independence,' followed by occupation. Interestingly, to make the 'invitation' to rule Gilgit-Baltistan formal, Pakistan signed the Karachi Agreement in 1949 with 'AJK,' without any representative from Gilgit-Baltistan.

Pakistan has divided the Kashmir territory under its control into two parts: 'AJK' and 'NA.' Both the regions have been decorated with different kinds of set up, which has been focused in later pages. 'AJK' is divided into two administrative divisions which in turn are composed of eight districts. Those are Bhimber, Kotli, Mirpur, Bagh, Muzaffarabad, Neelum, Poonch and Sudhnati. As per 1998 census its population was about 3 million. 'AJK' and 'NA' are predominantly Muslim. The population of 'AJK' includes Rajput, Sudhan, Kashmiri, Gujjar, Jat, Awans, Abbasi, Pashtuns, Mughal, Ansari, Malik, Rehmani, Khawajas, etc. The Hindko, Mirpuri, Pashto are the languages spoken by sizeable majority. The 'NA' has been divided into six districts— Gilgit, Skardu, Diamir, Ghizer, Ghanche and Astore. Its sparse population inhabits a vast area of 72,495 sq. kms. The ethnic groups are varied - Baltis, Shinas, Vashkuns, Mughals, Kashmiris, Pathans, Ladhakhis and Turks. People speak a number of languages such as Balti, Shina, Brushaski, Khawer, Wakhi, Turki, Tibeti, Pushto and Urdu.

References

1. Sumit Ganguly, *The Crisis in Kashmir: Portents of War, Hopes of Peace* (New Delhi: Foundation Books, 1997), p. 8.
2. Victoria Schofield, *Kashmir in the Crossfire: India, Pakistan and the Unending War* (New Delhi: Viva Books Pvt. Ltd., 2004), p. 24.
3. C. Dasgupta, *War and Diplomacy in Kashmir: 1947-48* (New Delhi: Sage Publications, 2002), p. 38.
4. V. P. Menon, *Integration of the Indian States* (Mumbai: Orient Longman Ltd., 1999), p. 453.
5. Jagmohan, *My Frozen Turbulence in Kashmir* (New Delhi: Allied Publishers, 2000), p. 85.
6. They included Hazara and Afridi tribesmen from Gilgit-Baltistan, paramilitary forces such as the Muslim League National Guards and regular Pakistani Army personnel, disguised as tribesmen. Sumit Ganguly, *Conflict Unending: India-Pakistan Tensions Since 1947* (New Delhi: Oxford University Press, 2002), p. 17.
7. V. P. Menon, n. 4, p. 461. Also see, Maurice Cohen, *Thunder over Kashmir* (Hyderabad: Orient Longman Ltd., 1995), p. 2.
8. Sumantra Bose, *Kashmir: Roots of Conflict, Paths to Peace* (New Delhi: Vistaar Publications, 2003), p. 34.
9. Balraj Puri, "Kashmiriyat: The Vitality of Kashmir Identity," *Contemporary South Asia*, vol. 4, no. 1, March 1995, p. 57.
10. Quoted in N. N. Raina, *Kashmir Politics and Imperialist Manoeuvres: 1846-1980* (New Delhi: Patriot Publishers, 1988), p. 11.
11. Quoted in F. M. Hassnain, *British Policy Towards Kashmir: 1846-1921* (New Delhi: Sterling Publishers, 1974), p. 61.
12. For various interpretations on this issue see Ahmad Hasan Dani, *History of Northern Areas of Pakistan* (Islamabad: National Institute of Historical and Cultural Research, 1991), pp. 349-352.
13. Quoted in Fakhar Mehmood Khan, "Gilgit-Baltistan's short Freedom." *http://www.balawaristan.net/GB.html.* Accessed on February 15, 2007.

2

Legal and Constitutional Setup

Kashmir across the LOC divided into two parts by Pakistan have different kinds of constitutional and political set ups. Pakistan sanctions notional *azadi* (freedom) to one part while it retains total control over another. While the relation of 'AJK' with Pakistan remains unclear the case of Gilgit-Baltistan is worse as it is devoid of any legal-constitutional status. Since beginning, Pakistan has followed a policy of 'calculated ambiguity' towards these areas of the undivided state of J&K. While it contests India's claim over the areas of Kashmir that are under its occupation, it also does not claim them despite maintaining total control thereby keeping the issue ambiguous. While it legally has no claim over undivided J&K and it fiercely advocates for the right to self determination of the people, its advocacy is dented by a clause in the interim constitution of 'AJK' which abides all the people living in the area to the ideology of accession to Pakistan. At the psychological level also the attempt in this context starts very early when even the books of primary school children teach 'Kashmir *banega* Pakistan.' In case of J&K the entity enjoys special status under Article 370 of Indian constitution and autonomy in many spheres.

The 'AJK' Constitution: Growth and Practice

With the establishment of a provisional government in October 1947, the 'AJK' entity came into existence in Poonch. With the signing of the Karachi Agreement in 1949 between the MC, Pakistan and the President[1] of 'AJK,' Islamabad established its control over 'AJK.' Besides providing broad rules for the governance of 'AJK,' the agreement empowered Pakistan to exercise full control over eight items including defence, foreign policy, negotiations with UNCIP, etc. Despite the claims by 'AJK' as well as government of Pakistan, and the prefix of *azad* in 'AJK', provisions such as president, prime minister and legislature, neither any nation nor international organization has so far recognized it as a sovereign state. The UN resolutions have recognized it only as a territory administered by local authorities until the Kashmir problem is resolved. The section A-3 of the UNCIP resolution on August 13, 1948 read, "Pending a final solution, the territory evacuated by the Pakistan troops will be administered by the local authorities under the surveillance of the Commission." Pakistan has never clearly defined its relations with 'AJK' and as a result the status of the entity remains ambiguous.

The Chief Plebiscite Officer of Pakistan, a joint secretary in Pakistan government, was the de facto ruler of 'AJK' from 1949 to 1968. He was not responsible to the 'AJK' government being an appointee of the Ministry of Kashmir Affairs that was formed in 1952 under the general supervision of the Home Ministry in Islamabad. Commenting on the autocratic control of the Kashmir Affairs Ministry over 'AJK,' the dismissed Finance Minister, Hamid Ullah Khan observed in 1953: "an ordinary clerk in Kashmir Affairs Ministry had a greater say in problems affecting Azad Kashmir than the President of the government of the territory." In fact, the president and the prime minister of 'AJK' enjoy only titular power. According to Major (retd.) Raja Abbas Khan, "Governments that came into being in Azad Kashmir virtually from its inception were all installed illegally by the Pakistan Government, first with the collaboration of Muslim Conference and then independently, although the people of Azad Kashmir were totally against establishment of such Governments."[2]

Until 1974 when the interim constitution was adopted under the supervision of Islamabad, 'AJK' remained devoid of a formal constitution. The tussle within the MC provided opportunity to Pakistan to enhance its control over 'AJK.' In May 1950, the MC President, Chaudhary Ghulam Abbas dissolved the government led by Mohammad Ibrahim Khan and in January 1951 formulated a Set of Rules for the conduct of government business in 'AJK.' Under the provisions of these rules, Abbas himself arrogated the position of supreme head of the region. In protest to Abbas, the Ibrahim group decided to form a parallel government with its headquarters in Poonch. However, the first major step to frame certain guidelines for governance called Rules of Business was adopted in 1952 in 'AJK' under the patronage of Ministry of Kashmir Affairs in Islamabad. Article 5 of the Rules stated, "the President of Azad Kashmir government shall hold office during the pleasure of the All Jammu and Kashmir Muslim Conference duly recognized as such by the government of Pakistan in the Ministry of Kashmir Affairs."[3] This article indicated the dominance of Pakistan and the MC in the affairs of 'AJK.' The Rules did not mention about any mechanism for the people to elect representatives. The state council (later converted into 'AJK' council), introduced under the Act of 1964, made the hand of Pakistan more powerful in controlling the affairs of the area. In 1970, the 'AJK' Government Act, promulgated by the government of Pakistan, provided for a 25-member legislative assembly and a president for 'AJK,' to be elected directly on the basis of adult franchise for a term of four years. This Act of 1970 was modified and re-enacted as the 'AJK' Interim Constitution Act in 1974.

Besides the preamble the interim constitution, as per its 1990 edition, has 59 sections and 4 schedules. It adopts parliamentary form of government for 'AJK.' The legislative assembly consists of 49 members, out of which 41 are directly elected on the basis of adult franchise, 5 women members are directly elected by members, one Islamic clergy directly elected by members, one overseas member and one among technocrats and professionals. Section 21 explains the dominant role played by Pakistan in the affairs of 'AJK.' The 'AJK' council (usually referred to as Kashmir council) consists of the prime minister of Pakistan, the president of 'AJK,' 5 members to be nominated by the prime minister of Pakistan from time to time from amongst ministers from his cabinet and members of Pakistani parliament, the prime minister of 'AJK' or a person nominated by him, and 6 members to be elected by the 'AJK' assembly from amongst state subjects in accordance with the system of proportional representation by means of single transferable vote. The prime minister of Pakistan is the chairman and the president of 'AJK' is the vice-chairman of the council. The president of 'AJK' is elected by the members of the joint sitting of the legislative assembly and 'AJK' council by the votes of majority of the total membership. The assembly elects one of its Muslim members prime minister of 'AJK.'

Section 19 (2) states that the government of 'AJK' has to comply with the rules made by the Kashmir council. The council is headed by the prime minister of Pakistan. Hence, the Kashmir council, supposed to be an upper house of 'AJK' legislature, has the Pakistan prime minister as chairman. This makes the subservience of 'AJK' government to Pakistan apparent. The judges of the supreme court and high court of 'AJK' are appointed by the president of 'AJK' on the 'advice' of the council. Important decisions are taken by the council and then those are implemented by the 'AJK' government. It would be worthwhile to mention that almost all the subjects of importance are kept in the purview of Pak prime minister led council, in which Pakistan has overtly an edge, to make laws. In total 52 items were kept in the council legislative list.[4] A study of these items, given below, clearly reflects that 'AJK' even lacks the powers which any local administration enjoys in a federal set up.

1. Subject to the responsibilities of the government of Pakistan under the UNCIP resolutions, nationality, citizenship and naturalization, migration from or into 'AJK,' admission into, and emigration and expulsion from, 'AJK,' including in relation thereto the regulation of the movements in 'AJK' of persons not domiciled in 'AJK.'

2. Post and telegraphs, including telephones, wireless broadcasting and other like forms of communicating; post offices, saving bank.

3. Public debt of the council; including the borrowing of money on the security of the council consolidated fund.

4. Council public services and council public service commission.

5. Council pensions, that is to say, pensions payable by the council or out of the council consolidated fund.

6. Administrative courts for council subjects.

7. Council agencies and institutions for the following purposes, that is to say, for research, for professional or technical training, or for the promotion of special studies.

8. Nuclear energy, including-
   a) mineral resources necessary for the generation of nuclear energy;

   b) the production of nuclear fuels and the generation and use of nuclear energy; and

c) ionizing radiations.

9. Aircraft and air navigation; the provision of aerodromes; regulation and organization of air traffic and of aerodromes.

10. Beacons and other provisions for safety of aircraft.

11. Carriage of passengers and goods by air.

12. Copyright, inventions, designs, trade marks and merchandise marks.

13. Opium so far as regards sale for export.

14. Banking, that is to say, the co-ordination with the government of Pakistan of the conduct of banking business.

15. The law of insurance and the regulation of the conduct of insurance business.

16. Stock-exchange and future markets with objects and business not confined to 'AJK.'

17. Corporations, that is to say, the incorporation, regulation and winding up trading corporations including banking, insurance and financial corporations, but not including universities.

18. Planning for economic coordination, including planning and coordination of scientific and technological research.

19. Highways, continuing beyond the territory of 'AJK,' excluding roads declared by the Government of Pakistan to be strategic importance.

20. Council surveys including geological surveys and council meteorological organizations.

21. Works, lands and buildings vested in, or in possession of, the council for the purposes of the council (not being military, naval or air force) works but, as regards property situated in 'AJK,' subject always to law made by the legislative assembly, save in so far as law made by the council otherwise provides.

22. Census.

23. Establishment of standards of weights and measures.

24. Extension of the powers and jurisdiction of members of a police force belonging to 'AJK' or any province of Pakistan to any area in such Province or 'AJK,' but not so as to enable the police of 'AJK' or such province to exercise powers and jurisdiction in such province or 'AJK' without the consent of the government of that province or 'AJK,' extension of the powers jurisdiction of members of a police force belonging the 'AJK,' or a province of Pakistan to railway areas outside 'AJK' or that province.

25. Election to the council.

26. The salaries, allowances and privileges of the members of the council and advisors.

27. Railways.

28. Mineral oil and natural gas; liquids and substances declared by law made by the council to be dangerously inflammable.

29. Development of industries, where development under council control is declared by law made by the council to be expedient in the public interest.

30. Removal of prisoners and accused persons from 'AJK' to Pakistan or from Pakistan to 'AJK.'

31. Measures to combat certain offences committed in connection with matters concerning the council and the government and the establishment of a police force for that purpose or the extension to 'AJK' of the jurisdiction of a police force established in Pakistan for the investigation of offences committed in connection with matters concerning the government of Pakistan.

32. Prevention of the extension from 'AJK' to Pakistan or from Pakistan to 'AJK' of infectious or contagious diseases or pests affecting men, animals or plants.

33. Population planning and social welfare.

34. Boilers.

35. Electricity.

36. Newspapers, books and printing presses.

37. State property.

38. Curriculum, syllabus, planning, policy, centres of excellence and standards of education.

39. Sanctioning of cinematograph films for exhibition.

40. Tourism.

41. Duties of customs, including export duties.

42. Taxes on income other than agricultural income.

43 Taxes on corporations.

44. Taxes on the capital value of the assets, not including taxes on capital gains on immovable property.

45. Taxes and duties on the production capacity of any plant, machinery, undertaking, establishment or installation in

lieu of the taxes and duties specified in entries 42 and 43 or in lieu of either or both of them.

46. Terminal taxes on goods or passengers carried by railway or air; taxes on their fares and freights.

47. Fees in respect of any of the matters enumerated in this list but not including fees taken in any court.

48. Jurisdiction and powers of all courts with respect to any of the matters enumerated in this list.

49. Offences against laws with respect to any of the matters enumerated in this list.

50. Inquiries and statistics for the purposes of any of the matters enumerated in this list.

51. Matters which under the Act are within the legislative competence of the council or relates to the council.

52. Matters incidental or ancillary to any of the matters enumerated in this list.

Like previous constitutional acts, the act of 1974 has also made the 'AJK' government totally subservient to the government of Pakistan. It seems that the framers of this constitution have overlooked some of the contradictions that appeared in the body of its text. The preamble to the 'AJK' constitution of 1974 reads: "... the future status of the State of Jammu and Kashmir is yet to be determined in accordance with the freely expressed will of the people of the State through the democratic method of free and fair plebiscite under the auspices of the United Nations as envisaged in UNCIP Resolutions adopted from time to time."[5] The section 4, sub-section 7 (2) of the constitution reads: "no person or political party in Azad Jammu and Kashmir shall be permitted to propagate against, or take part in activities prejudicial or detrimental to, the ideology of State's accession to Pakistan."[6] A cursory glance of these two provisions shows the contradiction that characterizes the constitution of 'AJK.' On the one hand the constitution says that the future of the undivided J&K is yet to be determined, on the other hand it says that the state's official policy is to accede to Pakistan. A closer analysis of this constitution reveals that there are many such provisions that belie the oft-repeated statements of the leaders of Pakistan that the Kashmir issue must be resolved according to the wishes of the people.

While section 9 reads, "every state subject shall have the right to freedom of speech and expression...." section 4, sub-section 7 (2) commits every person and political party in 'AJK' to subscribe to the ideology of the state's accession to Pakistan. In the pursuance of this principle, many parties have been debarred to take part in the assembly elections because they refused to subscribe to this ideology. Justice Abdul Majid Mallick, the former chief justice of 'AJK' high court, during his interaction with the authors[7] admitted that this provision is futile so far fundamental rights of the people of 'AJK' are concerned. In 'AJK,' a person with requisite merit cannot get into the government service unless he abides by the principle of accession to Pakistan. It would be interesting to point out that the oaths taken by the prime minister and president of 'AJK' bears the mark of contradiction just mentioned above. Before looking at the oaths it would not be out of context to mention that Pakistan has more than once advocated the right to self determination to the people of Kashmir but two issues remain crucial. First, Pakistan does not favour an independent Kashmir. During one of his visits to 'AJK' in 1973 the then Prime Minister of Pakistan, Z. A. Bhutto had said in a rally in Muzaffarabad that he is having key to the problems of 'AJK' in form of three proposals excluding the independence option. Those proposals include: (a) 'AJK' to remain as it is; (b) it could be a full fledged province of Pakistan; and (c) it could have a provincial status. Besides disfavouring the independence as an option, Pakistan obliges the people of 'AJK' to abide to the ideology of acceding to Pakistan or to lose democratic rights whatever. The authors have the information that the text books for the primary school students in 'AJK' contain phrases like 'Kashmir *banega* Pakistan' (Kashmir will become part of Pakistan). Sub section 3 of section 31 of 'AJK' constitution reads, "neither the Council nor the Assembly shall have the power to make any law concerning- (a) the responsibilities of Government of Pakistan under UNCIP resolutions; (b) the defence and security of Azad Jammu and Kashmir; (c) the current coin or the issue of any bills, notes or other paper currency; or (d) the external affairs of Azad Jammu and Kashmir including foreign trade and foreign aid."[8]

The first schedule of the 'AJK' constitution deals with the oath of offices of president, prime minister, ministers, speaker, deputy speaker, members of legislative assembly, member of the council, advisor and judges of the supreme court and the high court. The accession to Pakistan has been made an important principle in the 'AJK' constitution and gets reflected in the oaths undertaken by the high officials of the entity. One paragraph of the oath to all these offices, except that of the judges of the supreme court and high court, reads, "... I will remain loyal to the country and to the cause of accession of the state of Jammu and Kashmir to Pakistan." This brings into picture the stark contrast between the pledge of the highest office bearers of 'AJK' to 'provide ever fresh fillip to freedom struggle to the people in Occupied Kashmir' (preface to the constitution, November 1990 edition) and their official commitment to accession of undivided J&K to Pakistan. Some writers argue that the 'overuse of rhetoric and emotion' has pushed Pakistan to a corner by locking it into an all-or-nothing position.[9] The sentiment that 'AJK' can provide 'fresh fillip to freedom struggle' has been exploited by the leaders and in the process the local people express discontent for their policies. Oaths taken by all the prominent office bearers of 'AJK' put forward two interesting things one being a short term arrangement and other one a long term goal. The oath of the president provides ample evidence in this extent, "..... That, as President of Azad Jammu and Kashmir I will remain loyal to the country and to the cause of accession of the State of Jammu and Kashmir to Pakistan...." First, all the persons at the helm of affairs would remain 'loyal' to the country with a confusion that the country means either 'AJK' or Pakistan. If former is considered true, which in all probability is meant by the oath then the second loyalty that is demanded makes it a short term arrangement. In other words, the loyalty to 'AJK country' would be only until the people of the undivided J&K exercise their right to self determination and expectedly showing their long term loyalty by acceding to Pakistan. Although the interim constitution of 1974 has been amended several times, the ideology principle remains the basis of power exercised by the government of 'AJK' within limits set by Pakistan.

While in modern state system religion is kept at a distance from political affairs, in case of 'AJK' the religious principle is very much apparent in its politics and constitutional edifice.[10] Section 3 of the 'AJK' constitution states, "Islam shall be the State religion of Azad Jammu and Kashmir."[11] A non-Muslim can not become president or prime minister. This is in quite contrast to the J&K constitution that does not profess any such religious discrimination as to the selection to high political offices. Article 25 of the J&K constitution reads, among other things, that "the State shall ... seek to foster brotherhood and equality among all communities under the aegis of a Secular state." The constitution of 'AJK' preaches supremacy of religion over legal matters. Section 31(5) says, "no law shall be repugnant to the teaching and requirements of Islam as set out in the Holy Quran and Sunnah and all existing laws shall be brought in conformity with the Holy Quran and Sunnah."[12]

There is the provision of a council of Islamic Ideology which decides matters as to "whether a proposed law is or is not repugnant to the injunctions of Islam." One-third of the members of either the assembly or council have to refer the matter in order to obtain advice of the council of Islamic ideology, which is required to furnish the advice within fifteen days.

'AJK' has its own supreme court as highest court of appeal alongside a high court and other lower courts. All appeals against 'AJK' court go to the supreme court of Pakistan, which makes sure that nothing is adjudicated in the state contrary to the policy of Islamabad. In fact, there is a dual judicial system. Judicial offices in districts, high courts and the supreme court have parallel Islamic judicial system dispensing sharia law. These judges deal with criminal cases involving sharia law. Other criminal cases and civil cases are heard by the judges possessing the law degrees. The chief justice of the supreme court is appointed by the president on the advice of the council headed by Pak prime minister. But the question then arises in case of tussle between the supreme court and the Islamic council regarding jurisdictions there seems to be no clear cut guidelines as to which one would prevail.

Unlike the constitution of 'AJK,' the constitution of J&K makes clear the relationship between the state and the Indian federation. Article 3 of the constitution reads, "the State of Jammu and Kashmir is and shall be an integral part of the Union of India."[13] The constituent assembly of the state, constituting the representatives of the people of the state, abided by the sanctity of the Instrument of Accession (that led to accession of the state to the Indian Union). Article 4 defines the territory of the state and reads, "The territory of the State shall comprise all the territories which on the fifteen day of August 1947, were under the sovereignty or suzerainty of the

Ruler of the State." Article 370 of the Indian constitution though admits special status makes the state an integral part of India.

A crucial difference between Indian and Pakistan position is that while India openly admits Kashmir as its integral part and claims the territory with Pakistan, Pakistan neither admits Kashmir across LOC as its part nor recognizes it as an independent entity in substance but maintains tight grip, thus creating much confusion. While on one hand Islamabad's relations with Muzaffarabad are termed as that of a federal government with its unit (most of the Pakistani and 'AJK' leaders as also newspapers usually use these terms), the 'AJK' constitution talks about right to self-determination of the Kashmiri people and its contradictory ideology of accession of Kashmir to Pakistan. Interestingly, recently a member of the legislative assembly of 'AJK' questioned the rationale behind referring Islamabad based government as federal government. His objection was however dismissed on flimsy ground.

Gilgit-Baltistan

Gilgit-Baltistan, more than five times the area of 'AJK,' has no constitutional status. Pakistan's approach to this area's status, that is legally part of undivided J&K, is beleaguered with contradictions. There is no mention of the region in Pakistan's constitution, besides the area being kept bereft of a provincial or even provisional provincial status. 'Yet it also treats it, for practical purposes, as Pakistani territory.' For instance, in 1977 the military ruler of Pakistan General Zia-ul-Haq imposed martial law on Gilgit-Baltistan like rest of Pakistan but not on 'AJK.' Pakistan has ambiguously maintained that this region is part of the disputed territory of Kashmir but not the part of 'AJK.' Pakistan calls this region Federally Administered Areas. The rationale in keeping the legal and constitutional status of the areas ambiguous while decorating 'AJK' with all institutions and organs found in a sovereign country is beyond logic. The argument that those areas, being part of a disputed territory cannot be accorded any status, makes the things more confusing since the same logic should have been applied in case of 'AJK' as both the regions are parts of erstwhile princely state of undivided J&K. Syed Jaffar Shah, President of Gilgit-Baltistan PPP, is quoted by ICG asking "If AJK could get so much without anything untoward happening to Pakistan and the Kashmir cause, then why should all hell break loose if the Northern Areas were given the same status?"[14]

'AJK,' much smaller than the Gilgit-Baltistan, has been decorated with mechanisms like legislative assembly, supreme court, prime minister, president, etc. It seems to be natural on part of the people of Gilgit-Baltistan to raise voices of dissent. The Miskeen case is one such example, in which the legal wrangle between the people of the area and Pakistan came to a shoddy end. The area, like the 'AJK' is a part of the Kashmir problem, and as per the UN resolutions it too is a part of the disputed Kashmir. The Pakistan constitution too admits the region to be disputed. In this context it becomes logical to ask: how can a region, which is disputed even by Pakistan standards, be directly governed by Islamabad? Pakistan has not declared the area as its part, but continues to exercise all powers over the region. There appears to be a design behind this policy: first to admit the area to be disputed because the UN says so, but at the same time use this same yardstick to control the area till the dispute is resolved without giving even the basic rights to the people inhabiting it. It is pertinent in this context to see this issue as not only a case of legal ambiguity but also denial of basic rights. Unlike 'AJK,' Gilgit-Baltistan lacks indigenous leadership that could fight for the region's interests. Close cultural and linguistic ties with Pakistan has provided an edge to 'AJK' to bargain with Pakistan at least on some counts. Gilgit-Baltistan has nothing in common with the rest of Pakistan but religion. There are differences even on that count as Gilgit-Baltistan is a Shia majority area while Pakistan is Sunni dominant. A recent ICG report observes there is widespread belief among the people that one of the main reasons for which Pakistan does not allow them basic rights is its fear of the Shia majority in the area.

Despite keeping a tight control over the area and using it for promoting its interests, the map of Kashmir published by the Pakistan continued to show Gilgit-Baltistan as part of 'AJK' until 1987. The ambiguity over the status of the Gilgit-Baltistan could be partly attributed to the changing stances of Pakistan. On many occasions Pakistan has accepted the area being a disputed territory. First, it accepted holding of plebiscite in the area along with whole of undivided J&K as per the UN resolution. Second, in the boundary agreement with China it agreed that the sovereignty of the area does not lie with it and any agreement on this area would only be provisional. Both these instances show Pakistan has earlier conceded that along with 'AJK' the area of Gilgit-Baltistan too is part of the undivided J&K. Strangely enough in the Miskeen case Pakistan refused to agree that 'AJK' and Gilgit-Baltistan should be unified. To add to ambiguity many times Pakistan shied away from its stance that Gilgit-Baltistan is part of undivided J&K. Many a times it treated the area as its part. There lacks a clear cut policy on part of Islamabad towards this area. It wants to make the area as its part but at the same time apprehends that any such move would weaken its case regarding the Kashmir conflict. This dilemma of Pakistan is appropriately described by an IPS task group report in following words:

"Pakistan's official policy seems subject to confusion and uncertainty, particularly after 1980. The main reason being the strategic importance of the Northern Areas and hence a section of the government of Pakistan has always wished that the areas be merged with Pakistan. In particular about Gilgit Agency the Interior and Foreign Ministries have since November 1947, been thinking on these lines. The Interior Ministry argues that the Agency has not been under administrative control of Maharaja Kashmir. The British held and administered these areas like other political agencies of the tribal areas. Hence, with the British gone, Gilgit Agency gets automatically transferred to Pakistan. And, as the people of the area have themselves opted to join Pakistan, the legal requirement has also been met.... The Foreign Office did not agree to the proposal at that time. It felt that be it for only name sake, but Maharaja Kashmir exercised authority over Gilgit, it should not therefore be considered independent of the state of Jammu and Kashmir. Also, the possibility of plebiscite under the auspices of United Nations was still there. Then why should the Gilgit Agency's 'vote bank' be lost? The above dilemma still persists, and can be seen in the initiatives of various government organs in their respective spheres. Gilgit Agency is sometimes shown on the survey maps, as part of Pakistan while on some other occasions it is clubbed with the disputed state of Jammu and Kashmir."[15]

It is beyond doubt that this deliberate ambiguity has been part of the strategy adopted by Pakistan to not only keep the people of the area deprived of rights but also to use the area to pursue its regional interests without apprehending any kind of resentment. The most notorious instance in this context is ceding substantial chunk of the area to China in early 1960s. Since the area lacked any kind of representation at local level or at Pakistan assembly thus a part of this gifted territory to Pakistan (by 'AJK' leadership through Karachi agreement) was further presented by Pakistan to its neighbouring country i.e. China. Interestingly in both the cases of 'philanthropy' the people of the area were neither consulted nor even informed.

Pakistan's ceding part of Gilgit-Baltistan to China can be questioned on the ground of legality of its authority to conclude the boundary agreement. On March 2, 1963 Pakistan violated the UNCIP resolution as well as the UNSC resolutions by handing about 5,180 sq. km. of territory under its occupation to China. It gave away the entire area belonging to Hunza, south of the Mintaka Pass, known as Shaksgam-Muztagh valley. This agreement added further confusion. While Pakistan under this agreement agreed that it had no legal right over the region as it was disputed, it gave away a substantial portion of it to China. India lodged protest against the agreement through a letter dated March 16, 1963 addressed to the president of the UNSC. The letter argued that the agreement was a violation of the resolutions of the UNSC and the UNCIP. The then Defence Minster of India, Krishna Menon in his speech in the UNSC argued, "Over and above all this then has occurred the situation in which Pakistan today- not for any good reason, but merely for nuisance value and as an instrument to put pressure on us- has entered into negotiations and, I believe, has concluded agreements with the Central Government of the People's Republic of China. That agreement is in total violation of any rights or authority Pakistan may posses, for Pakistan has no sovereignty over this State; it is not Pakistan's to trade away or to negotiate about. Secondly, it was not necessary even for considerations relating to Pakistan's own security." [16]

India also sent protest notes to Pakistan and China in May 1962. The note to China read, "In lodging an emphatic protest with the government of the People's Republic of China for this interference with the sovereignty of India over the State of Jammu and Kashmir, the Government of India solemnly warns the Government of China that any change, provisional or otherwise, in the status of the state of Jammu and Kashmir brought about by third parties which seek to submit certain parts of India territory to foreign jurisdiction will not be binding on the Government of India and that the Government of India firmly repudiate any agreements, provisional or otherwise, regarding her own territories arrived at between third parties who have no legal or constitutional *locus standi* of any kind."[17]

Ignoring India's genuine complaints Pakistan and China made their friendship strong by trading a portion of the

Kashmir territory. Below is the text of the Sino-Pak Border agreement 1963 through which Pakistan illegally ceded parts of Kashmir to China.

The Government of the People's Republic of China and the Government of Pakistan;

HAVING agreed, with a view to ensuring the prevailing peace and tranquility on the border, to formally delimit and demarcate the boundary between China's Sinkiang and the contiguous areas the defence of which is under the actual control of Pakistan, in a spirit of fairness, reasonableness, mutual understanding and mutual accommodation, and on the basis of the ten principles as enunciated in the Bandung conference.

Being convinced that this would not only give full expression to the desire of the people of China and Pakistan for the development of good neighbourly and friendly relations, but also help safeguard Asian and world peace.

Have resolved for this purpose to conclude the present agreement and have appointed as their respective plenipotentiaries the following.

For the Government of the People's Republic of China; Chen Yi, Minister of Foreign Affairs.

For the Government of the Pakistan Zulfikar Bhutto, Minister of External Affairs.

Who, having mutually examined their full powers and found them to be in good and due form have agreed upon following:

Article 1

In view of the fact that the boundary between China's Sinkiang and the contiguous areas the defence of which is under the actual control of Pakistan has never been formally delimited, two parties agree to delimit it on the basis of the traditional customary boundary line including features and in a spirit of equality, mutual benefit and friendly cooperation.

Article 2

In accordance with the principle expounded in Article 1 of the present agreement, the two parties have fixed as follows the alignment of the entire boundary line between China's Sinkiang and the contiguous areas the defence of which is under the actual control of Pakistan.

(1) Commencing from its north western extremity at height 5,630 metres (a peak the reference coordinates of which are approximately longitude 74 degrees 34 minutes east and latitude 37 degrees 3 minutes north), the boundary line runs generally eastward and then south-eastward strictly along the main watershed between the tributaries of the Tashkurgan river of the Tarim river system on the one hand on the tributes of the Hunza river of the Indus river system on the other hand, passing through the Kilik Daban (Dawan), the Mintake Daban (pass), the Kharchanai Daban (named on the Chinese map only), the Mutsgila Daban (named on the Chinese map only) and the Parpik Pass (named on the Pakistan map only) and reaches the Khunjerab (Yutr) Daban (Pass).

(2) After passing through the Kunjerab (Yutr) Daban (pass) the boundary line runs generally southward along the above-mentioned main watershed upto a mountain-top south of the Daban (pass), where it leaves the main watershed to follow the crest of a spur lying generally in a south-easterly direction, which is the watershed between the Akjilga river (a nameless corresponding river on the Pakistan map) on the one hand, and the Taghumbash (Oprang) river and the Koliman Su (Orang Jilga) on the other hand. According to the map of the

Chinese side, the boundary line, after leaving the south-eastern extremity of the spur, runs along a small section of the middle line of the bed of the Koliman Su to reach its confluence with the Elechin river. According to the map of the Pakistan side, the boundary line, after leaving the south-eastern extremity of this spur, reaches the sharp bend of the Shaksgam of Muztagh river.

(3) From the aforesaid point, the boundary lines runs up the Kelechin river (Shaksgam or Muztagh river) along the middle line of its bed its confluence (reference coordinates approximately longitude 76 degrees 2 minutes east and latitude 36 degrees 26 minutes north) with the Shorbulak Daria (Shimshal river or Braldu river).

(4) From the confluence of the aforesaid two rivers, the boundary line, according to the map of the Chinese side, ascends the crest of a spur and runs along it to join the Karakoram range main watershed at a mountain-top (reference coordinates approximately longitude 75 degrees 54 minutes east and latitude 36 degrees 15 minutes north) which on this map is shown as belonging to the Shorgulak mountain. According to the map of the Pakistan side, the boundary line from the confluence of the above mentioned two river ascends the crest of a corresponding spur and runs along it, passing through height 6.520 meters (21,390 feet) till it joins the Karakoram range main watershed at a peak (reference coordinates approximately longitude 75 degrees 57 minutes east and latitude 36 degrees 3 minutes north).

(5) Thence, the boundary line, running generally southward and then eastward strictly follows the Karakoram range main watershed which separates the Tarim river drainage system from the Indus river drainage system, passing through the east Mustagh pass (Muztagh pass), the top of the Chogri peak (K-2) the top of the broad peak,

the top of the Gasherbrum mountain (8,068), the Indirakoli pass (names of the Chinese maps only) and the top of the Teramn Kankri peak, and reaches its south-eastern extremity at the Karakoram pass. Then alignment of the entire boundary line as described in section one of this article, has been drawn on the one million scale map of the Pakistan side in English which are signed and attached to the present agreement. In view of the fact that the maps of the two sides are not fully identical in their representation of topographical features the two parties have agreed that the actual features on the ground shall prevail, so far as the location and alignment of the boundary described in section one is concerned, and that they will be determined as far as possible by beginning survey on the ground.

Article 3

The two parties have agreed that:

(i) Wherever the boundary follows a river, the middle line of the river bed shall be the boundary line; and that

(ii) Wherever the boundary passes through a deban (pass) the water-parting line thereof shall be the boundary line.

Article 4

Once the two parties have agreed to set up, as soon as possible, a joint boundary demarcation commission, each side will appoint a chairman, one or more members and a certain number of advisers and technical staff. The joint boundary demarcation commission is charged with the responsibility in accordance with the provisions of the present agreement, to hold concrete discussions on and carry out the following tasks jointly.

(1) To conduct necessary surveys of the boundary area on the ground, as stated in Article two of the present

agreement so as to set up boundary markers at places considered to be appropriate by the two parties and to delineate the boundary line of the jointly prepared accurate maps.

To draft a protocol setting forth in detail the alignment of the entire boundary line and the location of all the boundary markers and prepare and get printed detailed maps, to be attached to the protocol, with the boundary line and the location of the boundary markers shown on them.

(2) The aforesaid protocol, upon being signed by representatives of the governments of the two countries, shall become an annex to the present agreement, and the detailed maps shall replace the maps attached to the present agreement.

(3) Upon the conclusion of the above-mentioned protocol, the tasks of the joint boundary demarcation commission shall be terminated.

Article 5

The two parties have agreed that any dispute concerning the boundary which may arise after the delimitation of boundary line actually existing between the two countries shall be settled peacefully by the two parties through friendly consultations.

Article 6

The two parties have agreed that after the settlement of the Kashmir dispute between Pakistan and India, the sovereign authority concerned will reopen negotiations with the Government of the People's Republic of China on the boundary as described in Article two of the present agreement, so as to sign a formal boundary treaty to replace the present agreement, provided that in the event of the sovereign authority being

Pakistan, the provisions of the present agreement and of the aforesaid protocol shall be maintained in the formal boundary treaty to be signed between the People's Republic of China and Pakistan.

Article 7

The present agreement shall come into force on the date of its signature.

Done in duplicate in Peking on the second day of March 1963, in the Chinese and English languages, both sides being equally authentic.

The Miskeen case

The Miskeen case is an important landmark in the history of Gilgit-Baltistan as far as its status is concerned. The filing of the petition, verdict of the case and the later happenings- all clearly portray ambiguity on part of Pakistan in defining the status of this area. In 1993 Malik Mohammad Miskeen and Haji Amir Jan from Gilgit-Baltistan, and Sheikh Abdul Aziz from Muzaffarabad in their petition to the 'AJK' High Court challenged the context due to which Pakistan was domineering the Gilgit-Baltistan area of undivided J&K and pleaded for its return to 'AJK.' It would not be out of context to have a look on some of the relevant portions of the detailed verdict of the 'AJK' High Court judges headed by Justice Mallick who later regretted the non implementation of the verdict in a personal interview with the authors. The verdict of handing over the area to 'AJK' was considered by Islamabad as an infringement of its sovereign right. The excerpts:[18]

The petition raises very crucial proposition in respect of administrative, political and geographic status of the Northern Areas. The settlement of the proposition is desired in the manner as to whether Northern Areas formed part of the State of Jammu and Kashmir, on August 15, 1947, at the time of emergence of Pakistan (independence of the sub-continent) and earlier. In case of positive answer, whether these areas should be annexed to Azad Jammu and Kashmir and be brought under the administrative control of the Azad Government of the State of Jammu and Kashmir, is the main relief sought in the petition. Resting the controversy on the aforesaid premises, it is desired that direction may be issued to the Government of Pakistan, through Secretary Kashmir Affairs and Northern Areas Division, Islamabad, to explain as to under what authority of law, it administered the said areas; to direct the Azad Government of the State of Jammu and Kashmir to take over administration of the areas and to create administrative and judicial machinery therein by providing due representation to the people of the areas in the Azad Jammu and Kashmir Legislative Assembly and the Council, and restoration of civil liberties and rights admissible to the people of Azad Jammu and Kashmir.

In support of the claim of the petitioners, it was stated that the geographical status of Northern Areas, for being integral part of Jammu and Kashmir State (as it existed on August 15, 1947 at the time of independence of the sub-continent and emergence of sovereign States of Pakistan and India), was acknowledged, among others, by the provisions of the Sino-Pakistan Agreement of 1963. Reference was made to the provisions of the constitution of Pakistan, 1973, to establish that these were not part of Pakistan.

It was further alleged that the Northern Areas formed part of Azad Jammu and Kashmir as defined in the Interim Constitution Act, 1974.... In that respect, reference was also made to the preamble of the Interim Constitution Act, 1974. It was claimed that the Northern Areas were being administratively controlled by respondent No. 1 (Pakistan) without any lawful authority and the State Subjects residing in those areas were being dealt with in an uncivic manner as no democratic institutions were established there. The Azad

Government of the State of Jammu and Kashmir, it was claimed, failed in its duty and constitutional obligations to acquire its administrative control of the areas and to provide civil facilities to its citizens living in the said areas. The petitioners also referred to their efforts in approaching the authorities in Pakistan and Azad Jammu and Kashmir for the redress of their grievance, without success, and claimed that they were constrained to invoke the jurisdiction of this court under aforesaid conditions.

The Azad Government of the State of Jammu and Kashmir, in its written statement, averred that the petition in the present form was not maintainable. It was explained that some unnecessary parties were impleaded, as such the petition was not maintainable for misjoinder of parties. It was admitted that the Northern Areas were historically part of Jammu and Kashmir State and the administration of these areas was being controlled by the Government of Pakistan in the light of the agreement entered into between the Government of Pakistan and the Azad Government of the State on April 28, 1949. It was further explained that the letters addressed by the President and Prime Minister of Azad Jammu and Kashmir and press statements issued by them, were a clear manifestation of the fact that the President of Azad Jammu and Kashmir was of definite view that the Northern Areas were part of Jammu and Kashmir. The written statement was signed by the Advocate General who was instructed through a letter, No. MQ/3518-24/91 of November 10, 1991.

(i) We have already partly analyzed the nature of the parties and the subject matter in issue. In absence of denial by the petitioners, it has to be accepted that the petition addressed by Qurban Ali and others is subjudice before the Lahore High Court, awaiting its decision. In such situation, it has to be settled whether the present petition is maintainable on not. Our answer to the objection is that the petition under consideration may not be thrown away simply on account of institution of another petition before another High Court.

It is relevant to state here that the subject matter relating to administrative control of Gilgit and Ladakh, as contained in the agreement, not been excluded expressly out of the purview of administration of the Government and the legislative authority of the Assembly (of 'AJK'). In other words, the Government of Pakistan has not retained the administrative control of Gilgit and Ladakh within the scheme of the Act 1974. In this view of the situation, the administrative control of the Northern Areas, ipso facto, reverted to the jurisdiction of Azad Government. That being the position, on enforcement of Act 1970 and thereafter the Interim Constitution Act 1974, the administrative control of the Northern Areas should have been automatically taken over by the Azad Government and the people of the Northern Areas should have been provided their share of representation in the Government, the Assembly, the Council and civil services. The omission on the part of the Government to take over administration by providing representation to the people of the Northern Areas in the aforesaid institutions, appears the result of inaptitude and lack of care.

The omission to include the administrative control of these areas within the purview of jurisdiction of Pakistan, to exclusion of Azad Government, was deliberate and purposeful, under these resolutions and acceptance of the same by the Pakistan Government. We have already analyzed that the Northern Areas are part of Jammu and Kashmir State. These areas were liberated by the people of the State in 1947 and this position was acknowledged by the government of Pakistan at all levels including its stance at the Security Council. The Security Council and the members of the United Nations Commission for India and Pakistan equally recognized such position of the Northern Areas, in their deliberations and decisions. Therefore, suffice it to say that the Act of 1974, by implication, repealed the agreement of 1949. That agreement carries no legal weight as such.

It is noticed elsewhere that in the written statement, the Azad Government and All Jammu and Kashmir Muslim Conference expressly averred that on enforcement of the Interim Constitution Act, it was enjoined upon the Government of Pakistan to restore the administrative control of the Northern Areas to the Azad Government. The averments supplemented our interpretation of the provisions of the Act and the agreement. All Jammu and Kashmir Conference being privy to the promulgation and enforcement of Acts 1970 and 1974, was in a much better position to appreciate the implications of conditions relating to distribution of administrative sphere of jurisdiction described in the aforesaid agreement. In its written statement, the Muslim Conference has taken a definite stand and averred that the administrative control of the Northern Areas was likely to revert to the Azad Government on enforcement of the Act 1970 and Act 1974. In support of its aforesaid view, a letter addressed by the President of Azad Jammu and Kashmir to the President of Pakistan was appended with the written statement. An identical stand has been taken by the Azad government. The stance taken by the Azad Government and the Muslim Conference is quite compatible and in agreement with the view of this Court.

The agreement, as it appeared in its scheme, phraseology used therein and division of spheres of jurisdiction, reflected its character as an ad hoc or transitional arrangement. It served its purpose till such time the Azad Government, with the approval of Pakistan Government, enforced its own Rules of Business, subsequently amended and superseded by Acts 1960, 1964, 1968, 1970 and 1974. A transitional arrangement relating to distribution of administrative jurisdiction and authority of

remains that these areas are admittedly not part of Pakistan. Likewise, the respondent has failed to explain as to why the residents of these areas may be kept deprived of the benefits of fundamental rights, civil liberties and right of their representation in the government and other national institutions. In absence of an express answer to the averment, it has to be believed that the respondent has impliedly admitted the claim of the petitioners in that respect.

We accordingly accept the petition and direct:

(i) (a) the Azad Government to immediately assume the administrative control of the Northern Areas and annex it with the administration of Azad Jammu and Kashmir;

(b) the Government of Pakistan to provide an adequate assistance and facility to the Azad Government in attainment of the said objective.

(ii) the residents (State subjects) of the Northern Areas shall enjoy the benefit of the fundamental rights conferred by the Act, 1974. They shall be provided representation in:

(a) the Government

(b) the Assembly

(c) the Council;

(d) the Civil Services; and

(e) other national institutions, in due course of law.

(iii) Azad Government shall take steps to establish administrative and judicial set up in the Northern Areas within the framework of the Interim Constitution Act.

The above mentioned excerpts clearly put forward that the area of Gilgit-Baltistan was part of undivided J&K. Interestingly, in the high court Pakistan not only refused to accept the authority of 'AJK' over Gilgit-Baltistan but also objected to the jurisdiction of the court hearing the case. It also denied the execution of the Karachi agreement though 'AJK' accepted the execution of the same in the court. 'AJK' government though objected the petition but admitted that Gilgit-Baltistan were historically part of erstwhile princely state of J&K. Nevertheless, the court observed that Pakistan has no jurisdiction outside its territory. Predictably, Pakistan opposed this verdict and as per its wishes the 'AJK' government appealed against the verdict in the supreme court, which annulled the high court's verdict declaring that the region is part of the undivided J&K but not that of 'AJK.' Announcing its decision on September 14, 1994, the court said, "no doubt, that Northern Areas are part of the state of Jammu and Kashmir – but not of Azad Kashmir. Therefore, the government need not take administrative control of these areas."[19] This judgment, though contradictory in itself, made clear that the areas are also not part of Pakistan and hence, the 'takeover of these areas is without legal or constitutional authority.'

Gilgit-Baltistan were put under direct control of Pakistan very next day of its declaration of 'independence' but later to legitimize its direct control Pakistan signed a dubious Karachi Agreement in April 1949 with 'AJK.' However, as mentioned earlier, Sardar Ibrahim publicly stated in the year 2003 that he did not sign the agreement. Even Islamabad has denied the signing of the agreement on more than one occasion thus creating doubts about the whole episode. Interesting enough there was no person from Gilgit-Baltistan as party or signatory to it. The deliberate omission of a representative from Gilgit-Baltistan at the time of the signing of the agreement might not appear surprising as Pakistan's design on this area became clear later. Neither 'AJK' government has any representation from the area in its government nor constitutionally is it empowered to represent the region. The question thus arises: how can the leaders from 'AJK' hand over Gilgit-Baltistan to Pakistan? Hence, the legality of this agreement is questioned. Asadullah Khan, a former president of the Gilgit-Baltistan Bar Association is quoted by an ICG report saying, "Who gave Azad Kashmir the right to determine our political destiny? The Karachi Agreement was nothing more than a sale of human beings, in which Pakistan and Azad Kashmir were customers, and we were the commodity on sale."[20] People of the area, objecting on the Karachi agreement, argue that 'it was an agreement among three non-native individuals who had no authority to take such a decision on their behalf.' Questioning the right of signatories to decide their fate, a leader from Gilgit-Baltistan argued, "Who are these people? The people of the Northern Areas don't know them. We did not cast a vote for Ghulam Abbas or Ibrahim. There was no Muslim Conference, and there is still no Muslim Conference in Gilgit. So how can the head of the Muslim Conference sign an agreement with Pakistan about that area?"[21] A letter was written by the president of 'AJK' to the president of Pakistan on March 17, 1989 wherein it was emphasized that there was a large scale discrimination faced by the people living in Gilgit-Baltistan. As per the letter, the area was handed over temporarily to Pakistan 'because of logistics problem; because of its geographical situation and because of Pakistan's security interest in view of the threat from communism.' Pakistan did not bother to give any heed to the letter asking for handing over the area back to 'AJK.'

Earlier 'AJK' assembly has also passed a resolution demanding the return of the area which had been taken over 'temporarily' by Pakistan under the Karachi Agreement, a demand Pakistan chose to ignore. The resolution read: "In the opinion of this House, it was a historical reality that Gilgit and Baltistan form part of the state of Jammu and Kashmir.... This House demands from the government of Pakistan, that Gilgit and

Baltistan be given representation in the Azad Jammu and Kashmir Legislative Assembly. To provide political and social justice to the people of the area, the Azad Kashmir High Court's jurisdiction be extended to Northern Areas so that the people of the area avail the benefit of freedom and enabled to shoulder future responsibilities."

The HRCP in its report titled *A Strong Yearning for Autonomy*, published in 2006, has observed that Pakistan did not define the constitutional status of Gilgit-Baltistan deliberately as part of its strategy on Kashmir. Authorities in Islamabad believe that in the event of a plebiscite the vote of the people of Gilgit-Baltistan could be crucial. The report observed, "The Pakistani establishment believes that if and when the plebiscite under the UN resolution is held, the votes of the people of the Northern Areas can play a decisive role because these areas were a part of the State of Kashmir under the Dogra maharaja."[22] Though the area is not expressly mentioned in the constitution of Pakistan, by virtue of Article 1 (2) (d) Gilgit-Baltistan is treated as its part for all practical purposes. Some of the recommendations of the report were:

(1) The area may be declared as a special area... with its own government, legislature, independent judiciary and guaranteeing the people certain fundamental rights that can not be taken away by ordinary legislation.

(2) Even if the people of the area are not given representation in parliament, the Gilgit-Baltistan council should be granted some legislative authority to begin with. The people of the area should be accorded some share in power, if not complete power.

(3) Participation in government would considerably decrease the sense of political deprivation and frustration that is currently fanning sectarian violence. It will broaden the vision of the local leaders and enable them to rise above

petty sectarian issues. The man in the street will also get a sense of participation.

(4) Administrators who view things differently and are concerned mainly with law and order are now dealing with sectarian clashes, but a democratically elected or representative authority would be in a better position to settle the issues.

(5) A high court should be established with writ jurisdiction similar to that provided under Article 199 of the Pakistani constitution complete with jurisdiction to enforce fundamental rights provided under the instrument itself. Judges should hold tenure posts and should be free of all kinds of executive pressures. The high court should exercise control and superintendence over all subordinate courts in the area.

In May 1999, the supreme court of Pakistan delivered a landmark judgment on the constitutional status of the area in response to Constitutional Petition 17 of 1994, which sought among others the declaration of the constitutional status of Gilgit-Baltistan. In its 42-pages judgment of May 28, 1999, the court directed the government of Pakistan to initiate appropriate administrative/legislative measures within a period of six months to make necessary amendments in the Constitution/ relevant statute/ statues/ order/ orders/ rules/ notification/ notifications, to ensure that the people of Northern Areas enjoy their fundamental rights, namely, to be governed through their chosen representatives and to have access to justice through an independent judiciary inter alia for enforcement of their Fundamental Rights.[23]

Yet, there was no genuine attempt from Islamabad to implement the judgment. With Bhasha dam controversy bringing forth the plight of the people of Gilgit-Baltistan to the forefront, as a face saving gesture it was announced in January 2007 that a package of constitutional reforms would be introduced in the area and the package is in the final stages of preparation. As per the reports, it was supposed to be approved immediately after its completion.[24] The passing months with no further information on the issue as also the apprehension about the extent Pakistan would allow Gilgit-Baltistan to taste democracy, freedom and identity; it seems that the things would remain obscure as earlier.

References

1. The then President of 'AJK', Sardar Ibrahim Khan is reported to have stated, "Please do not blame me for this sin...I did not sign it (the Karachi Agreement). I want to clear my name while I am alive." This has led to doubt regarding the authenticity of the Karachi Agreement. For his statement see, *The Kashmir Times*, May 5, 2003.
2. Raja Abbas Khan, *Real Azad Kashmir,* 1969, p. 3. (place of publication not mentioned).
3. Quoted in Prem Nath Bazaz, *The History of Struggle for Freedom in Kashmir* (Srinagar: Gulshan Publishers and Exporters, 2003), pp. 659-660.
4. *The Azad Jammu and Kashmir Interim Constitution Act, 1974* (Muzafarrabad: Azad Government of the State of J&K, 1990), pp. 49-52.
5. *Ibid.*, p. 1.
6. *Ibid*, p. 6.
7. Interview with Justice Mallick on August 6, 2006. For details of the interview see *Across LOC* , vol. 1, no. 2, pp. 11-13.
8. *The Azad Jammu and Kashmir Interim Constitution Act,* n. 4, p. 24.
9. Rashed Rahman, "Nothing left to lose." *http://www.himalmag.com/99May/lose.htm*. Accessed on April 25, 2007.

10. Debidatta Aurobinda Mahapatra, "Pakistan-Occupied Kashmir: Myth vs. Reality," *Across LOC*, vol. 1, no.1, April-June 2005, pp. 2-5.
11. *The Azad Jammu and Kashmir Interim Constitution Act,* n. 4, p. 4.
12. *Ibid.*, p. 24.
13. *The Constitution of Jammu and Kashmir* (Jammu: Law Department Codification Cell, 2003), p. 3.
14. "Discord in Pakistan's Northern Areas," *ICG Asia Report No. 131,* Brussels/Islamabad, April 2, 2007.
15. Khalid Rahman and Ershad Mahmud, "Northern Areas of Pakistan – Facts, Problems and Recommendations," *IPS Task Force Report*, p. 138.
16. Sisir Gupta, *Kashmir: A Study in India-Pakistan Relations* (New Delhi: Asia Publishing House, 1966), p. 428.
17. *Ibid.*
18. For details see the 'AJK' High Court Verdict on Gilgit-Baltistan.
19. *The News*, September 15, 1994.
20. *ICG Asia Report No. 131*, n. 14.
21. Interview of Nawaz Khan Naji. *http://www.hvk.org/articles/0304/116.html*. Accessed on October 29, 2005.
22. Human Rights Commission of Pakistan, *A Strong Yearning for Autonomy*, 2006.
23. "The Decision of Supreme Court of Pakistan," May 28, 1999, *Supreme Court Monthly Review*, vol. 32, p. 1401
24. Muhammad Yasin, "N. Areas representatives to get constitutional powers," *Dawn*, January 17, 2007.

3

Politics and Governance

As India and Pakistan have entered into the 'irreversible' peace process despite perceptible hinges, sooner or later the question of Kashmir will take the centre-stage. In this context it is important to keep in view that the Kashmir issue does not revolve around only the Kashmir valley or J&K but also include the parts across the LOC. The current discourse on Kashmir remains distorted as the happenings across LOC remain almost shadowed. While the happenings in J&K get a stymied focus in international fora, a little comes to light about the happenings in 'AJK' and Gilgit-Baltistan. It was the October 2005 earthquake which brought international attention to the region, till then it got scarcely focused as a haven of terrorists. To suit its strategic interests Pakistan divided the region in two parts. Gilgit-Baltistan, named 'NA,' remains deprived of basic rights. Another part, christened as 'Azad Kashmir,' continues to remain a dependency of Pakistan with a very ambiguous status. The legal constitutional aspects of these areas have been analyzed in the previous chapter. The present chapter endeavours to extend it further by focusing on politics and style of governance in the region. The 2006 elections in 'AJK' further necessitate such a study wherein people were not only denied right to elect their own government, but subjected to severe restrictions on other basic rights such as right to free expression of dissent. Even a cursory look at the political set up in Gilgit-Baltistan shows that things are far worse in the area.

History of Governance

The history of politics in 'AJK' shows that the survival of governments in the region depends upon Islamabad. It is said farcical elections are held in the area intermittently to buttress the fiction of its *azadi* (independence).[1] 'AJK' politics remains a closed one as those who do not religiously adhere to the lines of Pakistan find no place. The weak political system that prevails in the area alongside the strong hold of Pakistan is clearly reflected in a report published in *Viewpoint* published from Lahore. It reads, "Azad Kashmir's fractionalized political leadership seems incapable of evolving a political pattern that would give its people a reasonable good government; and even if they were willing to try it was not certain that Islamabad would let them do so for fear of losing control of the territory."[2] 'AJK' has been effectively governed through the KANA in Islamabad which was formed in 1952. Since 1947 till 1960 Pakistan appointed presidents from the MC cadre which followed the ideology of accession of Kashmir to Pakistan. The people of the area had no role in either their appointment or dismissal. With the commencement of interim constitution in 1974, the electoral process has been officially tagged to the ideology of accession.

The interim constitution provided for many provisions comprising a sovereign state, a legislative assembly, periodic elections, a prime minister, an indirectly elected president, an independent judiciary and local government institutions. All this notwithstanding, the area remain under Pakistan's strict control with virtually no real sovereignty of its own. Hence the electoral politics too is not only guided but guarded one wherein an elected government cannot dare go against wishes of Islamabad.[3] The area 'remains for all intents and purposes under Pakistan's strict control, exercising no real sovereignty of its own. From the outset, the institutional set up in the territory was designed to ensure Pakistan's control of the area's affairs.' Because of highly imbalanced division of power with Pakistan, the elected leaders of 'AJK' remain only titular heads while Islamabad enjoys the real power with the help of a compliant 'AJK' administration wherein all the high officials are at deputation from Pakistan. As per the HRW report, "Power in Azad Kashmir is exercised primarily through the Pakistani army's General Headquarters in Rawalpindi, just outside Islamabad, and its corps commander based in the hill station of Murree, two hours by road from Muzaffarabad. It is widely understood in Pakistan and privately admitted by virtually all politicians from Azad Kashmir that the corps commander in Murree is known to summon the Azad Kashmir prime minister, president and other government officials regularly to outline the military's views on all political and governance issues in the territory."[4] Since late 1980s the Pakistan military has virtually taken over 'AJK' with the government, irrespective of any party, obeying the formers' orders. Since the time when Pakistan launched a proxy war in J&K the 'AJK' government has been deprived of whatever little powers it enjoyed earlier. With 'struggle in Kashmir on' there is complete control of Pak military, ISI and ISI backed terrorist organizations in 'AJK.'

The politics in the area can best be characterized by pendulum of ambiguity wherein on the one hand elections are held in the area on an almost regular basis but the elected governments of this *'azad'* country are dismissed arbitrarily by another country, Pakistan. Under article 56 of the 1974 constitution, Islamabad can dismiss any elected government in 'AJK' irrespective of the support it may enjoy in the legislative assembly. It reads, nothing shall ".... prevent the Government of Pakistan from taking such action as it may consider necessary or expedient for the effective discharge of those responsibilities."[5] Since the commencement of the interim constitution in 1974, the main executive authority in 'AJK' rests with the council of which the Pakistani prime minister is the chairman. He dominates the council with the power of nominating six members. Each executive head of Pakistan, be it democratically elected or the military one, did exactly what they wanted in 'AJK.' The actions ranged from imposing martial law to formation of desired government; from suspension of political activities to sacking the elected president/prime minister. The history of 'AJK' electoral politics is replete with such instances. The observation of Shabir Chowdhary, Chairman of International Kashmir Alliance is noteworthy in this context. To quote him, "History of Azad Kashmir is witness to this fact that whoever has ruled Pakistan has also appointed a puppet of his/her choice in Azad Kashmir that he could look after interests of Pakistan. In fact the very first President of Azad Kashmir was installed as a president after abolishing 'Provisional Government' of Azad Kashmir on 24th October 1947; and according to first President's own admission late at night on 23rd October he was told by Commissioner for Rawalpindi and others that he would be President from tomorrow."[6]

Since the Karachi agreement of 1949 the 'AJK' president and the prime minister have enjoyed only titular power. It clearly gave an upper hand to Islamabad. A former president of 'AJK' quoted in the HRW report told that the governments of 'AJK' are 'by the Pakistanis, for Pakistan.' He also pointed to the striking continuity of the old princely system under British rule because of Islamabad's 'viceroy' role generally and the maintenance of the traditional *biradari* system locally.[7] The agreement of 1949 proved to be a milestone since it institutionalized the subservience of 'AJK' to Pakistan. The agreement between Pakistan and the MC handed over important matters to Islamabad with only minimal powers to 'AJK.' Residual powers were kept vague. The 'AJK' government was saddled with overseeing general supervision of the administration. The Chief Plebiscite Officer appointed by Islamabad and notified as the Chief Advisor to the Government of Pakistan, ex-officio, controlled all the levers of power in the initial stages. This Joint Secretary level officer was the de-facto ruler of 'AJK' for almost two decades, owing no responsibility to the 'AJK' government.

Most of the heads of government in 'AJK' were appointed and dismissed by Islamabad at will. A cursory look at the tenures of a majority of the heads of government is a testimony to this. The so called independent government of 'AJK' was announced on October 24, 1947 headed by Sardar Ibrahim Khan. When Chowdhary Ghulam Abbas, another prominent leader of MC also migrated to 'AJK' from J&K, a formula was evolved by Pakistan on the basis of which Sardar Khan continued as president and Chowdhary Abbas was appointed as the supreme head of the government. Thus, after so-called liberation in 1947, a presidential form of government was established but later on in 1948 Chowdhary Ghulam Abbas became supreme head. The Rules of Business in early 1950s were treated as constitution which provided that president and prime minister would be answerable to the supreme head and were to hold office at his pleasure. The executive and legislative authority was vested in the president, appointed by Islamabad. In October 1952, these rules were revised and, as per the revision, the president had to hold office during the pleasure of MC in letter and that of KANA in spirit. The office of supreme head that existed earlier and had the power to approve the legislation of 'AJK' was abolished in 1952 and president became the executive head. These rules were further amended in 1957. Ali Ahmad Shah replaced Sardar Ibrahim and remained in office from May 1950 to December 1951 as president. The government of Mirwaiz Yusuf Shah who took oath of president on December 5, 1951 lasted till June 21, 1952. Later Sher Ahmed Khan was sworn in as president who survived up to May 31, 1956 and again Mirwaiz Yusuf Shah was made president on June 1, 1956. He remained in office until September 6, 1956. On September 7, 1956 Sardar Abdul Qayuum Khan was appointed president and removed even before completing one year in office on April 13, 1957. Sardar Ibrahim Khan was sworn in as president on April 14, 1957. His government lasted up to April 26, 1959. Under the system that prevailed from 1947 to 1960, theoretically the person having the confidence of the MC was nominated president by Islamabad though in practice it was the choice of Islamabad tacitly agreed by the MC.

When General Ayub Khan took power and unseated president Iskander Mirza in Islamabad, political activities were banned in 'AJK.' Once confident enough of no opposition in implementing his rules, Ayub conceived the idea of basic democracies. This system provided that only people, who fulfil certain criteria like basic education, or income levels, should be allowed to exercise franchise, envisaged to keep the electoral politics in the controllable limits. The basic democracies were extended to 'AJK' in 1960 through the Azad J&K Basic Democracies Act. It provided for provision of presidential elections through the votes of basic democrats alongside a council that too was to be elected by indirect elections. For the first time, the 'AJK' president and the 'AJK' council were to be elected through the indirect means of basic democracies. The council consisted of 12 members elected by the people of 'AJK' and 'refugees,' state subjects settled elsewhere in Pakistan. It, however, remained a mere advisory body being subordinate to the chief advisor to the Ministry of KANA. It enjoyed no legislative powers. In 1964, the system was replaced by Azad J&K Government Act, 1964 whereby the eight out of 12 state councillors were to be elected by the basic democrats. Again in 1965, a provision of nomination of two members by president from amongst the 'refugees' was made. K. H. Khurshid who was appointed the president in April 27, 1959 was for the first time elected in 1961 through an electoral college of 1200 indirectly elected Basic Democrats in 'AJK' and another 1200 who represented 'refugees' in Pakistan. Khurshid was the first elected president of 'AJK.' He was forced to resign on August 5, 1964 by a mid-level police official and later jailed in Palandri and Dalai camp. He was replaced by Khan Abdul Hamid Khan on August 6, 1964. Khan remained in office up to October 7, 1969.

A new government Act of 1968 provided setting of new council consisting of twelve members among which 8 were elected from 'AJK' region and 4 from among the 'refugees.' The refugee members were not elected but nominated by the chief advisor on the recommendation of 'AJK' president. The chairman of the council elected by the councillors was also the ex-officio president. Ayub Khan resigned in April 1969 and succeeded by General Yahya Khan who imposed martial law in Pakistan. Accordingly, government changed in 'AJK' and Brigadier Abdul Rehman succeeded Hamid Khan. Later elections were announced under Act of 1970. This Act for the first time after more than two decades provided for adult franchise to the people of 'AJK' to elect the legislative members and the president. Under the new directions from Islamabad the practice of presidents' selection was abolished and a provision of 25-member assembly, comprising 24 elected members and one nominated women member, was introduced. The elections under this arrangement led to the election of MC candidate Sardar Abdul Qayuum Khan as president. Sardar Qayuum became president on November 12, 1970 and remained in office until April 16, 1975 after Yahya Khan introduced presidential form of government. Direct elections of president of 'AJK' were held on October 30, 1970. Qayuum is 'credited to raise the status of 'AJK' government from municipal level to that of provincial level.'[8] He was later dismissed during Zulfikar Ali Bhutto's government from 1972-77 in Islamabad. On April 16, 1975 the 'AJK' legislative assembly passed a vote of no confidence against the president and he was succeeded by Manzar Masood, Speaker of the house. He held office until May 29, 1975 when Sardar Ibrahim was made president and Abdul Hamid Khan prime minister.

In June 1974 in a meeting chaired by Bhutto a new interim constitution of so called Azad Kashmir was passed that made the prime minister the executive head. Since then prime minister is elected by the members of legislature. Under the interim constitution, the prime minister is the chief executive and the president is the constitutional head. It provided for legislative assembly of 42 members. Also, a council was formed, with the prime minister of Pakistan as chairman and the 'AJK' president as vice-chairman. Islamabad could nominate five members to the council who had to be essentially members of the Pakistan national assembly. The chairman, along with these five federal nominees, gave Islamabad leverage in the council.[9] This council has rightly been described 'supra power' body by the high court of 'AJK' in spite of parliamentary form of government in the region. The council's decisions are final and not subject to judicial review. 'AJK' followed a multi-tiered system of local governance with 202 Union Councils, ten Town Committees, fifty Markaz Councils, two Municipal Corporations, eleven Municipal Committees, nineteen sub-divisions, and 1,646 villages. All key administrative offices are but manned by Pakistani officials. These include the office of the chief secretary (the principal bureaucrat), the inspector-general of police, the accountant-general and the finance secretary. Sardar Karamdad Khan, a Muzaffarabad-based lawyer, was quoted by the HRW, "The Pakistani bureaucracy is the real administrative power, the ISI and the Pakistan army exercise coercive power. And under the constitution, the elected representatives are subservient to the Kashmir Council controlled by Pakistan. High Court and Supreme Court Judges can only be appointed by approval of the Ministry of Kashmir Affairs in Islamabad. The Minister of Kashmir Affairs can dismiss the PM, as can the Chief Secretary—another Islamabad appointee. Under Article 56, the President of Pakistan can dissolve the legislative assembly. Surely, this is a truly unique form of self-rule."[10]

May 1975 witnessed first assembly elections in the region under the interim constitution that has largely clarified that the electoral politics in 'AJK' would be officially managed by Pakistan. It also officially set the stage for the pattern ritualistically followed since then wherein whosoever is in power in Islamabad decides the course of electoral politics in 'AJK.'

The elections also initiated the process of allegations of rigging, use of Pakistan army to change the course of elections in favour of the party supported by Islamabad, non-participation of large number of electorate in the elections, etc. The 1975 elections brought PPP to power that was also in power in Islamabad. The MC boycotted the 1975 elections and later alleged large scale rigging by PPP. According to Urdu daily *Nawa-i-Waqt*, of the 1, 45,000 listed voters only 60,000 exercised their voting right in 1975 assembly elections.[11]

The PPP government in 'AJK' could not complete even half of its tenure due to change of regime in Islamabad after military coup by Pakistan's Army Chief General Zia-ul-Haq. He imposed martial law in Pakistan in July 1977. Following the ritual of his predecessors General Zia dismissed the PPP government in 'AJK' and dissolved the legislative assembly on August 10, 1977. Sardar Ibrahim Khan continued as president upto October 30, 1978 and then through a proclamation of General Zia, as chairman of the 'AJK' council, a serving brigadier Mohammad Hayat Khan was nominated president with all the powers. Almost all political parties opposed the dismissal of the assembly and arbitrary appointment of new president contending that the region was not under the martial law unlike in Pakistan. All the protests went in vain. They only resulted in arrests and detentions. General Zia also targeted non-political bodies including legal institutions. The chief justice of high court was sacked allegedly for accepting the petitions regarding the constitutional validity of appointment of Hayat Khan as president.

On July 31, 1979 martial law order was issued suspending all political activities. Political activities remained suspended till mid-1985 in the region. Since August 1977 to June 16, 1985 there was no elected government even for the name sake in 'AJK.' The mass demonstrations in this period, however, became more prominent. Showing its insensitivity to the aspirations of the people of area for restoration of elected government Islamabad only replaced Hayat Khan with a retired army official, Maj. General Abdul Rahim Khan. Hayat remained in office till February 1983. Later he was made to resign and was succeeded by Rehman on February 1, 1983 who remained in office till October 1, 1985. The 1985 general elections to the assembly restricted only to registered political parties, thus disqualifying the PPP, brought the MC to power with Sikandar Hayat Khan as prime minister and Abdul Qayuum Khan as president. Despite the fact that seven political parties attempted to confront the MC by forming an alliance, the results favoured the latter. The post-election scenario was marred by allegations against favourable attitude of Islamabad towards the MC. It was alleged that proximity to Islamabad was the only positive point in favour of MC and it did not enjoy the popular support. There was great deal of dissatisfaction among people on the corrupt role of the MC and an agitation started against it. Following the death of the K. H. Khurshid on March 11, 1988, the opposition leaders in the assembly ended the movement with an agreement among MC, PPP, Liberation League, Tehrik Ammal and Azad Muslim Conference.[12]

The change of regime in Islamabad and coming of PPP in power in 1988 again cast its shadow on the future of 'AJK' government. Amidst threats of dismissal the MC government completed its tenure. The general elections of May 21, 1990 brought Raja Mumtaz Hussain Rathore of PPP to power with the support of PPP-led government at Islamabad, thus perpetuating the same party rule both at Islamabad and Muzaffarabad. Sardar Qayuum continued as president after the election on August 27, 1990.

For Rathore, the boat of power could not sail smoothly for long mainly due to two reasons. First, President Sardar Qayuum was from another political party, the MC. He used his power to ensure that the making of Rathore government was not smooth by refusing to administer the oath of office to members of the winning party, which was performed by the speaker of the assembly. Qayuum kept the Rathore government at its toes on one or the other issue for long time. Second, the coming of Nawaz Sharif of PML in Islamabad in 1990 revived the old memories of regime change in 'AJK.' While Rathore accused the government of Nawaz Sharif of unnecessary interference in the affairs of 'AJK,' Nawaz Sharif government accused him of corruption and misrule. After a tussle of power politics, the region again witnessed elections in mid-1991 wherein MC won the majority with the support from Islamabad amidst huge complaints of rigging. Rathore refused to accept the results and on expected lines was sacked under Section 56. Later he was arrested and imprisoned. Benazir Bhutto during her next turn in power from 1993 cautiously chose not to dismiss Sardar Qayuum led 'AJK' government.[13] On anticipated lines in the 1996 elections, however, PPP snatched power from the MC. After the elections in June 1996, the President of 'AJK,' Sikandar Hayat Khan, was removed through a voice vote in the assembly. In 2001, Sardar Qayuum was not allowed to form the government despite the MC securing 30 out of total 48 seats to the 'AJK' assembly for his supposedly 'mistake' in eulogizing the peace initiative undertaken by then Prime Minister of India, Atal Behari Vajpayee at Agra, and in appealing the terrorists to favour peace.[14]

When the Nawaz Sharif government was dismissed after 1999 coup by General Pervez Musharraf, 'AJK' politics too witnessed changes. In 2001 elections, MC secured 29 seats out of 40 directly elected seats in the legislative assembly. Sikandar Hayat Khan was made the prime minister and the relatively unknown Major Gen. (retd.) Sardar Muhammad Anwar Khan was appointed president in August 2001. It is argued that the decision to bring Anwar Khan, a former army Major General who retired just days before his election as president, was reached in Islamabad. Controversially, his appointment was facilitated by an ordinance issued by Musharraf that waived the restriction on government employees accepting any political post succeeding two years after retirement.[15]

The making and unmaking of governments at the behest of the government of Pakistan has remained a stark reality in 'AJK.' Pakistan dismisses governments that do not suit its interests. Till 1982, i.e. within 35 years of the formation of 'AJK,' 22 regime changes took place. Authorities in Islamabad seem to be content to promote frictions within political leaders and parties in 'AJK' so that intervention and manipulation of the political process can be made easy. Similarly, Islamabad is indignant of any leadership in 'AJK' who tries to assert themselves over its dictates. K. H. Khurshid, the first President of 'AJK' became the first victim when he was dismissed in 1964 for trying to assert himself. After his dismissal the *Outlook* of Karachi wrote on August 14, 1964: "The uncomfortable truth is that the Ministry of Kashmir Affairs has acquired a vested interest of its own. It treats 'Azad Kashmir' territory and Gilgit-Baltistan areas as its own domain that a Joint Secretary controls as Chief Advisor. His overlordship is supreme and without such checks and balances as are applicable to areas of Pakistan. The possibility of friction between the 'AJK' government and the Ministry of Kashmir Affairs has always been there. The Ministry likes to deal with puppets, not with the Presidents who take their position too literally."[16] In contrast, due to its special status, J&K enjoys more powers than the other states of Indian federation. Article 249 of the Indian constitution, which allows the upper house of the parliament to initiate law in matters of state list, is not applicable in case of J&K.

The setting up of an interim constitution and granting of electoral rights per se does not portray genuine democracy. While the 'AJK' constitution in its preamble holds supremacy of the wishes of the people in deciding their future, another provision section 4-7(2) subjects individuals to an ideology that favours its non-existence as an independent entity. This provision curbs the fundamental right of the individual to express their views on a political platform freely. The provision declares that unless the individual subscribes to the ideology of the state's accession to Pakistan, they would be ineligible to contest elections to the popular bodies. In 1996, 31 JKLF candidates were debarred to contest election to the legislative assembly on this ground. When the JKLF leader Amanullah Khan protested against this move, he was arrested along with 300 supporters. Similarly, 25 candidates were barred from contesting polls in July 2001 after refusing to sign the accession form. Thus, pro-independence parties such as the Kashmir Muttahida Mahaz, the JKLF and the Jammu and Kashmir National Awami Front are disqualified from participating in 'AJK' elections as they refuse to swear allegiance to Pakistan. The Chairman of the APNA, a group of 12 political parties, Arif Shahid argues "to contest elections, we have to sign a form saying that Kashmir is a part of Pakistan. We refuse to sign, or cross it out and sign, and so the Pakistan government rejects our candidature."[17] In the July 2006 more than 60 candidates were debarred from contesting the election on the same criterion.

The 'AJK' administration, on analysis, looks like a junior partner to Islamabad so much so that it is dubbed as the fifth province of Pakistan. In a famous judgment by the 'AJK' High Court, Justice Manzoor Geelani ruled that the autonomous status of 'AJK' is only a myth. He observed, "Azad Kashmir government was no 'powerful' than any other Pakistani provincial government."[18] Yet, as overall set up indicates it seems in many matters 'AJK' is even less powerful than the Pak provinces. The joint secretary at the Ministry of KANA in Islamabad is in the charge of 'AJK' government and can be rightly called the real head of it.[19] Unlike the legislative assembly of J&K, the assembly in Muzaffarabad requires Islamabad's prior approval for all enactments of statutory rules, appointments, public property, budget, loans, taxes, internal security and civil supplies. Administrative justice in 'AJK' is handled by the Kashmir council that is dominated by Islamabad.[20] While in the case of a large-scale disturbance police force can be brought in from Pakistan, the 'AJK' police cannot be sent to Pakistani cities. Similarly, Pakistani police can directly pursue fugitives from the area, but the local police cannot directly pursue fugitives from Pakistan. Moreover, as already mentioned, all the high posts in the area are reserved for the Pakistan officials. It does not seem that there is no requisite calibre in 'AJK' to fill the high positions but it is likely suspicion on the people of 'AJK' that motivates the appointments to be made from Islamabad. Liaquat Hayyat writes, "the underlying reason behind this (appointment of high officials from Islamabad) is that there is mistrust about the loyalties of Kashmiris. That is why the rule is enforced through these non-Kashmiris."[21] Similarly, the earthquake-related matters are directly dealt with by Islamabad through Earthquake Reconstruction and Rehabilitation Authority, which directly distributes funds and does not trust 'AJK' government, dubbing it incompetent and ineffective.[22] In contrast, J&K government has dealt with the earthquake in its territory with assistance from India. The local government's relief and rehabilitation effort in collaboration with Indian army has been appreciated by the people.[23] There is also resentment regarding Pakistan's utilization of the 'AJK' resources for its domestic use. The International Kashmir Alliance chief, Syed Nazir Gilani claims Pakistan has used the Kashmir issue for its water interests and domestic concerns.[24] Pakistani authorities claim that the poor region of 'AJK' cannot be developed without active financial support from Islamabad, thus justifying a culture of dependency. However, there is no dearth of dissenting voices in this context though their voice is not allowed to reach the masses. To the Pak argument that almost 50 per cent of its budget is sanctioned from Islamabad, they counter that the pending royalty from the Mangla hydel dam would suffice to meet its budgetary requirements. This *azad* entity contributes positively to Pakistan's national economy in terms of foreign currency but remains highly dependent on Pakistan.

The opposition parties have time and again questioned the interference of Pakistan in the internal affairs of 'AJK.' The MC that played important role in the formation of 'AJK' and is pro-Pakistan in its approach has also many times expressed dissatisfaction at the manner Islamabad treats 'AJK.' Its leader and incumbent Prime Minister, Sardar Attique Khan had cautioned Pakistan against treating 'AJK' as a 'private estate' or as a 'municipal committee.'[25] His warning is couched with the advice if Pakistan does not address the popular concerns, the negligence may give rise to popular unrest. While Attique complains of negligence, his father Sardar Qayuum criticizes the dominating role of Pakistan bureaucracy in the Kashmir Committee that was formed to counter the negative fall outs of the 9/11 on Pakistan's position on Kashmir.

2006 Elections

While the intervention from Islamabad is complained by many political parties as the recent elections in July 2006 revealed, the elections in J&K in 2002 was accepted as free and fair not only by the local people but also by other countries. The 2006 elections in 'AJK' were marked by controversies regarding timing of elections and preparation of electoral lists in post-earthquake situation, and inter-party rivalries. As in earlier elections, the post- election scenario this time also witnessed controversies regarding manipulation of elections results and extreme interference by Islamabad. The elections were held on July 11, 2006 to directly elect 41 members of 49-seat legislative assembly (one seat was increased recently). Out of 41, 29 members are elected from the 'AJK' electoral territory and 12 members from the Kashmiri 'refugees' settled in Pakistan. Five seats are reserved for women and one each for an Islamic scholar, technocrat and overseas Kashmiri. For these reserved seats the 41- members of the assembly indirectly elect candidates.

The recent elections witnessed entrance of some new political parties into the fray to get the power. Besides the MC, other main parties in the elections included PPP, People's Party Jammu Kashmir, PML and MQM. Two religious parties, the JI and Jamiat Ulema-e-Islam formed part of MMA. 369 candidates contested the elections. 40 candidates of MC, 37 of PML, 36 contestants of PPP, 33 of MMA, 23 of MQM, 28 candidates from other parties and 172 independents were in the electoral fray. Nearly 2.5 million people had the voting right. 1,112 polling stations were set up in Pakistan for the 12 assembly seats and 4,858 polling stations with 7,214 booths for voting in 'AJK.'

Kashmir issue remained the focal point during campaign for most parties including the ruling MC. PML tried to woo voters by proclaiming that it has raised the Kashmir question at all national and international fora for early resolution 'as per the aspirations of the people.' The developmental activities and rehabilitation too remained an important issue. Some other issues such as the opening of routes across the LOC also surfaced during the campaign. The religious parties asked for votes for their 'prominent' role in rehabilitation after the earthquake. Some parties also tried to secure votes by criticizing the failure of ruling MC in properly handling the post-earthquake situation. Setting all apprehensions aside, the ruling party retained its power position. The electoral results witnessed the pro-accession MC returning to power by having 31 seats. The party won 21 seats in direct elections and seven of the eight reserved seats as well. Apart from these, three independent candidates also joined the party giving it a two-third majority in the legislative assembly. Sardar Attique Khan, son of Sardar Qayuum Khan, was elected prime minister on July 24, 2006 by the eighth legislative assembly since 1970, and the seventh since the formation of an interim constitution of 'AJK' in 1974. The government formation process was completed with the election of Raja Zulqarnain Khan as the 21st president in the last week of July and oath taking of 16-member cabinet on August 7.

The chief election commissioner of 'AJK' declared the elections were held in a free, fair and peaceful manner and no untoward incident was reported. While the later part of the statement may be lauded the former appear incredulous. Various quarters from within 'AJK,' Pakistan, India and the international community have questioned the much vaulted transparency in conducting elections. The elections were marred by both pre and post election controversies and criticism.

Two major issues remained controversial before the election: the timing of the election and preparation of electoral lists.[26] In the aftermath of 2005 earthquake that brought a trail of death and destruction to the region, the argument in favour of postponement of the elections so that the rehabilitation task remains a priority held humanitarian ground. In this context, questioning the time and calling elections 'like rubbing salt on the wound' and 'inviting a bereaved family to a grand feast' may not appear surprising. The pre-election scenario too witnessed a prolonged controversy regarding preparation of electoral lists. The then acting chief election commissioner Justice Manzur-ul-Hassan Gillani, judge of supreme court of 'AJK,' favoured preparation of new electoral lists for conducting the elections. But the assembly adopted a joint resolution recommending utilization of updated old lists. The resolution blocked the preparation of fresh electoral rolls. The acting chief election commissioner then tendered his resignation. Justice Riaz Akhtar Choudhry, chief justice of the 'AJK' high court was thereafter appointed chief election commissioner.[27] Doubts were raised in this context since it was apprehended that there was possibility of manipulation of electoral rolls as thousands of voters perished under the debris due to earthquake. It would also not be out of context to mention that many political parties, keeping in view the fact that the existing ones were prepared a decade ago, demanded revision of the electoral rolls. In the post election scenario it was alleged that many voters could not cast their votes due to errors in the voters list or for not possessing identity cards.

The electoral rule that every candidate has to sign the affidavit submitting to the ideology of accession of Kashmir to Pakistan became the focal point of criticism. This rule operating in the region since decades debars from contesting those who do not sign the affidavit. A person gets disqualified to contest if, "He is propagating any opinion or acting in any manner prejudicial to the ideology of Pakistan, the ideology of the State's accession to Pakistan or the sovereignty, integrity of Pakistan or security of Azad Jammu and Kashmir or Pakistan, or morality, or the maintenance of public order, or the integrity or independence of the Judiciary of Azad Jammu and Kashmir or Pakistan." It also debars those who "ridicule the Judiciary of Azad Jammu and Kashmir or Pakistan, or the Armed Forces of Pakistan." In the 1996 elections, those who wished to participate on the platform of independence and refused to sign the declaration calling the region's accession to Pakistan were denied the right to contest. In 2001 and 2006 elections the same thing was repeated. Though this clause existed earlier yet the issue of exclusion of those from contesting who refused to accede to the ideology of accession of Kashmir to Pakistan drew attention only in the recent times.

Amanullah Khan, the leader of JKLF, questioned the rule in the backdrop of Pakistan's proclamation of Kashmir being 'a disputed territory.' The leader of APNA, Sardar Muhammed Shabir Kashmiri in a press conference on June 26, 2006 not only questioned the legality of the accession clause but also charged Pakistan as pursuant of a policy of double-speak. He argued, "Pakistan has always been crying hoarse that whole Jammu & Kashmir is disputed and its people have yet to decide their future, and that Pakistan is the champion of their right of self-determination, freedom and independence. But what does she mean by self-determination, freedom and independence of the people of Jammu Kashmir? Just voting for the accession of the State of Jammu Kashmir to Pakistan and not otherwise!"[28] He announced observing the election day as black day. The HRW too castigated Pakistan on this issue. Brad Adams, its

Asia Director observed, "The electoral law undermines Kashmiris' basic political rights by barring them from seeking office if they oppose Kashmir's accession to Pakistan....The restrictions on political participation and the harassment and persecution of Kashmiri nationalists in Azad Kashmir violate international standards on free expression and expose the Pakistani government's hypocrisy about Kashmir." Indian foreign office on June 12 stated that the elections would be 'a replay of earlier exercises.' The disqualification of all political parties and candidates who failed to meet the condition of declaring their allegiance to the accession of Kashmir to Pakistan exposed the 'insincerity of Pakistan's proclaimed policy that the future of Kashmir should be decided by its people.' The spokesperson of Indian foreign ministry pointed out that this disqualification is particularly glaring in the light of the proposal made by Pakistan President General Musharraf of introducing self-governance in Kashmir.

The controversy involving the accession clause became more prominent keeping in view the assurance from the ruling party leaders that the clause could be repealed. Before the election process started, in May 2006 the Chief Election Commissioner had called an all-parties meeting. The clause was questioned and the then president and prime minister of 'AJK' had given an assurance that they would repeal the same. Then Prime Minister Sardar Sikandar Hayat Khan in reply to a question from an Indian journalist during a South Asian Free Media Association visit too had assured that his party would amend the constitution to abolish the accession clause. The abolition promise ended in air and those who did not sign the accession affidavit were debarred from contesting the elections.

Pakistan denied its role in the debarring of candidates arguing that 'AJK' elections were determined by its own constitution. JKLF termed the denial as a misrepresentation, arguing that the interim constitution had been vetted by Pakistan before it came into operation. The organization argued that the preamble to the constitution mentions that the government of Pakistan had approved the constitution and later the 'AJK' government was authorized to introduce it in the legislature. Differences among local parties also crept in regarding the choice of electoral procedure. While some parties favoured phased elections, others opposed it. PPP on February 16, 2006 rejected phased polls by saying that it would provide an opportunity to Islamabad to manipulate the elections. Speaking at a press conference in Muzaffarabad, the party president, Sahibzada Ishaq Zafar, said his party was opposed to the postponement of elections as well as holding of snap polls. He called for delegating the powers of the 'AJK' cabinet to the judiciary with the announcement of the election schedule so as to avert the possibility of rigging.

Commenting on the elections M. A. R. K. Khaleeque, spokesperson of APNA observed, "These elections are no different to the ones held in the past in POK. In Pakistan occupied Kashmir, democratic institutions have always remained in the subordination of the military, the bureaucracy and its agencies. And, this will continue."[29] The parties like APNA remained outside the electoral process. Those who abided to the condition of agreeing to the accession clause too have criticized the whole process. Amidst the claim by MC that they won the election on the basis of their performance and their ideology of accession to Pakistan, rigging and manipulation seem to acquire centre stage in the election. In fact, the whole electoral process turned into a battle between the Islamabad-backed MC and others. All the opposition parties, whether liberal or religious ones, termed the exercise as farcical. Reportedly large-scale rigging took place in many constituencies and almost total manipulation of the results of 'refugee' seats in Pakistan. To quote PML leader Barrister Sultan Mehmood Chaudhry, "The rigging in the Kashmiri refugees' constituencies was naked whereas here ('AJK') it was selective and organized."[30] It is alleged that the voters were intimidated with the use of force and the officials of law enforcement agencies stamped the ballot papers illegally in favour of the MC candidates.

MMA 'AJK' president, Sardar Ijaz Afzal Khan refused to accept the results. He alleged that the ruling class in Pakistan has 'hijacked the mandate of people by seizing polling stations.' It is argued that the 'refugees' seats have been always 'allocated' rather than elected. To quote Islamabad based writer Ershad Mahmud, "these seats have become, simply, a tool of manipulation in the hands of the ruling government in Islamabad, and particularly Punjab, which has eight and a half seats in its territorial jurisdiction. There is no doubt that successive federal governments have been gifting these seats to their allies. The ruling parties always use their leverage to ensure their allies' victory. Additionally ... a huge number of non-Kashmiris are registered as voters."[31] The parties like PPP called the elections as a demonstration of the next general elections to be held in Pakistan. Ishaq Zafar, president of PPP contended there had been rigging at many polling stations. Immediately after the elections, Mian Raza Rabbani, Leader of the Opposition, Senate of Pakistan and Deputy Secretary General, PPP issued a press statement saying, "the manner in which the elections have been conducted leaves no room for doubt that the next elections in Pakistan will be manipulated and rigged to achieve the political agenda of the regime."[32] Rabbani accused the government of intimidating voters and forcibly acquiring their identity cards, which they later allegedly used to fill the ballot boxes, after 'throwing the opposition out with the help of the local administration.'

JI leader, Qazi Hussain Ahmad too contended that the result of elections was a 'trailer of upcoming engineered' general elections to be held in Pakistan. PML Chief Barrister Chaudhry was one of the strong critics of the whole episode. He issued on August 11 a white paper on the elections arguing that the ruling MC bagged 450,127 votes and its opponents secured 735,340 votes but both secured an equal number of seats. Terming the election as black period in the political history of 'AJK' he demanded an impartial probe into the matter. To quote him, "Despite rigging, manipulation, use of force and violence and a carrot and stick policy, the ruling party secured far fewer votes than the Opposition parties who take the identical stance that these were bogus elections."[33] Commenting on the role of Pakistan in the election Shabir Chowdhary noted, "It is established fact that Pakistani governments meddle with the affairs of Azad Kashmir, and outcome of the 'elections' is always according to desires of Islamabad. However there is a big difference between the present interference and the previous ones. In the past Pakistani governments did everything from behind the scenes."[34]

Questions were raised on the participation of Islamabad appointed administrators in the election campaigns of the MC candidates. The meeting of President Pervez Musharraf with Sardar Abdul Qayuum Khan and Sardar Attique Khan a week before the elections too was alleged to be a signal to the officials to support the MC candidates. This was termed as pre-poll rigging of the 'AJK' elections in favour of the MC, facilitated by Pakistan. Rigging during the assembly elections and the results clearly indicate that only those political parties can stake claim to power which have the blessings of Islamabad.

Both Pakistan and 'AJK' government were termed corrupt by various political parties. Referring to the embezzlement of millions of rupees in Kashmir Liberation Cell funds during 1991-96, Barrister Chaudhry said that the MC was the best choice for Pakistan since its leaders have a record of loot and plunder. Alleging that the people too were displeased by the whole episode, PP-'AJK' leader Chaudhry Abdul Majeed argued, "General Musharraf has annoyed 80 per cent population of this state by pleasing 18 percent....He has become a controversial personality in Kashmir."[35] Majeed questioned Musharraf's claim of promoting self-governance in Kashmir. He alleged that ballot papers were distributed in the MC dominated constituencies without the signatures of presiding officers. He demanded fresh elections in the wake of 'proven rigging.' Shafqat Inqalabi, spokesperson of the BNF, commented 'there was no election in POK; there was only a selection of MLAs by Pakistani Government agencies and the Army.'

Besides Pakistan and 'AJK' ruling party, the roles of the election commission, armed forces as also the ISI too were severely condemned. Addressing a joint press conference, Barrister Chaudhry and JKPP leader Sardar Khalid Ibrahim condemned the role of armed forces by arguing that 'the way they intervened in the elections has put their integrity at risk.' It was also alleged that the ISI and other agencies were used openly to influence the results. PPP charged the election commission to be a 'silent spectator' to the rigging.

The opposition parties used many kinds of tactics to register their discontent. The PML launched a mass contact campaign to apprise the people about the electoral malpractices. It also prepared a booklet carrying the partisan statements of Pakistan officials before elections, reports of national and international media on incidents of rigging as well relevant statements of the polling staff. Many elected candidates did not even take oath on the prescribed day to protest the rigging. It is reported that to prevent any mass protest arbitrary arrests were carried out. The secretary general of PPP, Chaudhary Mohammad Yasin was arrested on July 13. Yasin had made serious charges of manipulation in the elections by arguing that he was winning the elections by a lead of 9,000 votes, the results were however changed overnight. 'AJK' Prime Minister Sardar Attique Ahmed Khan has rejected the opposition's demand for fresh elections. Interestingly he termed the elections as 'model of fair polls' and asked the opposition to accept the 'verdict given by the people.'

The pattern of one party dominant system that is congruent with ideology of accession of Kashmir to Pakistan prevails in 'AJK.' Political parties in 'AJK' can be put into four categories on the basis of their place of origin and ideology. First, the local parties favouring the ideology of accession. In this category comes the MC, one of the major parties in 'AJK' since the area was occupied by Pakistan. Second, the local parties who favour establishment of an 'independent Kashmir.' Most of these parties like JKLF however are kept away from the electoral politics because this principle is unacceptable to Pakistan. Third, the national parties of Pakistan that were, of late, allowed to operate in 'AJK.' In this context the prominent one is PPP that succeeded to dethrone the MC for more than once. Fourth category comprises of those local and Pakistan national parties that are extremist in their ideology with religion being their sole play card. JI comes in this category.

The electoral politics in 'AJK' is yet to commensurate with the genuine principles of democracy and human rights. The history of elections vindicates this assumption and the recent election further corroborates it.[36] Interestingly since mid-1980s, in quite contrast to elections in Pakistan, elections in 'AJK' are held almost regularly. However, considering it as a sign of functioning democracy becomes imprudent in the wake of the fact that Pakistan's control over the area is nearly total. It may be interesting to ask how can Pakistan, which champions 'self-determination' for the Kashmiri people, devise means to trample the basic democratic rights of the very people. Section 4 of 'AJK' constitution is symbolic of Pakistan's designs to subjugate the people of the region. Another important feature of 'AJK' politics is its subservient character to the dictates of Islamabad. Pakistan not only makes and unmakes governments at Muzaffarabad at wish but also prepares the theatre for the electoral game to be played under its own direction. Whether it is the first 'AJK' President K. H. Khurshid or Mumtaz Rathore, or any other 'AJK' leader, their ominous fates are decided by all-powerful Islamabad. In this whole election jamboree, it is not the people of 'AJK' that matter but the combination of political establishment at Islamabad, the Pakistan army and the ISI. The politics in 'AJK,' hence, is under the tutelage of Pakistan.

The recent election does not appear to reflect the wishes of the people. The open confession of the incumbent prime minister that his party won on the basis of its support to the accession ideology corroborates this point of view. The hurry to conduct elections after the devastating earthquake without adequately addressing the humanitarian concerns and the use of old electoral rolls further complicated the already complex scenario. The conduct of election, after all, appears to be condescending for those forces in Kashmir across LOC, which support Pakistan policies in the region. Instead of being a democratic exercise the election in 'AJK' has only served the objectives of Pakistan.

Gilgit-Baltistan

Since separating the administration of Gilgit-Baltistan from 'AJK', Pakistan has successfully carried out its policy to keep the politics of two areas segregated. In an interview with ANI Television, Shabir Choudhry disclosed that Islamabad would not like people of Gilgit-Baltistan and 'AJK' to get united. "Because if they do, that means they would be asking for their rights, not only democratic rights but also asking for the unification and independence of the state. The Pakistani authorities would very much like the attention to be on the Indian side of Kashmir." Lack of direct road linkage between 'AJK' and Gilgit-Baltistan fosters this segregation further. Quite contrary to 'AJK' the area of Gilgit-Baltistan was governed by FCR that were introduced by British in 18th century to curb criminal activities in the tribal areas. The regulation that remained in the area for around three decades not only obstructed the free movement of the locals but also forbade any kind of political activity in the region. This law thus consequently helped Pakistan to govern the area without even tokenism. The lack of political institutions and ban on all political activities played a significant role in keeping the people of the area apathetic towards the overall scenario. However, this cannot be concluded that there was no resentment against such a move. It was only that there were no institutions or organizations to give voice to the resentment. The area remained a 'colony' with no legal-constitutional as also political set up for a long time.

A political agent was appointed by Pakistan in November 1947 to administer the area. Later he was placed under the political resident of the NWFP. Following the Karachi agreement the administrative control of Gilgit-Baltistan was handed over to Pakistan. After briefly being under control of a political agent, in 1950, the area was placed under the direct control of KANA. In 1952, a mid-ranking civil servant based in Karachi was appointed political resident for the areas. Despite dramatic changes in the international and local political scene KANA remains the ultimate decision maker for the area, though recently some token institutions have been introduced.

It was only as late as 1967 that political resident was re-designated as resident and also relocated from Islamabad to Gilgit. This re-designation and relocation notwithstanding, the non-native resident continued to be all powerful in all terms-administrative, legislative, financial and judicial. The resident appointed was also entrusted with the powers of high court and revenue commissioner. To make his work easier, the resident was assisted by two political agents. These agents, one each for Gilgit and Baltistan agencies, exercised enormous powers simultaneously in their capacities as- district and sessions judge; district magistrate; revenue collector; commissioner for FCR; inspector general of police; chairman of district council; and controlling officer of cooperative society.

For the first time elections were held in the area as late as in 1970. The elections led to constitution of a 16 member Northern Areas Advisory Council. Interestingly, this council with all members from the area was first headed by resident and later by Minister of KANA. As named, the council was merely advisory in function. Alongside some substantial changes were also carried out in the first half of 1970s in the form of abolition of FCR, according the status of districts to Gilgit and Baltistan agencies, constitution of new districts-Diamir, Ghanche and Ghizer, re-designation of resident as resident commissioner and that of political agents as deputy commissioners. The Northern Areas Advisory Council was later replaced by a Northern Areas Council, the members of which were to be directly elected by adult franchise. Despite these changes, the areas remained devoid of any democratic structure.

General Zia-ul-Haq during his tenure allowed a representative from the area to sit as observer in the Pakistan assembly. In 1982, three members from the area were granted observer status in the Federal Advisory Council of Pakistan made by the military ruler. Yet it did not last long. This token representation could not be seen as some benevolent attempt but the one to bring the areas under the constitutional paradigm of Pakistan. The 1977 martial law in Pakistan was also extended to Gilgit-Baltistan which added to the confusion regarding the status of the area. Zia-ul-Haq also spoke on more than one occasion that the area was part of Pakistan though on some other occasions he denied the same. As per a report, in April 1982, Zia stated that Gilgit, Skardu and Hunza were not 'disputed' areas, but part of Pakistan. Again in May 9, 1982, he said: 'Kashmir has been a disputed issue, but so far as the Northern Areas are concerned, we do not accept them disputed.' On another occasion he said, 'I am not talking of Kashmir; I am talking about the Northern Areas, which make part of Pakistan.' Changing his public statement later in an interview with Indian journalist M. J. Akbar, General Zia conceded that 'Gilgit -Baltistan were not part of Pakistan and were as much disputed as the rest of the Kashmir.'[37]

In 1994 LFO was adopted for the area. Schedule II to the LFO listed the matters with respect to which the council may make laws. As per the order no bill passed by the council could become law unless approved and signed by the chief executive. Islamabad may also by order make laws with respect to matters not enumerated in the schedule. As per the provision of LFO the Northern Areas Council was again re-designated as the NALC. The membership of the council was enhanced to 26 with a provision for direct elections. These cosmetic changes, however, in no way changed the power position of this representative body. It continued to have only advisory role with all the powers entrusted in KANA. A significant change was that political activities were allowed in the area to be carried out by local and national parties of Pakistan. Interestingly, the political parties from 'AJK' including the MC that had gifted Pakistan the area of Gilgit-Baltistan by Karachi agreement were denied the right to carry out activities in these areas. A statement by Sardar Mohammad Ibrahim in this regard is worth noting. He said: "As and when we tried to go there (in Gilgit-Baltistan), we were blocked. Such actions by the Ministry of Kashmir Affairs were considered to mean that people of the two areas ('AJK' and Gilgit-Baltistan) should not be let to forge close relations."

The Northern Areas Rules of Business, 1994 provided in Rule 5 (c) that the chief executive shall exercise the powers of the 'Federal Ministry of Finance' in relation to the approved budget for Gilgit-Baltistan. Interestingly, the Rules define government as the chief executive, the deputy chief executive and the chief secretary with no mention of the council. The council set up and controlled by KANA provided little scope for the local people to have self-rule. The chief executive is minister of KANA, chief secretary is appointed by Islamabad and all other ministers by the chief executive. The council elects deputy chief executive who is from the area. The non-representative and non-native chief executive has no accountability to the NALC. In his absence the chief secretary holds all the powers. The area continues to be ruled by KANA with the help of six non-local officers appointed by Islamabad. These officers are the chief executive officer, the commissioner, the deputy commissioner, the inspector general of police, the judicial commissioner and the chief engineer public works.

According to Bashir Ahmed Jehangiri, a former Pakistan Supreme Court justice, ' whole of the NA were being governed by the section officers of Kashmir Affairs Ministry.... There is no law in the Northern Areas whatsoever.' It is argued that the bureaucrats appointed by the Islamabad have more powers than the 'democratically elected members' of NALC. Consequently the concept of self-governance in Gilgit-Baltistan seems to be a mockery of democracy. Interestingly, Pakistan, which claims to have 'championed' the cause of people of J&K, has not allowed the people of Gilgit-Baltistan to be governed by their own representatives. The report of HRCP on Gilgit-Baltistan quoted a member of the council as saying that he was not even allowed to meet the chief executive.[38] The members also do not have any direct link with Islamabad, KANA being the only bridge. KANA is responsible for finance, administration, as also law making in the area notwithstanding the presence of NALC. The budget for the area is allocated as per the demands put forward by KANA.

The main function of councillors is said to be 'receiving dignitaries from Pakistan.' NALC is termed as 'impotent' and 'a leisure club for private contractors.' The region is ruled by KANA wherein the Islamabad based bureaucrats do not bother to even pass a single glance at whatever occasional resolutions are passed by the NALC. Some unanimous resolutions adopted by the NALC in its sessions held in Gilgit could be mentioned as example:[39]

- A resolution was passed in the fourth session of the NALC, from September 18 to 23, 2000, for approval of the procedure and conduct of business rules 2000, and submitted to the chief executive. There was no response.
- There was a proposal for renaming the Bhasha dam as Diamir dam, and construction of a substitute road for the affected people of the Karakoram Highway. This was passed during the November 2000 session, and submitted to the chief executive. Some actions in this matter were taken only after mass protests in the area.
- Right of self-rule in the light of supreme court of Pakistan judgment, dated May 28, 1999. No response.

- Abolition of Supreme Judicial Council comprising of bureaucrats to ensure independent judiciary. No response.
- Bringing the chief court of Gilgit-Baltistan at par with the high court. No response.
- The question of grant of compensation, to those affected by border firing in Qamari and Minimarg areas of Diamir, was raised during the November 2000 session. No action was taken.
- A resolution on taking up development activities through the NALC was adopted. No action was taken.
- A proposal for inclusion of development schemes in the annual development programme, until such time that the people of area are granted legal and democratic rights, was adopted. No response.
- On November 20, 2000, the NALC passed a unanimous resolution, and demanded that the reign of the area be handed over to them, rather than chief executive who is an outsider. The result of this demand was that NALC members were banned from entering any government offices.

Gilgit-Baltistan witnessed the first party-based elections to the council, comprising 26 members in October 1994. It was announced on March 31, 1995, that the members would have the same status, emoluments and privileges as the members of the NWFP legislative assembly, thereby giving it pretence of a provincial legislative assembly. PPP bagged the seat of deputy chief executive. The five advisors were from PPP, Tahrik-i-Jafaria and Muslim League (Junejo group). Reportedly, all of them i.e. advisors as well as deputy chief executive generally complained that they have no powers as those are exercised by the bureaucracy at Islamabad.

The Pakistan supreme court ruling of 1999 directed Islamabad that people of this area are 'entitled to participate in the governance of their area and to have an independent judiciary to enforce, inter alia, the Fundamental Rights.' It emphasized the need for 'proper administrative and legislative steps' to ensure the extension of the fundamental rights enshrined in the constitution of Pakistan including the right to self-governance to Gilgit-Baltistan within a period of six months. Even many years after this judgment, the directions from the court are still waiting to be implemented in letter and spirit and as the amendments in the LFO of 1994 made in July 2000, mentioned below, show the future does not appear encouraging in this context. The tight grip of Islamabad on the area is intact as before. Main features of the amendments were:[40]

- NALC was authorized to legislate on 40 items;
- Council's membership was raised to 29. Five seats were reserved for women – one from each district indirectly elected;
- Chief executive was not supposed to be from amongst the council members;
- Speaker, elected by the council members, was given the authority to preside over council's meetings;
- Council members were deprived of their earlier power to approve development schemes;
- Deputy chief executive was authorized to transfer officers of grade 18, but not the deputy commissioner or the superintendent of police that were appointed by Pakistan. For that he will have to get prior approval of the chief secretary, an Islamabad appointee.

Elections to the NALC were held in November 1999 and in December 2004. The breach of privileges of the members of the NALC touched new height in March 2007. A local NGO made the 'mistake' of arranging a series of capacity-building workshops for the NALC members at the interim facility of the Pakistan Institute for Parliamentary Services at Parliament Lodge in Islamabad. The ministry of KANA, as reported in the local press, disapproved of the idea of NALC members getting any sort of training in Islamabad, and reportedly advised members to skip the training opportunity.[41] Robert Templer, the ICG's Asia programme Director, observed that genuine democracy in the area remains a distant dream. He pointed out, "Islamabad sees the region (Gilgit-Baltistan) as a card to play in negotiations with India about Kashmir, and unless the government empowers locally elected representatives instead of governing through a viceroy from Islamabad, it will continue to lose its legitimacy at a fast pace."

It is not that there were no attempts by the local people to highlight their problems, most of them could not sustain for long to have any substantial impact. Amanullah Kahn in his book mentions three important attempts in this context.[42] Gilgit League was established in 1957, but banned following the imposition of martial law in 1958. In sixties Gilgit and Baltistan Jamhoori Mahaz tried to plead the case of the people of the area by using all democratic methods ranging from media to protests. This organization, credited for the 1973 resolution of 'AJK' assembly regarding the handing over of Gilgit-Baltistan to 'AJK,' also became defunct in early 1973. In 1973 another organization named Gilgit and Baltistan Students Federation was formed in Karachi. It also remained active only for a while and ceased all activities in 1976.

References

1. Sultan Shaheen, "How Azad is Azad Kashmir." *http://www.jammu-kashmir.com/insights/insight990902.html*. Accessed on July 19, 2006.
2. *Viewpoint*, July 11, 1991.
3. Debidatta Aurobinda Mahapatra, "Electoral Politics in AJK," *Across LOC*, Vol. 2, no. 1, January-March 2006, pp. 1-4.
4. "With Friends Like These...," *HRW Report*, vol. 18, no. 12 (C), September 2006, p. 29.
5. *The Azad Jammu and Kashmir Interim Constitution Act, 1974* (Muzafarrabad: Azad Government of the State of J&K, 1990), p. 43.
6. Shabir Choudhry, "Musharraf Factor in Azad Kashmir Elections" *http://www.gaash-online.com/articles/90/1/*

Musharraf-Factor-in-Azad-Kashmir-Elections.html. Accessed on September 22, 2006.

7. *HRW Report*, n. 4, p. 28.
8. M. Sharif Tariq, *Kashmir in strangulation* (Mirpur: Mohd. Sharif Tariq, 2003), p. 20.
9. Debidatta Aurobinda Mahapatra, "Some Reflections on AJK Constitution," *Across LOC*, Vol. 1, no. 2, July-September 2005, p. 4.
10. *HRW Report*, n. 4, p. 31.
11. Cited in Samuel Baid, "Politics in "Azad Kashmir,"" in Jasjit Singh, ed., *Pakistan Occupied Kashmir Under the Jackboot* (New Delhi: Siddhi Books, 1995), p. 112.
12. M. Sharif Tariq, n. 8, pp. 13-21.
13. *HRW*, n. 4, p. 30.
14. Samuel Baid, "Political Crisis in PoK," *Daily Excelsior*, April 1, 2004, p. 6.*http://news.bbc.co.uk/1/hi/world/south_asia/1468287.stm*. Accessed on August 26, 2006.
15. Susannah Price, "Ex-general elected to Kashmir post," BBC News Online, August 1, 2001. *http://news.bbc.co.uk/1/hi/world/south_asia/1468287.stm*. Accessed on August 26, 2006.
16. Quoted in "A Comprehensive Note on Jammu & Kashmir." *http://www.indianembassy.org/policy/Kashmir/Kashmir_MEA/POK.html*. Accessed on October 12, 2005.
17. Ibid.
18. Hashim Qureshi, *Kashmir: The Unveiling of Truth* (Lahore: Jeddajudh Publications, 1999), p. 265.
19. Leo Rose, "The Politics of Azad Kashmir," in Raju G. C. Thomas, ed., *Perspectives on Kashmir: The Roots of Conflict in South Asia* (Oxford: Westview Press, 1992), p. 246.
20. "Azad Kashmir" and "Northern Territories" or Pakistan Occupied Kashmir (POK)?" *http://members.tripod.com/~INDIA_RESOURCE/pok.html*. Accessed on March 30, 2006.
21. Liaquat Hayyat, "Politics of 'Azad' Kashmir: Behind the Scene Facts," *The Kashmir Times*, June 23, 2006.
22. Ershad Mahmud, "New Dispensation in Azad Kashmir," *The Kashmir Times*, August 3, 2006.

23. Debidatta Aurobinda Mahapatra "J&K and POK: A Comparison," *Across LOC*, vol. 2, no. 3, July-September 2006, pp. 3-5.
24. *The Kashmir Times*, January 24, 2005.
25. *Greater Kashmir*, January 30, 2005.
26. Seema Shekhawat, "Elections in AJK: A Balance Sheet," *Across LOC*, July-September 2006.
27. For details see *Pakistan Observer*, July 4, 2005.
28. *The Kashmir Times*, July 2, 2006.
29. *http://in.news.yahoo.com/060710/139/65rt9.html*. Accessed on August 10, 2006.
30. *Greater Kashmir*, July 19, 2006.
31. Quoted in Nirupama Subramanian, "What the Elections in PoK Mean," *The Hindu*, August 15, 2006. Ershad Mahmud, "Azad Kashmir's struggle for fair polls," *The News International*, May 15, 2005.
32. *http://www.ppp.org.pk/news_events/Jul06/13-7-2006.html.* Accessed on July 18, 2006.
33. *Daily Times*, August 12, 2006.
34. Shabir Choudhry, n. 6.
35. *Greater Kashmir*, July 25, 2006.
36. Debidatta Aurobinda Mahapatra, "Other Kashmir Elections," *Kashmir Images*, July 22, 2006.
37. Khalid Rahman and Ershad Mahmud, "Northern Areas of Pakistan – Facts, Problems and Recommendations," *IPS Task Force Report*, pp. 128-129.
38. "HRCP mission to the Northern Areas," *Report of Fact Finding Mission of Human Rights Commission of Pakistan,* August-September 2005.
39. Abdul Hamid Khan, "If we had a choice between India and Pakistan, we would not be part of Pakistan." http://www.tehelka.com/channels/currentaffairs/2001/dec/3/ca120301abdul2.htm. Accessed on January 22, 2005.
40. Bahadur Ali Salik, "Northern Areas Package a Joke with People," *The Nation*, June 15, 2000.

41. M. Ismail Khan, "Justice needed with or without chief," *The Kashmir Times*, March 14, 2007.
42. Amanullah Khan, *Jehde Musalsal* (Rawalpindi: S.S. Combined, 1992), pp. 77-80.

4

Sectarian Turbulence

Unrest in Gilgit-Baltistan has received sparse attention in informed circles. As mentioned in an earlier chapter, the area not only lacks constitutional status, but even modest demands such as reformed legal system and providing some teeth to the so called legislative council have been met with apathy and sometimes with batons. Low literacy rate, extreme poverty and lack of democratic culture have not only led to growth of unrest but also increased the rank of religion-fed fanatics. And this culture of fanaticism is further spurred by divide and rule policy promoted by Islamabad from time to time. The sectarian violence in the region suits the interests of Islamabad as it provides various sects fodder to keep them engaged, thus letting the issues such as fundamental rights subside from their attention. As a result, no unified voice could emerge from the muffled people. Pakistan also uses the volatile situation to pursue its interests such as ceding a significant portion of territory to China without any provocation or using the area to train terrorists. Though at the surface level the situation seems to be managed at the will of Pakistan, in reality the things have outmanoeuvred the designs of the ruler. It seems that the sectarian genie has come out of the bottle with no clue to make it return back. Besides sectarian turbulence the other most serious problem that Pakistan has to grapple with is the movement for independence by the local people. All these developments might have serious implications for the whole South Asian region, the glimmerings of which have already been felt. The acute sectarianism alongside the utter neglect of the area since past six decades with unavailability of even minimal necessitates of life, the dissenting voices have become quite vocal wherein the demand for independence of the area from the clutches of Pakistan has become a dominant force.

The Beginning

The region, slightly smaller than NWFP of Pakistan but more than six times the size of 'AJK,' is sparsely populated with a population of just around 870,000 as per the 1998 census. It has a conglomeration of numerous ethnic groups and tribes. F. M. Khan gives the complex breakdown of the sects in the region: Hunza, Punial, Yasin, Ishkoman and Gupis (100 per cent Ismaili), Nagar (100 per cent Shia), Chilas and Darel/ Tanger (100 per cent Sunnis), Astor (90 per cent Sunni, 10 percent Shia), Baltistan (96 per cent Shia, 2 per cent Sunni, 2 per cent Nurbakhshi) and Gilgit (60 per cent Shia, 40 per cent Sunni).[1] As per latest available estimate, the population of the area is approximately 1.5 million with around 39 per cent Shia, 27 per cent Sunni, 18 per cent Ismaili and 16 per cent Nurbakhshi. The district wise breakdown as per Manzoom Ali's 2004 estimation is Gilgit (54 per cent Shia, 27 per cent Ismaili and 19 per cent Sunni), Skardu (87 per cent Shia, 10 per cent Nurbakhshi and 3 per cent Sunni), Diamer (90 per cent Sunni, 10 per cent Shia), Ghizer (87 per cent Ismaili, 13 per cent Sunni) and Ghanche (87 per cent Nurbakhshi, 8 per cent Sunni, 5 per cent Shia).[2] The district of Astore, made in 2005 comprises 70 per cent Sunni and 30 per cent Shia. The region have a high percentage of Shia, some tribal in their ethnic origin and many Ismaili Shias, the sect led by the Agha Khan and considered heretics by hard-line Islamists.[3] Major languages spoken in the region are Shina, Balti, Brushaski, Wakhi, Khowar and Domski.

Sectarianism is rife in this sparsely populated but ethnically and linguistically diverse region. Five districts of the region are dominated by one sect, consequence being rare sectarian strife though in the recent years the menace has spread all over. The biggest trouble prone area is Gilgit, the administrative centre of Gilgit-Baltistan. Traditionally, the people of Gilgit-Baltistan are peace loving. There are reports of many inter-ethnic and inter-tribe marriages in the region. Ethnic ties and tribal loyalties surpassed sectarian identities. Things have drastically changed in the area since they came under the rule of Pakistan, especially since late 1980s. Today the entire population is divided on the sectarian basis. The situation has reached such a stage in the last two decades that petty issues are enough to spark bloody sectarian clashes. Recent decades have witnessed many such bloodbaths resulting in innumerable men and material losses. In most of the incidents of sectarian violence Shias are at the receiving end. In fact, many analysts consider the region a battleground for Pakistan's sectarian agenda. It is argued that at the behest of Islamabad, members of the Sunni sect attack the Shias at every available opportunity. Every Sunni attack results in a tit-for-tat Shia response thereby putting the area in a vicious circle of violence. HRW in its annual report released in January 2006 noted that intelligence agencies of Pakistan are to be blamed for the sectarian violence in the area.

The history of the ongoing sectarian violence in Gilgit-Baltistan dates back to 1960s and 1970s when the religious leaders of Sunni and Shia sects started invectives against each other. The international scenario in the form of the Iranian revolution and the Afghanistan war further contributed to sectarian troubles in late 1980s and 1990s. It is argued that the increased activities of religious extremists in the wake of Pakistan's involvement in the Afghan war coupled with the freedom given to religious groups have vitiated the atmosphere in this Shia majority area. The LeT gained influence in the area during the Kargil War in 1999 thereby putting the last nail in the coffin on the once common harmonious style of living. The sectarian tensions and killings in Pakistan too contribute directly to sectarian tensions in the region. Portentously, the recent period has witnessed emergence of a vicious circle wherein the sectarian violence in Pakistan have a direct impact on the region and vice versa. Pakistan's use of religious groups for internal and external policy objectives is a major reason for the current sectarian situation in the country.[4] It is, thus, not hidden that the basic dynamics of sectarianism in Gilgit-Baltistan is also a replica of the situation in Pakistan, being the offshoot of the policies of the same rulers. The deliberately kept ambiguity over the status of the area accompanied by a strong control from Islamabad based military dictators has played a key role in spreading this menace. To quote an ICG report, "By denying the Northern Areas a constitutional identity, administering it through a highly centralized bureaucracy and depriving its residents of political rights and recourse to justice, Pakistan has created an environment in which increasing numbers, particularly youth, have no outlet to express themselves except through sectarian violence. 'Sectarianism has provided a convenient outlet for releasing the frustration engendered by political neglect,' said the local PML-Nawaz leader, Hafeez-ur-Rehman. 'Wherever there is a lingering sense of deprivation, the eventual outcome can only be chaos and destruction.' An NALC member added: 'Religious extremism always emerges from the womb of military rule.'"[5]

The first reported sectarian clash in Gilgit-Baltistan took place during Zulfikar Ali Bhutto's reign in the mid-seventies when Sunnis raised objections over the Shias' making a stage in the middle of a road and delivering speeches. Acting on the objection, Bhutto deprived Shias of this right. The consequent resentment of Shias resulted in firing by police, injuring many. Things deteriorated during the tenure of General Zia-ul-Haq in Pakistan in 1980s. After coming to power, under the slogan of Nizam-e-Mustafa he obligated sharia, largely anti-Shia, in order to legitimize the military rule and to promote jehad in

Afghanistan and more prominently in J&K with the help of Sunni Islamist parties and Deobandis. The Zia era witnessed creation of extremists groups like the anti-Shia Sipah-e-Sahaba and in reaction to that Tehreek-e-Nafaz-e-Fiqah-e-Jafria was formed by Shia extremists. In 1990, the Sipah-e-Sahaba created another extremist wing, the Lashkar-e-Jhangvi and the Shias formed the Sipah-e-Muhammad. In an editorial Gilgit was described as 'an old sectarian trouble spot, with many past tragedies to its name' fitting in the 'prognosis that such aggression is always targeted at a minority which is concentrated in any area.'[6]

The major brunt of aggressive Sunni Islamization drive initiated by Genderal Zia was borne by Shia dominated Gilgit-Baltistan region. The importance given by Islamabad to the ulemas and the politics played by the regional administrative officers appointed by Islamabad have been responsible for fuelling sectarian clashes.[7] To quote an editorial published in Pakistani daily *Dawn*, "The seeds of this violence were sown during the period of General Zia-ul-Haq in the backdrop of the Afghan war and Islamabad's overt support of Deobandi Islamist groups like Gulbuddin Hekmatyar's Hezb-e-Islami.... Since then thousands, mostly Shiite, have fallen prey to the Sunni-Deobandi sectarian frenzy."[8] Besides, it was always in the interest of army in Pakistan to keep the Gilgit-Baltistan divided on sectarian lines to keep its tight control over the strategically important area from where it can operate its activities in J&K as also to maintain relations with China. This policy has seriously affected peace in the area.

Since the region remains deprived of substantial powers and as all high officials are from Pakistan from Sunni sect, it is no surprise that the area has become a hub of sectarianism and Shias are targeted repeatedly. The dependent and fragile political set up along with the toothless judicial system has further led to the growth of this menace. Poor economic conditions and lack of educational facilities also contributed their share in making the region hub of communal strife. In absence of government educational institutions Gilgit-Baltistan has witnessed mushroom growth of madrasas that preach hatred. The economically weak people send their children to these madrasas. As per a report the area is an ulema producing industry. As per another report Gilgit-Baltistan has the lowest GDP growth rate in comparison to Pakistan or its provinces, but very high GMP (Gross Mullah Product) and GJP (Gross Jehadi Terrorist Product) growth rates. The local madrasas in the area produce the third largest number of mullahs after the NWFP and Balochistan provinces of Pakistan and the third largest number of jehadi terrorists after Punjab and the NWFP.[9] The ulemas along with the jehadi terrorists instigate sectarian hate, leading to frequent violence.[10]

The deliberate policy of Islamabad of changing the demographic balance of the Shia dominated Gilgit-Baltistan since Zia era by settling outsiders in the area too contributed to the unrest. This part of Kashmir, known for demographic sanctity since outsiders were not allowed to settle down in the area, paid a heavy price under the Pakistan occupation. It is reported that as of January 2001 the old population ratio of 1:4 (non-locals to locals) has now changed to 3:4 (non-locals to locals). The Shia pockets of Skardu and Gilgit are witnessing a constant increase in the population of non-Shias. Abdul Hamid Khan, Chairman of BNF argues, "The Pakistani administration has also been involved in efforts to alter the demographic profile of Pakistan-occupied Gilgit-Baltistan, reducing the indigenous people to a minority. In the Gilgit and Skardu areas, large tracts of land have been allotted to non-locals. Other outsiders have purchased substantial stretches of land since they are economically better off than the locals. The rapid induction of Punjabi and Pushtun outsiders has created a sense of acute insecurity among the locals."[11] The *Friday Times* of October 15-21, 1992 quoted Muzaffar Ali, a Shia leader and General Secretary of the Gilgit-Baltistan Bar Association, as saying: "Pakistan is instigating violence to suppress our genuine demands. In Pakistan, three Supreme Court Judges have to confirm a sessions judge's verdict. Here... a single senior judge from down country (Pakistan) confirms a verdict functioning as an autonomous judicial commissioner. He is at times even junior to the local sessions judge. The State Subject rules remained enforced in Indian Kashmir after 1947.... We have ended up without a constitution, representation, even without civil or judicial rights ...." This policy of bringing Sunni settlers from outside got a boost after the construction of the Karakoram Highway and the opening of trade through the China border. The people from Kargil, who went Gilgit-Baltistan to meet their relatives, told the authors that most of the business in the area is in hands of the outsiders settled there.[12]

Easy availability of arms in the area is another reason for the sect-based violence. Despite scores of checkpoints, arms and narcotics flow unabated in the area. The setting up of training camps for the jehadis to fight for 'independence' of Kashmir has made the area a place to buy weapons easily. It is argued that sophisticated weaponry, including AK-47 assault rifles and rocket launchers are easily available in the market, thus making the society more violent. Reportedly, 'approximately 12,000 Kalashnikovs have been stored in Skardu city for terrorism, 64 double-door pick-ups are used to supply weapons for Baltistan alone ... the ISI has turned the whole region into a military depot, which could explode anytime.' Use of this territory for training the jehadis to 'fight for independence of Kashmir' since late 1980s and early 1990s proved disastrous for the area. Many local Sunnis who had fought erstwhile Soviet Union as jehadis in Afghanistan returned home after the Soviet withdrawal in late 1980s, and joined anti-Shia sectarian groups. It is reported that in most of the Sunni dominated areas there was mushroom growth of the training camps where Sunni jehadis were given training with arms and ammunition, reaching the area in the unprecedented number. The period also witnessed return of many local Shia graduates from Iran's religious schools. It was told to authors by those who have visited the area that many of the Shias go to Iran from Gilgit- Baltistan for Islamic education and employment. 'With Iranian financial backing and support,' they formed Shia militant organizations to counter the Sunni extremist groups. The retired Shia officials from Pakistan army also started training the youth. Both groups being armed and trained the situation is easily imaginable.

The Kargil war also had an adverse effect on the already volatile situation. The use of an extremist anti-Shia LeT alongside the regular troops during the Kargil intrusion of 1999 further fuelled the cycle of sectarian violence. It is reported that since then the extremist organizations like JeM, Al-Ikhwan and Harkat-ul-Mujahideen have opened their branches in the area thereby making it a 'hub of Sunni jehadi training and anti-Shia activism.' According to Hamid Khan, many terrorist training camps has been established in Gilgit-Baltistan by Pakistan including Tangir and Darel, Astore, Darul-Uloom, Juglote, Gilgit, Madrasa Nusratul-Islam, Konodas, Skardu city, and Ghowadi village near Skardu. There is also a big camp near Mansehra of NWFP on the Karakoram Highway. Following the announcement of President Musharraf of dismantling the entire terrorist training infrastructure in POK in January 2005 it was expected that the situation would improve. Instead, it is widely reported that despite the ban on many of these groups, they still operate freely under pseudo names.

Turmoil Turning Gory

First major sectarian clash took place when anti-Shia riots broke out in May 1988 over the sighting of the *ramzan* moon. When Shias in Gilgit celebrated Eid-ul-Fitr, Sunnis, still fasting because their religious leaders had not sighted the moon, attacked them. This led to violent clashes between the two sects. Following intervention by the local leaders the situation settled down. After a brief calm of nearly four days, reportedly the military regime of Pakistan used Afghan and Pakistani wahabis from NWFP and local Sunnis, jointly called *lashkar* (army), to 'teach a lesson' to Shias that led to hundreds of killings. For three days, the *lashkar* killed and looted with impunity. This was despite the presence of contingents of the paramilitary Frontier Constabulary.[13]

The official complicity in the attack becomes clear from the fact that the army of extremists with arms had travelled a long way to reach Gilgit but were not stopped at any point. As per the ICG report, "The attack was entirely government sponsored, or how else could the invaders have been, first, allowed unhindered passage from NWFP right up to Gilgit and, secondly, permitted to commit the carnage that they did?,' asked a Shia religious leader from Jalalabad, one of the villages razed to the ground. Sunnis deny government complicity and insist both sides were at fault. 'The administration did nothing to prevent the riots of 1988 but to say that it was actively involved would be untrue. It was more a case of gross negligence than active complicity,' a Sunni leader maintained. However, he conceded: 'Zia let the Sunni mosques say and do what they pleased and allowed the Sunni mullahs to fill the power vacuum in the region.'"[14] To quote Mohammad Shehzad, "On the fifth day, a huge *lashkar* of 80,000 Sunni extremists was sent by Zia-ul-Haq's government to annihilate the Shias. Villages inhabited by the Shias- Jalalabad, Bonji, Darot, Jaglot, Pari, and Manawar were completely ruined. Even their animals were slaughtered. The *laskhar* had travelled a long distance from Mansehra to Gilgit and the government did not stop it. Instead, it put the blame on RAW (Research and Analysis Wing, an Indian intelligence agency) and CIA (Central Intelligence Agency, US intelligence Agency)."[15] According to a *Herald* report of May 1990, "In May 1988, low-intensity political rivalry and sectarian tension ignited into full-scale carnage as thousands of armed tribesmen from outside Gilgit district invaded Gilgit along the Karakoram Highway. Nobody stopped them. They destroyed crops and houses, lynched and burnt people to death in the villages around Gilgit town. The number of dead and injured was put in the hundreds. But numbers alone tell nothing of the savagery of the invading hordes and the chilling impact it has left on these peaceful valleys." Similarly in a report published in *Dawn* on December 21, 2002, K. M. Ahmed gave the details regarding the sending of *lashkar* by Zia in the area. The report pointed, ".... the raiders, who were tribals and mujahideen elements, could not have reached this remote place from Peshawar without someone's blessing. The Frontier Constabulary, whose check-posts dot the Swat-Besham road and the Besham-Gilgit highway, did not act to intercept the raiders."[16]

Since the initial clashes ended with a truce between local community leaders, Shias were unprepared for the attack. As per unofficial reports, there was killing of about 700 Shias.[17] It is also said that none other than Osama bin Laden led the wahabi Pushtuns.[18] Some experts believe that the mysterious air crash in which General Zia died was an act of sabotage done by a Shia crew member accompanying Zia to avenge the carnage. Though this sectarian clash is mainly blamed on Sunni Islamization policies of General Zia, yet the subsequent governments largely failed to bring an end to the deadly clashes between the two sects. In fact, the reliance on jehadis for its proxy war in Kashmir has continued to fuel the flames of sectarian violence in the region. Places like Chilas and Gilgit have become hub of Sunni jehadi training and anti-Shia activism.[19]

During the democratic interlude of the 1990s in Pakistan, representative institutions ensured an uneasy peace in the area with Shias attempting to unite themselves on a political platform to assert demands. To quote the ICG report, "Disillusioned with Islamabad and motivated by the need to unite on a common platform to ensure their collective survival, Shias in the region supported the Tehreek-e-Nafaz-e-Fiqah-e-Jafria (TNFJ), initially a religious organization but transformed, through sheer numbers, into a formidable political force. The TNFJ, and the Shia community as whole, boycotted elections to the Northern Areas Council in 1991, accusing KANA minister Sardar Mehtab Abbassi of redrawing constituencies in Gilgit to favour the Sunnis. In 1994, however, soon after the passage of the LFO and concerned about Shia alienation, Islamabad held early elections in which the TNFJ won ten of 24 seats and was included in a coalition government. Although Islamabad's decision to make concessions to a local religious party, rather than strengthening moderate political forces, was troublesome, it did help to lessen Shia alienation."[20]

To assume that the situation turned better would be to close eyes to the reality. According to figures cited in the ICG report there was a steady increase in sectarian related killings between 1990 and 1992, with seven in 1990, twelve in 1991, and 30 in 1992. Gilgit was in firm grip of sectarian violence in 1992 following the assassination of Gayyasuddin, a Sunni leader on May 30, leading to at least 30 killings. This was followed by local attempt to bring peace by organizing peace talks which could not bring fruitful results. The conciliatory talks ended when Latif Hassan, a Shia leader was shot dead on August 4, 1993, again leading to clashes claiming more than two dozen lives. In 1993 sectarian riots 20 Shias reportedly lost their lives.

The Rizvi Episode

Violent tension again swallowed up the area with the murder of Agha Zia-ud-din Rizvi, a prominent Shia leader in January 2005. An attempt on his life was made on January 8, 2005, critically injuring him. One of the assailants killed by his bodyguards was later identified as a member of Lashkar-e-Jhangvi, known for its anti-Shia ideology. The assassination attempt was followed by a violent reaction by Shias. A large number of public and private properties were set on fire and a number of officials attacked. A Sunni district forest officer and six others were burnt alive in the house of former. The Sunni director of the health department was also killed in his office. More than a dozen people were killed and uncounted injured before troops were deployed to restore law and order. Curfew was imposed in the area. The death of injured Rizvi in less than a week led to fresh wave of vicious circle of violence. The news of his death enraged his supporters and they embarked on a violent reaction.

Many people again became the victims of sectarian violence. The area continued to simmer for weeks after the incident. The curfew remained in place for one month in Gilgit and Skardu, but failed to bring back normalcy with incidents of shooting continuing. The Karakoram Highway was blocked, thus obstructing movement of people and goods. The reaction to the killing of the Shia cleric also reached Karachi in Pakistan where a Sipah-e-Sahaba cleric was shot dead by unidentified gunmen. Another attempt to kill an Islamabad Sunni-Deobandi cleric failed. After two months in March, a former Gilgit-Baltistan Sunni police chief, Sakhiullah Tareen, who was in charge of the area at the time of assassination of Rizvi, was shot dead along with his guards.

Islamabad suspected that a 'foreign agency' had killed Rizvi to fuel sectarianism in Pakistan. In fact it has become a trend in Pakistan that whenever there is some untoward incident a foreign hand is blamed. To quote an editorial published in *Dawn,* "No place, from Gilgit in the north to Karachi in the south, is safe from this menace (sectarian violence).... Every time there is a sectarian attack in Pakistan, religious leaders and officials accuse foreign intelligence agencies of committing the atrocity. The fact, however, is that every time the police catches the culprits, we find that they belong to one or the other half-dozen sectarian groups that have held this country hostage to their agenda. Evidence also proves that the violence has been perpetrated by zealous Muslims rather than by foreign elements.... This is not a happy scenario. And it won't do us any good to follow the line of clerics who try to sweep this violence under the carpet by blaming it on foreign hands. We will have to accept that the sectarian bug has bitten us and the fever is running high. Only then can we begin to cure it."[21]

The Text Book Controversy

It is widely believed that the real cause of killing of Rizvi was his struggle in favour of a separate syllabus for Shia students. The killing of Rizvi intensified the textbook controversy that rocked the area for more than five years. The trouble started in 1999 when Islamabad introduced amended textbooks, produced by the Textbook Board of Punjab province of Pakistan. According to Shia leaders, the curriculum promoted Sunni beliefs and practices, excluding theirs. The Shia community started a campaign for changes in the curriculum, particularly in textbooks for religious studies that allegedly presented only a Sunni version of the Islamic history. The distortions were not only limited to Islamic studies but also highlighted in textbooks of other subjects such as Urdu, History, English and even the drawing books. In an interview, Rizvi had warned the government of serious consequences if the issue was not resolved. To quote him, "The government has failed to address it to our satisfaction. The textbooks promote Sunni thought and totally neglect ours. We want the books redesigned or the consequences will be extremely dangerous."[22] The Shia leader said the Islamic textbooks have been deliberately distorted to promote sectarian hatred between the two sects. A senior Education Ministry official at Islamabad was quoted saying that the government was considering re-writing the controversial portions of textbooks. Despite initial assurances to look into the matter the administration later backtracked.[23] The issue remained unresolved, giving a hint that the government was not serious. In an area known for sectarian violence the move of changing the curriculum, tilted heavily towards the ideology of one sect, without first trying to build a consensus cannot be categorized as an attempt to modernize the education system. Despite knowing possible Shia backlash, the government's series of assurances followed by denials lend credence to the suspicion that the move for curriculum change was a calculated one to keep the flame of sectarianism burning.

On expected lines Shias resented the apathetic attitude of the authorities. Shia and Sunni students in a Gilgit high school clashed in 2001. Agha Zia-ud-Din called for a boycott of the schools. Since 2001 Shia students started school boycotts and occasional clashes became common between the two sects. Gilgit witnessed widespread unrest for a fortnight commencing from the last week of June 2001. Instead of sincerely attempting to resolve the issue Islamabad terminated all movements between Gilgit and the rest of Pakistan. Reportedly, a strict censorship was imposed on the publication of details of the unrest. In February 2003 unidentified gunmen killed at least nine Shias and wounded eight, all from Gilgit-Baltistan, as they headed to evening prayers in Karachi. In May 2004, a local attempt was made to resolve the curriculum issue and all the sects of the region agreed to the settlement on a three-point formula:

1. In Shia majority areas, instead of the controversial aspects of the curriculum, the one suitable to the Shia faith would be taught.
2. In Sunni majority areas, the curriculum would be taught as it is.
3. In the areas where there is mixed population, the curriculum would specify the faith of both the sects.

The utterly insensitive administration, however, rejected the proposal that could have restored peace in the area. The situation again aggravated. There were large-scale arrests of school children as well as the top Shia leadership. In response, the Shia community announced observation of strike on June 3, 2004. However, a curfew was imposed early in the morning on the same day to make the strike attempt a failure. The Shias defied the curfew and protested strongly against the arrest of their leaders. The consequent violent clashes with security forces led to heavy men and material losses. There were half a dozen killings. Many were injured and property worth millions of rupees was destroyed. Despite critical situation, the Minister for KANA, chief executive of Gilgit-Baltistan, visited the area only once for two hours, to get a briefing from the local administration. Surprisingly aftermath of the terrible violence the local government agreed to enforce the formula, which it had earlier rejected, put in place by the two sects to calm down the situation. Following violent riots, an editorial in *Daily Times* blamed not only Islamabad but also the media for being criminally apathetic towards the happenings in Gilgit-Baltistan. It wrote, "The syllabus issue in Gilgit continues to hang fire. …Sporadic news has been coming out of Gilgit about the syllabus problem for the past one year. We know that the Shias there are unhappy over certain passages and pictures in the officially prescribed Islamiat textbook. But it is a measure of the failure of the mainstream press that most newspapers have not bothered to dig up the facts. Every story talks about the unrest and refers to the syllabus, but no attempt has been made to provide details of what exactly is wrong with the textbook.… This is in line with the treatment we have meted out to the Northern Areas over the past four decades. In the 1980s, the Pakistani state under Gen. Zia-ul Haq made a deliberate attempt to infuse Sunni-Deobandi cadres of a sectarian party in order to put down the Shia. The problem of syllabus we now encounter in Gilgit and also elsewhere is the product of the state's enterprise of backing a particular brand of Islamic exegesis. Of course, there are other factors, not least the rampant corruption in the region by officials of the state and lack of development and employment opportunities. But the ground reality is that the area is sitting atop a time bomb and the syllabus is the trigger that could activate it. That is why it is surprising that despite the issue festering for so long the federal (Pakistan) government has done nothing visible to address it."[24]

Islamabad's argument that the violence was instantaneous had been challenged. The Musharraf government, as per news reports, was forewarned about the possibility of violence spreading when in the year 2003 there were protests against the prescribed textbooks. There were also complaints that clerics were coming from 'outside' the area and delivering flaming sermons. But no heed was paid to these serious developments. 'The incidents were not treated as a series of connected happenings leading up to a climax.' The Syllabus Issue Committee unanimously agreed to withdraw the textbooks containing controversial contents unacceptable to either sect. On April 26, 2005, Pakistan's Minister for Education, Lt. General (retd.) Javed Ashraf Qazi chaired a high-level committee meeting in Islamabad, which had three representatives from Gilgit-Baltistan, to resolve the issue. It was decided to replace the contentious books by those of NWFP Textbook Board and the National Book Foundation that were acceptable to both the sects. It was also assured that all controversial contents from textbooks would be withdrawn in the revised curriculum.[25] Despite passing of more than two years the assurance is still waiting to be fulfilled. The old textbooks are still used in the region, although the controversial chapters are not taught. In absence of a permanent solution to the curriculum issue Shias contend that there can never be a compromise on commonly acceptable syllabus especially after the 'martyrdom' of Rizvi, the main advocate for a separate curriculum.

List of some of the Objections

(i) The incident of wahee (revelation) has been described in a ridiculous manner that shows the Prophet himself was not sure about his prophet-hood. Islamiat, 4th grade, 22; Social Studies, 4th grade, 115; Urdu, 8th grade, 14.

(ii) Abraham's father Azar has been described as worshipper of idols. Islamiat, 6th grade, 62.

(iii) The Prophet is said to have missed his prayer during the battle of Khandaq. Islamiat, 5th grade, 43.

(iv) The Prophet's wife Ayesha has been projected as superior to all other women of the prophet's family through fake ahadiz (sayings of the Prophet). Urdu, 7th, 9-10.

(v) The Sunni caliphs have been presented as Khulfa-e-Rashideen unopposed by Shias. [The Shias do not recognize the first three caliphs as Khulfa-e-Rashideen.] Urdu, 3rd grade, 89; Arabic, 7th grade, 46; Social Studies, 7th grade, 12-14.

(vi) The Caliphs [that are not recognized by Shias] have been eulogized through titles such as Siddique-wa-Amirul Momineen [the First Caliph Hazrat Abu Bakar Siddique] and Farooq-wa-

Amirul Momineed [the Second Caliph Hazrat Umar Farooq]. Shias claim such titles are only for Hazrat Ali [the Fourth Caliph]. Urdu, 4th grade, 77; Islamiat, 4th grade, 25; Arabic, 8th grade, 27.

(vii) The Sunni Caliphs have been glorified through special chapters that pay them a rich tribute. No such tribute has been paid to the Shia Caliphs.

(viii) It is a fabricated statement that the Prophet asked the First Caliph to lead the prayer when he [the Prophet] was ill. Islamiat, 5th grade, 59-60. Islamiat, BA, 294.

(ix) The contribution and sacrifices of Hazrat Ali have been faded out deliberately.

(x) Yazid has been totally exonerated from Karbala and the entire blame has been shifted to Ibn-e-Ziyad. Urdu, 8th grade, 105.

(xi) Khalid bin Walid has been praised more compared to Hazrat Ali. It is untrue that the Prophet had bestowed him (Walid) the title of Saif Ullah. Urdu, 7th grade, 30-33.

(xii) Sunni procedure of ablution has been featured in Islamiat, Urdu, 9-10th grade, 157.

(xiii) The addition of prayer is better than sleep. Islamiat, grade 8th, 8.

(xiv) Sunni procedure of prayer is featured. Islamiat, 2nd grade, 15; Urdu, 3rd grade, 57.

(xv) A picture that depicts Sunni style of saying prayer. Urdu, 2nd grade, 18.

(xvi) Such sayings of Prophet have been quoted that have been told by the Sunni historians.

(xvii) The Islamiat of 12th grade promotes the Sunni school of thought.

(xviii) Prophet's uncle Hazrat Abu Talib has been described as non-Muslim. Islamiat, BA, 231.

Source: http://www.sikhspectrum.com/082003/textbooks.htm

The recent history of the area is proof enough that even if a solution to the textbook issue could be finally found the sectarian gulf in the area is not going to end. While Islamabad was proudly announcing the 'amicable' solution of the textbook problem, four Shias were shot during Eid Milad-ul-Nabi celebrations. The incident took place when Shias were returning home after celebrating the Prophet's birth anniversary. To avoid counter reaction Section 144 was imposed for two months in the area. In October 2005, Gilgit again witnessed bloody clashes between Shias and all Sunni Pakistan Rangers, a paramilitary force of Pakistan deployed in Gilgit-Baltistan. The upsurge of violence in Gilgit followed an armed clash between Rangers and civilians, claiming twelve lives. The area remained under curfew since October 13 for a long time. On December 7, 2005 an editorial published in the *Daily Times* reported that intelligence agents had discovered Lashkar-e-Jhangvi and Sipah-e-Sahaba groups planning to use suicide-bombs to target Shia members of the Gilgit-Baltistan legislative council. The editorial apprehended another bout of sectarian attacks in the wake of the disclosure that extremist groups are attempting to recruit members from the quake hit areas of 'AJK' and NWFP by distributing publications like Zarb-e-Momin for this purpose.[26]

On September 21, 2005 Islamabad formed a *jirga* (traditional tribal assembly), headed by the NALC Speaker, Malik Muhammad Maskeen and included representatives from both the sects to bring peace in the area, without involving the other NALC members in the process. Despite the fact that the *jirga* signed a peace agreement, the area remained anything but peaceful. The extremist leaders of both sects have continued their preaching of hatred. To quote the ICG report, "Sunni Tehreek Ahl-e-Sunnat Wal Jamaat Chief, Qazi Nisar Ahmed has warned 'if the Shias continue to publicly hold offensive rituals and disparage our revered religious personages, then one should not be surprised if a Sunni takes up his gun and retaliates.' Sheikh Nayyar Abbas, leader of the Shia Anjuman-i-Islami insists there are no moderate Sunnis in Gilgit, only Wahhabis who denounce Shias: 'When we are called infidels and people who are detestable to us are publicly venerated, what do you expect us to do? We cannot abandon our core beliefs simply for the sake of peace.'"[27]

Highway Turned Battleground

Karakoram Highway, linking China to Pakistan, has become a battleground for sectarian strife. Travelling on this road is considered 'nightmare.' This all-weather road stretching about 840 kilometres runs through a predominantly Sunni area from Gilgit to Rawalpindi where instances of firing on passenger buses have taken several times, claiming many lives. It also passes via Shia dominated Nagar valley onwards to Hunza, where incidents of selective killings and ambushing the buses are not uncommon.[28] Pakistan appointed Sunni inspector general of police - highest-ranking police officer in the area - was assassinated along with his bodyguards on March 23, 2005 while travelling between Gilgit and Hunza. Two Shias travelling on the highway were also shot in the same month. On July 17, 2005 an attack on a bus near Chilas led to killing of four passengers and injuring others. This incident led to a spree of tit-for-tat killings. Six more deaths were reported in revenge attacks. Later a Union Council chairperson and three others were gunned down. On July 22, 2005 sectarian hatred reignited clashes between rival groups in the area leading to killing of ten people. The seriousness of situation can be gauged from the fact that people are reluctant to travel on the roads running through the areas inhabited by the rival sect. To avoid passage through the Shia dominated Ampheri area Sunnis residing in the Basin area have constructed a bridge over river Gilgit to reach Gilgit city via Konodas. Shias have to pass through Sunni dominated Kashrot area as they have no alternative to reach airport without an ominous risk.[29]

Insensitive Administration

According to the figures given by the Institute for Conflict Management 81 people had lost their lives till October 28, 2005. As per another estimate there were around 100 deaths in sectarian violence between June 2004 and October 2005 in the area.[30] As per a report of HRCP more than sixty-seven people were killed till July in Gilgit-Baltistan since January 8, 2005. The report held the local administration, the Pakistan army and Islamabad responsible for failing to take action in time to tackle the situation. The insensitivity resulted in huge loss of lives and property thereby making all sects suspicious of the role of government.[31] In its 2006 annual report the commission again showed its concern by lamenting that the area continues to remain in the grip of sectarian riots.

Despite such a tragic situation the authorities have failed to neutralise the menace of sectarianism effectively. Rather, the volatility is gaining strength despite the government claims to the contrary. The information regarding violence in the area reaches outside only sporadically. There is little documentation about the arrest and punishment of those responsible. Either no arrests were made, or if so there have been no convictions. In most cases no judicial enquiry was done. Even when some inquiry was done, such as the one to investigate Rizvi's murder, the report was not made public. The committee set up to investigate October 2005 sectarian incidents submitted its report to Islamabad in January 2006 but the report has not been made public even after more than one and half years passed.

There have also been large-scale arbitrary arrests of the leaders of a particular sect. In 2005 a Shia leader, Sheikh Ghulam Mohiyuddin was arrested at a gathering. Police claimed that he was apprehended for breaching peace. Hundreds of his followers witnessed his arrest. Earlier, another religious leader, Sheikh Nasir Hussain Zamani, had also been arrested on the same charge. The Imamia Council of Gilgit said the police move was to sabotage peace talks currently underway to reduce sectarian tensions.[32] The administration has shown lack of understanding and sensitivity towards the majority population not only in matters like curriculum but also in the appointment of officials. In 2005, Pakistan government installed a Sunni to the post of chief commissioner in Gilgit that created large-scale resentment. To quote an editorial of *Dawn*, "The ministry concerned appointed a fundamentalist Sunni as chief commissioner despite its awareness that the Shias of Gilgit panic at the appointment of officers holding extreme Sunni views. What it ignored was the message contained in the earlier murder of a retired Sunni I G Chief Commissioner Major (retd.) Nadeem Manzur, a hardcore Sunni officer ... carries no blot but his almost fanatic observance of Sunni faith should have alerted the ministry to his unsuitability. In the event, he proved ineffective and has recently been recalled. Why was he sent to Gilgit in the first place? One fears that the ministry itself could be infected with sectarian passions."[33] The local leaders have time and again charged Islamabad for its sectarian based administrative arrangement in the area that as per their version keeps the flame of the sect based violence burning. The political arrangement as per the BNF website has been always motivated by sectarianism. The arrangement as per the website was as follows:[34]

- Chief Executive - Non local Shia Minister of Pakistan.
- Deputy Chief Executive - Mir Ghazanfar Ali Khan, a local Hunza Ismaili, with real powers if any; in the hands of his non local Sunni wife.
- Speaker - Malik Maskeen. A 1988 Government sponsored sectarian attack hero, who is a Sunni like his predecessor.
- Deputy Speaker - Syed Asad Zaidi, Secretive Agency Shia man, who initiated Shia-Sunni conflict in Gilgit.

The real powers are in the hands of following ruling military cabal:-

- Commander Frontier Constabulary: Always a Wahabi oriented Sunni.
- Brigadiers and Colonels: Always non local Wahabi oriented Sunnis.
- Corps Commander 10 Corps : Non-local Sunni.
- DG of ISI and other Agencies: All non-local Sunnis always.
- The real Chief Executive: General Pervez Musharraf. Abdul Hamid Khan, fighting for the independence of the

area, charges Islamabad of a direct role in the sectarian violence in the area. He argues, "One of the major issues that we are today faced within Balawaristan is the growing menace of sectarian rivalries. For this Pakistani occupants and their agents are to blame, masters that they are of the art of 'divide and rule', pitting Shias and Sunnis against each other. Pakistani agents paid Sunni and Shia clerics to spew venom against each other and thus divide our people. There is evidence to suggest the direct involvement of Pakistani soldiers and Afghan militants in promoting this increasing strife. As a result, many of our people have been killed in what are euphemistically termed 'Sunni-Shia' conflicts. Whenever efforts were made to breach the divide between the Sunnis and the Shias, Pakistani occupants attempted to stoke the flames of sectarianism even further. On April 9, 1993, when sectarian strife was at its peak, a conference of all political, religious and nationalist parties of Balawaristan was organized by the BNF. Hardliners belonging to both the Shia and the Sunni sects were also attending the conference, and so the local administration was requested for security. The police present was near the conference venue usually, but was deliberately withdrawn while the conference was going on. The intention of the occupying forces was quite clear. They wanted to see the murder of rival groups, but fortunately nothing untoward happened. The conference concluded peacefully, demanding political, democratic and human rights for our people and the withdrawal of the Pakistani administration. The participants unanimously expressed their anguish against the Pakistani occupation....The Inter-Services Intelligence, the Pakistani secret services' agency, has also played a central role in promoting sectarianism in Balawaristan. And so have the judiciary as well as the head of administration and Police."

Pakistan's policy of nurturing the extremist elements has taken its toll wherein the sectarian monster has grown to its fullest extent, engulfing not only Gilgit-Baltistan but also whole of Pakistan. To quote an editorial, "Unfortunately, the state of Pakistan has been unable to stem this (sectarian) growing trend because of its past involvement with the jehadi militias who were trained out of the Sunni seminaries.... Sectarianism is the outcome of the process of national-security driven 'nation-building' by the military in Pakistan for many decades....Either the state is too weak or too scared to name and take on all such sectarian organizations or it still hopes to 'use' some of them for dubious 'national security' purposes in the future or, as is more likely, it is a bit of both."[35]

Many analysts argue the denial of rights to the people and underdevelopment has led to the spread of sectarian violence. To quote Gulmina Bilal, "When rights are denied to people, when justice fails them, when they don't have a political voice, conflicts will arise and they will be settled by the gun barrel rather than political negotiation."[36] Here a question needs to be raised: if the concerns are raised at the discriminatory role of the administration as found in unprecedented change of demographic composition in the area, is blaming only underdevelopment and ambiguous status for sectarian violence justified? At the same time, it is also admissible that these factors along with illiteracy have contributed largely to the growth of Frankenstein's monster called sectarianism. In fact, as already mentioned, there is official complicity in the sectarian incidents. It is suspected the administration occasionally stirs it up to divert the public attention from the political issues. This development has given rise to widespread suspicion that Islamabad pays *ulema* to start clashes. Attempts to suppress popular aspirations by enforcing draconian laws and changing the demographic pattern corroborate this viewpoint.

The administration uses coercive tactics such as deploying troops, imposing curfew and giving shoot-at-sight order to control the situation. The imposition of curfew leaves travellers stranded, besides bringing plethora of problems for the locals. People have to stay at home without sufficient food and fuel for days altogether. All public activities too come to a halt. Unfortunately these coercive means that need to be used as last resort have become a norm. On an average curfew was imposed every fortnightly after the Rizvi episode. The coercive tactics, however, only brings a facade of normalcy. Violence keeps erupting from time to time. Criticizing the official response in form of curfews, slapping Section 144, calling in the troops, cordons and arrests an editorial in *Daily Times* condemned the lack of attempt to address the causes of sectarian unrest, the obvious result being frequent recrudescence of violence.[37]

The Cost

The cost of sectarian violence in Gilgit-Baltistan is manifold.[38] First, killings and counter killings have become routine. The soured Shia-Sunni relations have claimed thousands of lives. The persisting culture of sectarian hatred has made the lives of the innocent wretched. There is a constant threat of being shot merely because of being born into a different sect. The incidence of refusal by three Pak appointed Sunni police officers to join duty at Gilgit despite the risk of facing disciplinary action is an indicative of the grave situation. This has raised a pertinent question that if the police officers of high rank prefer dismissal to serve, what would be befalling the common people who have no option but continue living amidst the insecure environment. Second is the issue of ever-widening mistrust between the two sects wherein the Shias are at the receiving end. The Shia officials are kept out of decision making higher posts. Keeping out of the Shia officials from security arrangements during visit of General Musharraf in August 2001 exemplify the deep mistrust amongst the Sunni dominated authorities towards a particular sect. Third, it has led to forced migration. One unofficial estimate suggests that more than 30,000 Gilgit residents have fled the city and its suburbs since

2000, in the wake of rising incidents of sectarian strife. Linked with this is the issue of increasing ghettoization. A large number of families have abandoned their ancestral homes and properties to move into areas populated by their respective sects. People divided on sectarian lines prefer to live in ghettos to counter any untoward situation in a united manner. The areas dominated by the 'rival' sect are designated as no-go zones. Fourth, properties worth millions have been destroyed in the seeming unending violence. Fifth, it has also led to disruption of even the minimal available infrastructure. The frequent disruption of educational and health services have long term implications for the people. During the curriculum controversy, complete academic year of thousands of students was wasted due to closure of schools. Sixth, sectarian violence has engulfed the area so tightly that the united demand for empowered representative political institutions is not even heard. It seems the fractured people have more to settle on sectarian grounds against each other than on the political one wherein they have to jointly stand against Islamabad. However, the movement for independence from Pakistan by the alienated people has become quite perceptible in recent years.

References

1. For details see, F. M. Khan, *The History of Gilgit, Baltistan and Chitral: A Short History of two Millennia* (Gilgit: Eejaz Publishers, 2002)
2. For details see, Manzoom Ali, *Atlas of the Northern Areas* (Gilgit, 2004).
3. Stephen Philip Cohen, *The Idea of Pakistan* (New Delhi: Oxford University Press, 2005), p. 222.
4. Zaigham Khan, "Gilgit on Fire," *The International News*, January 15, 2005.
5. "Discord in Pakistan's Northern Areas," *ICG Asia Report No. 131,* Brussels/Islamabad, April 2, 2007.

6 "War within Pakistan," *Daily Times*, February 1, 2007.

7. Status of the Northern Areas, *Selected Clippings from the Pak Media (1990-94)*, May 10, 1994, p.3.
8. "Another Sectarian Atrocity," *Dawn*, February 11, 2006.
9. B. Raman, "Unrest in Gilgit-Baltistan." *http://www.saag.org/papers13/paper1241.html*. Accessed on December 12, 2006.
10. Ershad Mahmud, "Challenges before the New Government in NAs," *The International News*, December 11, 2004.
11. Abdul Hamid Khan, "Pakistan's Heart of Darkness." *http://www.atimes.com/atimes/South_Asia/DH22Df03.html*. Accessed on December 17, 2006.
12. The authors have made surveys to study the prospects of opening of Kargil-Skardu route and issue of divided families in Ladakh region in July 2006 and May 2007.
13. A. H. Sorbo, "Paradise Lost," *The Herald*, June 1988.
14. *ICG Asia Report No. 131*, n. 5.
15. Mohammed Shehzad, "Textbook Controversy in Gilgit." *http://www.sikhspectrum.com/082003/textbooks.htm*. Accessed on January 12, 2007.
16. Khaled Ahmed, "Islamic Extremism in Pakistan." *http://www.southasianmedia.net/magazine/islamicextremism_Pakistan.htm*. Accessed on August 23, 2006.
17. *Public Opinion Trends*, Pakistan Series, vol. 33, no.166, July 14, 2005.
18. B. Raman, "Pakistan: The Shia Anger." *www.saag.org/papers9/paper810.html*. Accessed on March 5, 2006.
19. "The State of Sectarianism in Pakistan," *ICG Asia Report No. 95*, Brussels/Islamabad, April 18, 2005.
20. *ICG Asia Report No. 131*, n. 5.
21.. "Another Sectarian Atrocity," n. 8.
22. *http://www.pakistan-facts.com/article.php?story=20030708125240298*. Accessed on January 18, 2007.
23. Farman Ali, "Studied Silence," *The Herald*, February 2006.
24. "The plight of the Northern Areas," *Daily Times*, June 4, 2004.
25. *Dawn*, April 27, 2005.

26. "Failure to Tackle Gilgit Violence is Unforgivable," *Daily Times*, December 7, 2005.
27. *ICG Asia Report No. 131*, n. 5.
28. Ahsan Wali Khan, "Gilgit's Continuing Tension," *The News International*, August 7, 2005.
29. *Ibid.*
30. Safdar Khan, "Gilgit's Sectarian Conundrum," *Dawn*, October 30, 2005.
31. "HRCP Mission to the Northern Areas," *Report of Fact Finding Mission of HRCP,* August-September 2005.
32. *http://www.westernresistance.com/blog/archives/001343.html*. Accessed on February 21, 2006.
33. "Failure to Tackle Gilgit Violence is Unforgivable," n. 26.
34. Ghulam Mehdi, "What a Beautiful Sectarian Political Arrangements in Northern Areas." *http://www.balawaristan.net/sectwise.html*. Accessed on September 30, 2006.
35. "War within Pakistan," *Daily Times*, February 1, 2007.
36. Gulmina Bilal, "While Gilgit burns," *The News*, November 22, 2005.
37. "Take Gilgit Violence Seriously!," *Daily Times*, April 29, 2005.
38. Seema Shekhawat, "Sectarian Violence in Northern Areas: An Analysis," *Across LOC*, July-September 2005, pp. 8-9.

5

Movement for Independence

Suffocation of popular aspirations, persistent refusal to grant the basic rights, enforcement of draconian laws and deliberate demographic change have resulted in large scale discontentment in Kashmir across the LOC.[1] The 'time has stood still' for the local people since the area came under Pak control, owing to complete neglect and apathy of successive regimes. The widespread discontent among the people is quite apparent in recent times. This discontentment has now gone beyond the earlier demands for accommodation and taken the shape of demand for independence from the control of Pakistan. There are strong voices both in 'AJK' and Gilgit-Baltistan who want freedom from Pak control. The people of Gilgit-Baltistan prefer to call the area Balawaristan, instead of using the ambiguous term Northern Areas. "We want Freedom from Pakistan's illegal occupation, Pakistan must quit Balawaristan (Occupied Gilgit-Baltistan) by complying UNCIP Resolution. No package, no Pakistan, we want free Baltistan, slavery is a curse, join and help BNF for freedom." This is the message flashed in the website of BNF.

The Background

Besides sectarianism, the spreading of discontent among the people in Gilgit-Baltistan can be attributed to a number of other factors which have been focused in this section, though they have been dealt with in tidbits elsewhere in the book. For about 60 years, the area has been administered by Pakistan although they are not legally part of it. There is little possibility of Pakistan ever agreeing to give up control of the area, either to form part of an independent state of J&K or as an independent state in its own right.[2] The area is neither a part of Pakistan nor an independent entity or part of 'AJK.' It is deprived of any legal and constitutional status. *K2*, Gilgit-Baltistan's weekly newspaper carries on its masthead, *Sarzamin-Be-Ain Ki Awaz* (the voice of the constitution-less). Frustrated over the years with the dilly-dallying tactics of the government of Pakistan over granting a status to Gilgit-Baltistan, Malik Miskeen and others had filed a writ petition with the 'AJK' high court in 1990. In its 1993 verdict the court declared that the area is a part of the territory of Kashmir and thus the administration of the area should be in the hands of the 'AJK' government. Refusing to accept the judgment, the government of Pakistan said in a statement issued on March 11, 1993, "The Azad Jammu and Kashmir Government has no jurisdiction over the NA, which are under the administrative control of Pakistan and historically had been administered by the Central Government. There is no question of passing on the administrative jurisdiction of the NA to the AJK Government." Islamabad challenged the verdict in the supreme court. The court adhered to the stand of Pakistan and asked it to grant some kind of local administration to the area. Thus, despite the attempts by the people, the area continues to remain deprived of a status. This ambiguous situation has been used by Pakistan for pursuing its own strategic interests like ceding some parts of the territory to China in 1963 and offering US to build a military base. Such kind of steps has made people suspicious of Pakistan's intentions. The area is ruled directly from Islamabad through KANA with no real powers resting in the elected NALC. A recent European parliamentarian Baroness Emma Nicholson's report entitled "Report on Kashmir: Present Situation and Future Prospects" has strongly criticized Pakistan for the absence of representative democratic institutions and political atrocities in 'AJK' and Gilgit-Baltistan.

The people of the territory have no political and socio-economic rights like right to be represented in Pakistan's parliament, the right to control budget through elected representatives, etc. Since its illegal occupation in late 1940s, the area has been under virtual Martial Law. Till late under the Frontier Crime Regulations, framed by the British during the colonial days for dealing with the 'criminal tribes' of the areas bordering Afghanistan, every resident of the area was supposed to report to the local police station about his movements. Those violating the rule were liable to punishment. The people remain without recourse to basic human rights. The freedom of speech and expression is absent. There is only a negligible presence of newspapers, radio or TV stations in the area that too are not free to report, being subjected to tight control. The publications not adhering to the lines of the administration are frequently shut down. All copies of a local magazine, *Balawaristan Times*, were confiscated and banned in 1994. *Gilgit Digest* was banned in 1998. The authorities banned the weekly K-2 many times on the charge of publishing the 'subversive' demands like human rights, democracy, etc. It was banned in the year 2000 for carrying a news report that mentioned Pakistan's independence day was celebrated as *yaum-e-siyah* (black day) in Gilgit-Baltistan. Its editor, Raja Hussain Khan Maqpoon, imprisoned twice for not adhering to the dictates of Islamabad, laments, "it is ironic that the world is more worried about the falling trees; they are sad that our white leopards are vanishing day by day; the dead bodies of our Markhor frightens them; they are going all out to preserve our eco system. But nobody ever thinks of the people of this land."[3] The HRCP in its special study of the area revealed that the rights of the people for free movement, speech and expression are constrained to the maximum. The situation of the common people could be well gauged by an incident narrated by Sultan Shahin, a New Delhi based journalist, during his trip to the area wherein an elected member of the district council, Mohammad Javed Mirza, of the Karakoram National Front, expressed his inability to give his residence telephone number since the telephone connections of all political activists are tapped.[4]

There is no high court or supreme court in the area. Nobody is allowed to file a writ on human rights violation or appeal against the decision of the chief court, the chairperson of which is nominated by Islamabad. It has the power to award death sentence to the people. Disclosing the deplorable condition, Abdul Hamid Khan, BNF leader, in a faxed statement to the international media said, "We are not only deprived of fundamentals and constitutional rights but we do not have rights that animals enjoy in some countries."[5] The HRCP's monthly newsletter for January 1994 reported, "The Judicial Commissioner does not have writ jurisdiction and, as the people of the NA do not have any fundamental rights, the Judicial Commissioner does not have jurisdiction to enforce them. The Judicial Commissioner has no say in the appointments and the transfers of subordinate court judges, which are done by the KANA division. ...By a notification, order 39 of the civil procedure code was amended, taking away the powers of the civil courts to grant temporary injunctions.... By another notification, the Speedy Trial Courts Act, 1992, was made applicable to the NA with the amendment that in appeal from the trial court, any differences of the opinion between the two judges of the Appellate court will be settled by the chairman of the court. Such arbitrary application of laws is particularly unfair because not only do the people have no forum to protest against or amend these laws, but also because the courts have no writ jurisdiction or the people any fundamental rights." S. M. Agha, leader of the BNF has once said that law in Gilgit-Baltistan was operating to 'suppress rather than reform or redress.' Abdul Hamid Khan in a letter to the UN charged Islamabad and its agencies of attempting a deliberate demographic change in Gilgit-Baltistan. Comparing General

Musharraf to General Zia, he estimated that more than 900 youth had been killed, 1,000 had became disabled or wounded, while 40 were still missing and several civilian buildings were destroyed due to Pakistan sponsored 'genocide.' He also called upon the UN and the International Court of Justice to book General Musharraf and other Pakistani generals as 'war criminals for the genocide' carried out by them in the area.

The neglect of the area also gets clearly reflected by the fact that despite being very rich in natural resources it remains one of the poorest. In 1998-1999, the total allocation for development works in Gilgit-Baltistan amounted to only Pakistani Rs. 3,09330 (US $1,500), according to then prevailing rate. Despite governmental claims of having increased annual budgetary allocations, reportedly three-fourth of its population continue to live below the poverty line. The area lacks basic infrastructure like piped water supply, electricity, health services, etc. There is just one doctor for 6,000 people. The educational facilities too are minimal. There are only 12 high schools and two regional colleges, with no postgraduate facilities. Literacy remains very low. As per statistics available, adult literacy in the area is 14 per cent for males and 3.5 per cent for females. Apart from the Karakoram highway no new road construction has been undertaken so far. There is no industry except a few brick kilns. The economy is mainly dependent on agriculture. The area provides water for agriculture in Pakistan's provinces, but there are no adequate irrigation facilities for its own agriculture. Moreover, most of the land is owned by a privileged few in this mountainous area. In absence of any other opportunity, the principal means of livelihood for the local people were from tourism and by joining the Northern Light Infantry. However, the recruitment of the people in the army has been reduced considerably following the air crash of 1988 killing General Zia, allegedly engineered by a Shia. The tourism industry has been severely affected due to the 9/11 terrorist attacks in the US. Lack of educational institutions has practically closed all avenues of government jobs. Very few locals, who are able to secure government jobs, reportedly are paid 25 per cent less than non-locals. Only low level jobs are open to the locals with all first class jobs reserved for outsiders. Whatever little development is visible in the area is credited to the Agha Khan Foundation.

Summing up the appalling condition Nawaz Khan Naji, leader of BNF argues, "...We are foreigners, actually. It is completely an occupation. We have no president, prime minister, parliament, courts, and the Pathans are buying property and our cities are becoming Pathan-majority cities, where our locals are becoming minorities. We have no right to cast votes in Pakistan, nor in Azad Kashmir. Like a no-man's land. We are the last colony in the world."[6] *The Friday Times* of October 15-21, 1992 quoted Mohammad Yahya Shah, Chief Convener of the Hunza-Nagar Movement, a Shia organization, who bemoaned, "we were ruled by the whites during the British days, but we are now being ruled by the browns from the plains. The rapid settling-in of mostly Punjabis and Pushtuns from outside, particularly the trading classes, has created a sense of acute insecurity among the local Shias and resulted in antagonistic perceptions between the locals and the outsiders. The genie is out of the bottle. Political reform has been abandoned in favour of extremism which the Government is abetting in order to prolong its unconstitutional militarization. The economic and environmental plundering continues unabated." "Gilgit Baltistan is a colony of Pakistan and we don't even have rights that equal the rights of slaves of middle ages. This unique region that has endured a crucial period in history is forced to live like a state in the medieval times.... One of our great comrades Ghazi Anwar committed suicide in front of UN offices in Kabul in protest against the human rights violation in Gilgit and Baltistan," said advocate Mohammed Iqbal of the Karakoram National Movement to IANS in an email interview.[7]

The frustration has hit the highest point wherein people feel neglected not only by Pakistan but also by media and human rights organizations. To quote a resident of the area,

"The plight of minorities and women in Pakistan is known to everyone. The people of Balochistan have become enemy combatants in their own state. But I envy them all. The women have the likes of Asma Jahangir defending them on every forum. The minorities have their moral support from the western media. The Balochis have their fearless leader, Akbar Bugti. We, the people of Gilgit Baltistan, are the political orphans without any forceful voice to speak for our rights. The media is silent since the large newspaper groups do not find a large readership in these mountainous regions where majority of the people are illiterate. The human rights organizations have not found any fertile ground for donor agencies here. Not so recently, the Human Rights Commission of Pakistan sent its team to investigate the living conditions of the people there. Till now, its action has been limited to a press conference and a hurriedly written report. Still we have to be thankful to Asma Jahangir and Iqbal Haider for taking this rare initiative unknown in the recorded history of Pakistan. Even the World Social Forum ignored us. No representative from this region was invited."[8]

Despite such a long history of resentment the movement in Gilgit-Baltistan has not been able to draw attention of scholars as the gravity of the situation would demand. It seems that the turmoil has remained concealed by a calculated design. The international attention is apparently lured to those political concerns that appear in international media. The western press is not much concerned with a peaceful struggle that the local are currently adhering to, because 'only when a struggle turns into an armed struggle does it attract media attention.' The debarring of foreign journalists and human rights activists to enter the area and report freely has also shielded the realities and instead, a contorted version of developments in the region has been propagated. 'If at all anybody does risk entering Balawaristan, the ISI and other agencies monitor the activities of that person very closely,' writes Abdul Hamid Khan. In a letter to the Urdu daily, *Jasarat*, Amir Humza Qureshi, founder of the Gilgit-Baltistan Jamhoori Mahaz, writes: "It is a fact that people of this region are facing more human rights violations and whenever the official (Pakistani) media talks of repression in (Indian) Kashmir, people with strong hearts laugh at this hypocritical attitude, and people with weak hearts cry."

Demand for Freedom

The first organization to raise voice against Islamabad was Tanzeem-e-Millat led by Johar Ali Khan in Gilgit in 1971. In 1974, it called for a strike that took a violent turn. The organization was banned later and it could not bring any succour to the people though it set the stage for further intensification of the movement. Since 1999 the demand for independence has become quite perceptible. The accumulated dissent has led to the demand for an independent republic of Balawaristan, comprising the areas of Gilgit, Baltistan, Chitral, Shhenaki Kohistan. Though the Balawaristan movement proposes to include the areas of Leh and Kargil districts in J&K yet the primary goal is independence of Gilgit-Baltistan from Pakistan. As a first step, the emphasis currently is to draw attention at various levels to the atrocities committed by Pakistan, besides challenging the authority of Islamabad to rule the area. The leaders of the movement argue that if the people of the region cannot vote for the parliament of Pakistan, then how can and why should Pakistan apply its laws in the area? Those favouring independence fiercely argue that nothing short of independence is acceptable since 'the people of this region are treated by Pakistan as virtual slaves and have been deprived of all basic human rights.'

The prominent organizations which steer the freedom movement include BNF, the J&K People's National Party, Gilgit Baltistan United Action Forum for Self Rule, Muttehda Quami Party, Gilgit-Baltistan National Alliance, Karakoram National Movement, Gilgit-Baltistan United Front for Self-Rule, the Gharib Avaam Quami movement, the Gilgit-Baltistan Thinkers Forum and Baltistan Students Federation. Many other groups reportedly remain underground since any overt expression of political aspirations leads to arbitrary arrests. The movement is currently divided between those who are demanding independence of the entire Kashmir and those who are calling for the independence of Balawaristan. There has been a dramatic shift in the people's demand for merger with Pakistan to independence in a decade or so. As per a local journalist "ten years ago nobody here wanted to hear the name 'Kashmir,' everybody was for merger with Pakistan. Today, the mood has changed to one of self-determination rather than merger."[9] Abdul Hamid Khan argues, "We were not against Pakistani occupation by birth due to unawareness situation created in the area. We were sympathizers of Pakistan till the last of 1980's because of lack of knowledge and non-existence of political environment in Balawaristan.... We realized the ugly behaviour and satanic intention of Pakistan, when late general Zia the dictator and godfather of terrorists managed to attack our innocent Shia brothers by terming them as infidels by using Afghan terrorists in 1988. We can say it is not the US, which has been victimized by terrorists first, we the people of this disputed region first came under attack of terrorism in 1988 much before Sep. 11th in 2001."[10]

The frequent protest demonstrations and various efforts, almost non-violent, by the local people in an attempt to attract international attention has become common. The local organizations have for the present been confining their activities by taking up their cause with international organizations, media, India and the Kashmiri leaders. As the dissatisfaction of the disgruntled people mount day by day, the possibility of an armed movement in near future cannot be ruled out. Abdul Hamid Khan faxed a statement to the international media from Karachi a couple of years ago, demanding independence. He had said then, "The people of Gilgit and Baltistan have been betrayed by Pakistan and made slaves in their own land. We no longer have the rights that we had been under the Dogra rule which we struggled so hard against. We do not have the political freedom people have either in Indian Kashmir or POK (meaning 'AJK'). So we want the fourth option, which is to liberate our people from all foreign occupation." The BNF presentation at the Geneva conference on human rights in 2000 also made a plea for international attention to the plight of the people. Among other issues, the presentation made the following important points: [11]

1. Gilgit-Baltistan is reeling under the stifling control of the armed forces of Pakistan and its security agencies like the ISI. Innocent people are being treated as subjugated slaves. They have been deprived of all basic human, economic, cultural and political rights due to the worst colonial system imposed by Pakistan in the name of religion. As a result, the simple folks are living like animals in this civilized world even at the dawn of 21st century.
2. A number of local people have been brutally killed by Pakistan forces. But this area is the only part of the world where the highest court works on the basis of the contract and where no written petition is allowed against any human rights violations.
3. Pakistan intelligence agency ISI has been forcibly sending the innocent youth across the LOC for terrorist activities. Those who refuse to work for ISI are picked up and killed. In 1999 alone Pakistani occupation forces used our innocent people as cannon fodder against India in its Kargil misadventure. More than 400 young men of locals lost their lives, about 1,000 were wounded and approximately 40 are still missing.

A document distributed at the Conference provided list of names and addresses of those youth from Gilgit-Baltistan who were sent by the ISI across the LOC in 1998-99 and those who were killed on refusal. The apathetic attitude of Islamabad for Kargil dead led to further growth of discontent among the people. Since General Musharraf had projected those who occupied the Kargil heights as Kashmiri mujahideen and not regulars of the Pakistan Army, the dead and injured mainly from Gilgit-Baltistan were disowned. There was no open acknowledgement of deaths or announcements for compensation for the families of the deceased. Inadequate compensation to the families of those who had enrolled themselves in the Northern Light Infantry further incensed the feeling of alienation. Just like in 'AJK' wherein the television pictures of Indian army doing its best to help the common people in J&K aftermath of 2005 earthquake has confused the locals as to if all the propaganda against the atrocities in J&K by India is false, the people in Gilgit-Baltistan too were emotionally touched by the pictures of Indian army giving the Islamic style burial to their dead whose bodies were refused by Pakistan to be taken back. In fact it is argued by many analysts that the movement for independence got renewed impetus following the Kargil episode.

The leaders leading the movement have written letters to several politicians and social activists in J&K calling for help. They have also written letters to Indian leaders to seek their help. It would not be out of context to mention a letter written by Abdul Hamid Khan to then Prime Minister of India, Atal Behari Vajpayee.[12] The letter pointed that the people of Gilgit-Baltistan are deprived of all their basic human rights, political and economic rights, and are subject to incessant oppression by Pakistan. They suffer untold miseries at the hands of the Pakistan Army and its intelligence agencies, which are deployed in strength to subdue the nationalists of our area. Because the people of Balawaristan have been demonstrating their anger about, and rejection of, the Pakistani occupation, they continue to be targeted and eliminated silently. More than 100 political leaders and workers are facing state treason charges (Pakistani section 124 A), while there is no single person who faces such charges in J&K instead of their anti-India campaign. In the light of the above mentioned atrocities and evil designs of Pakistan, the letter argued, local people do not want to become a votary of Pakistan in any way if plebiscite or referendum is held. There were requests to invite the people of Gilgit-Baltistan and 'AJK' to participate in the dialogue and to allow them to fill the 25 vacant seats in the J&K legislative assembly. This would enable them to represent their areas and reveal the oppression perpetrated against them.

To the surprise of not only those struggling for independence in Gilgit-Baltistan but also of the interested circles aware of Pak atrocities as well as the propaganda against India, New Delhi has only rarely raised the issue of Gilgit-Baltistan with Pakistan. After the objection of 1963 when Pakistan ceded a sizeable junk of the area to China there is no record of India protesting the excesses committed by Islamabad in Gilgit-Baltistan that it has always claimed to be its integral part. In a significant shift from the past policy, the Indian Ministry of External Affairs did express concern over the 'severe repressive measures being taken against legitimate protests and demonstrations,' as well as on the building of Bhasha dam in the recent times.

There has been a rising crescendo of alienation as Islamabad continues to follow an ostrich like policy to the developments in the region. In a cover page article on Gilgit-Baltistan carried in 1988, *The Herald* described the area 'the world's last colony.' After about twenty years of this depiction nothing has practically changed. Popular support for movement for independence has grown tremendously in the past decade. The constant increase in the number of protestors in the rallies, the increase in number of rallies and protest demonstrations all speak for themselves. Besides, the silent support in wake of the strong control of Islamabad too cannot be overlooked. As a leader demanding independence argued, "if Pakistan is in control obviously people will not speak against Pakistan. If the peoples' views are ascertained through some independent agency, such as the UN, who is to say what they would choose?" Pakistan's military rulers have employed coercive tactics to suppress the mass movement. Gilgit-Baltistan Thinkers Forum Chairman, Wajahat Khan was subjected to harassment for holding a press conference in Islamabad to disclose the atrocities committed on the people in Gilgit-Baltistan. Many journalists were not allowed to enter the press conference venue. Arbitrary arrests of the independence seekers take place frequently. As per reports more than hundred supporters of the movement are charged with treason and sedition. The attempts to wage a unified political battle have been thwarted by the ban imposed by Islamabad on anyone contesting the elections unless he/she signs a pledge that the area is an integral part of Pakistan. Yet, the attempts of ruthless suppression have not been able to suppress the revolutionary spirit of the suffering people. General Musharraf announced grant of an additional rupees of 20 crores to the development budget of Gilgit-Baltistan on March 4, 2000. Though Islamabad claims to have increased the annual budgetary allocations for the area, it is unlikely to make any positive impact since after suffering for a long period the people are in no mood to get contented by piece-meal concessions. The slogan 'no package, no Pakistan' is gaining more and more support. The leaders of the movement claim that nothing short of self-rule is acceptable.

General Musharraf's proposal for a solution of the Kashmir by dividing it into seven components, with Gilgit-Baltistan being one of them, and by reaching an agreement with India for the withdrawal of the forces from these parts to be followed by an exercise to determine the wishes of people on their future has been welcomed by the movement supporters. It was for the first time Islamabad had admitted that the future of this region is still to be determined, pointed the supporters of the movement. However, Musharraf went back on it following a furore in Pakistan, thus bringing the situation back to square one.

The situation in 'AJK is no less dismal than in Gilgit-Baltistan, but the main difference between the two is that in the case of the former Pakistan's policy of carrot and stick has worked to the optimum. The reports of HRCP as well as the EU Parliament have continuously harped on the fact that total check on freedom of speech and expression is the hallmark of Islamabad's policy in 'AJK.' The ideology of accessic. incorporated in the 'AJK' constitution seems to have served a brilliant barrier against the rise of any dissent. As mentioned in earlier pages, the dissent raised by parties and organizations like Jammu and Kashmir Independence League, APNA, JKLF has been met with coercion.

The undemocratic nature of Islamabad in exercising power over 'AJK' is clearly tangible. While it suppresses dissent raised in a peaceful and democratic manner, it provides enough leeway to terrorist organizations which undertake violent activities in J&K and elsewhere in the world. The chapter on earthquake has focused on this issue that how during the tragedy the terrorists had a free rein in the area. It would be interesting to point out here that it is Islamabad which proclaims itself as champion of rights of Kashmiri people, but when the very people demand those rights their demands are met with batons and bullets.

The loyalty oath, denial of which forbids the chance of participation in elections, getting government jobs, etc. reflects limitation on freedom enjoyed by the people in the area. Arbitrary detentions and torture are widespread. Some of the people of the region the authors met complained, on condition of anonymity, of the coercive policies of Islamabad. But, most of them maintained deadly silence when asked about the freedom enjoyed by the people. Kotli Press Club President, Mirza Zahid Baig who visited Jammu via Poonch-Rawalakote route, maintained a studied silence on the issue of human rights when asked by the authors.[13] Similarly, Raza Hussain who visited to Poonch through the same route was almost evasive on the issue.[14] The all pervading control of ISI on the people, both in and out, hence, is well imaginable. The communication facilities are under strict surveillance. Till recently, the only radio station allowed to operate in the territory was the 'AJK' radio, a subsidiary of the state controlled Radio Pakistan. The print media is obligated to not only seek permission from the

'AJK' council headed by Pak prime minister and KANA but also have to mandatory take the loyalty oath towards Pakistan. The complete control on the media, print as well as electronic has further choked the voice of the people to come out in open.

It would not be out of context to reproduce excerpts of interview of Muhammad Saeed Asad, a government servant in 'AJK' and author of numerous books on Kashmir, conducted by HRW. Asad's three books have been banned reportedly for being 'anti-state.' These included Shaur-e-Farda that was banned in 1996, a book on the Mangla dam controversy that was banned in 2002, and another one on Gilgit-Baltistan that was banned in 2004. He was also suspended for his 'anti-state' activities. To quote him, "... My books have been banned because they talk of Kashmiri rights and Kashmiri nationalism....I was suspended from my government job for writing on the Mangla Dam issue. The ISI called me upon publication of the book. It was a major in the ISI. He verified that I had compiled the book and had not been forced into writing it. The book represented the views of Kashmiris on Mangla and indicates that Pakistan was exploiting Kashmir for its own gains. Two weeks after publication, I had a three-hour-long meeting with Pakistan's Military Intelligence. They told me that this was a sensitive matter and I should not have written about it. 'The public does not know why you have brought this into the public domain,' the officer said. I replied that people had a right to know what Mangla dam was and who derived advantages from it. It was my national duty, as a Kashmiri, to bring this out. 'This is precisely your crime,' the officer said... 'You should avoid writing such books. We are placing you under surveillance' one said. But, I made it clear to them that I would keep on writing and they could keep on banning my work. They keep giving me trouble by stopping pay raises, suspending me from the job periodically and posting me from district to district in order to make life difficult. But, I am determined to keep on writing and to keep on working. The government of Pakistan is willing to fund books and propaganda to the tune of millions of dollars to propagate its own views and stance. Why can't we exert our individual efforts to disagree? They brook no dissent and want total and complete control. The Pakistan government just wants to suppress the Kashmiris. I have been repeatedly offered advancement if I support Pakistan. Endless youth in Kashmir who have masters and professional degrees are unemployed because the government knows they are pro-independence. This is how the Pakistanis, our so-called friends, treat us."[15]

References

1. Seema Shekhawat, "Movement for Independence in Northern Areas," *Across LOC*, October-December 2005, pp. 7-10.
2. Victoria Schofield, "Pakistan's Northern Areas Dilemma Resentment is growing over the Local Population's Lack of Political Status." *http://news.bbc.co.uk/1/hi/world/south_asia/1491179.stm.* Accessed on October 22, 2005.
3. B. Raman, "Gilgit & Baltistan, China & North Korea." *http://www.saag.org/papers3/paper289.html.* Accessed on October 30, 2005.
4. Sultan Shahin, "Across the Divide: Gilgit Valley Searches for Identity," *Asia Times*, December 18, 2004.
5. Quoted in Hamid Mandozai Khan, "Free Balawaristan from Pakistani Occupation." *http://india.indymedia.org/en/2003/02/3306.shtml.* Accessed on October 29, 2005.
6. *http://www.rediff.com/news/2004/mar/16inter.htm.* Accessed on October 29, 2005.
7. "After 21 Days of Freedom, 60 Years of Colonization." http://www.nerve.in/news:25350043769. Accessed on April 30, 2007.
8. Syed Ali, "People of Gilgit Baltistan: The Political Orphans." http://www.chowk.com/show_article.cgi?aid=00006997&channel=civic%20center. Accessed on July 30, 2006.
9. Quoted in Siddharth Varadarajan, "Gilgit Leaders Deny they're Indian Agents," *Times of India*, March 28, 2002.

10. Abdul Hamid Khan, Chairman of Balawaristan National Front: An Interview with South Asia Analysis. Group. *http://www.stratmag.com/page05.htm*. Accessed on July 25, 2006.
11. Sultan Shahin, "Free Balawaristan Movement Gains Momentum." *http://www.jammu-kashmir.com/insights/insight20000206b.html*. Accessed on October 21, 2005.
12. *http://www.indiareacts.com/smallpages/thelastcolony.htm*. Accessed on December 23, 2006.
13. Personal Interview, December 22, 2006.
14. Personal Interview, April 26, 2007.
15. "With Friends Like These...," *Human Rights Watch Report*, vol. 18, no. 12 (C), September 2006.

6

Water Issues

In 2000 Islamabad launched ambitious Vision 2025, envisaging construction of dams, water reservoirs, raising the existing ones, etc. Besides major producers of renewable energy, dams also supply water for agriculture, industry and domestic uses and act as an important means for flood control. However, large dams also adversely affect ecosystem, socio-cultural and economic lives of people. Dam-construction, hence, is a controversial topic in global discourse on sustainable development. Every state has right to cater to the needs of its people and prosper economically by exploring prospects of dam construction, and Pakistan is no exception to this imperative. But question arises whether a state has right to build dams in a territory which does not belong to it and when the local people are against it. The Mangla dam built in 'AJK' and Diamir-Bhasha dam to be built in Gilgit-Baltistan are some issues which need attention in this context. If Pakistan considers the Kashmir under its control disputed how can it use the territory for its interest? The argument that the military regime proposed increase of height of Mangla dam and construction of Diamir-Bhasha as national consensus on proposed construction of other dams such as Kalabagh could not evolve has its own weakness. If Pakistan could not evolve national consensus i.e. approval from the national parties and all the four provinces to use land within its own territory, how far is it justifiable on its part to use the 'disputed' territory for the same purpose? The construction of Bhasha dam is the latest provocation to fuel discontent among the people against Islamabad, thus providing a fresh fillip to the demand for independence. This chapter makes an attempt to study both the dams, the discontent among the local people and the locus of Pakistan in whole scenario.

Diamir- Bhasha Dam

The site of Diamir-Bhasha dam (generally referred to as Bhasha dam in the book) is on Indus river about 315 km upstream of Tarbela dam, 165 km downstream of the Gilgit and 40 km downstream of Chilas in the Diamir district. The dam would have a maximum height of 270 m, and impound a reservoir of about 7.4 MAF, with live storage of more than 6.4 MAF. The mean annual discharge of Indus at the site being 50 MAF, the dam will impound 15 per cent of the annual river flow. The dam project would cover an area of 110 km and extend 100 km upstream of the dam site up to Raikot bridge on Karakoram highway. In Vision 2025 the WAPDA has estimated US $ 6.60 billion its total cost. The authority also indicated that the completion of the project could take 7 years. It is estimated that the dam would inundate 32 villages, thousands of acres of fertile land and parts of the Karakoram highway. (See Table 1)

Table 1

Dam Type	Zoned earth-rockfill with central core
Location	Chilas on the River Indus
Height	200 metres (660 ft.) (above river bed)
Length of crest	3,018 feet
Reservoir Area	27,700 acres
Catchment Area	152,100 km^2
Gross Head	145 m (476 feet)

Average Flow	1,970 m3/sec (69,600 ft3/sec)
Design Flood Discharge	19,300 m3/sec (682,000 cusecs)
Total Storage Capacity	9.0 km3 (7.3 MAF)
Live Storage Capacity	7.0 km3 (5.7 MAF)
Total Volume of Dam	58 million yards
Total Volume of Fill	44 million m3
Installed Capacity for Hydropower	3,360 MW from 12 units
Energy Generated	14.1 GWh
Spillway Type	Overflow, with concrete lined chute,flip bucket and plunge pool
Spillway Gates	6 - 16.6 x 20 metres (54.5 x 65.6 ft)
Cost	$ 6.7 billion
Potential Financer	World Bank (subject to examining its feasibility report and detailed engineering geological and economic studies.)
Estimated Period	7 years
Approximate Life	100 Years
Villages inundated	32
People displaced	30, 000
Land inundated	31,580 acres of barren land and 1600 acres of arable land.

Source: http://www.waterinfo.net.pk/pdf/fs2br.pdf

In early 2006 Pakistan decided to build five dams– Kalabagh, Bhasha, Akori, Munda, and Kurram Tangi – by the year 2016 to meet the water shortage of about 20 million acre feet of water. The construction of Bhasha dam along with other dams in the pipeline is considered as a necessity for Pakistan on three related basis. First, Pakistan has agriculture based economy. As one of the world's fastest growing population it is facing serious shortages in food grains due to lack of large river regulation capability through sizeable storages. Hence, there is an urgent need to build water storages for augmenting agriculture production. Second, the sedimentation has led to loss of about 5 MAF as far as Tarbela, Mangla and Chashma reservoirs are concerned, which would likely increase to 6 MAF by the year 2012. Third, the current demand of electricity in Pakistan is above 17,000 MW. This is estimated to cross 22,000 MW by the year 2010. Hydropower can provide the required electricity at an affordable price. Pakistan argues that multiple benefits ranging from local to national would accrue by building these dams. First, the dam would make available about 6.4 MAF annual water storage for augmenting irrigation supplies. Second, it would lead to harnessing of renewable source of clean and cheap energy. Third, it would reduce dependence on thermal power, thus saving foreign exchange. Fourth, it would also provide employment opportunity, particularly to the locals, during construction and operation. Lastly, the infrastructure in the area of construction would lead to betterment of life of the local people.

On January 17, 2006 in a televised address Pak President General Pervez Musharraf announced the construction of five multi-purpose water storages during next 10-12 years. Bhasha dam was proclaimed as a priority project to be built in the first phase, postponing a decision on Kalabagh dam until a consensus is developed among all the four provinces of Pakistan. While announcing the construction of the Bhasha dam on priority basis it was informed that all the political parties are supporting this project and the chief ministers of the four provinces have agreed to it. The feasibility report is prepared and there are no obstacles to this project. Senior NWFP Minister Sirajul Haq has said that instead of wasting energy and focusing on controversial Kalabagh Dam, Islamabad government should start work on the uncontroversial Bhasha Dam. "The chief ministers of the four provinces have already agreed that the construction of Bhasha Dam should be started. Its feasibility report is prepared and there are no obstacles to this project. All the political parties are supporting this project,"[1] said the minister. It was also termed to be the best project among the proposed ones in terms of minimum human displacement, land submergence and higher power production capacity. Since quite some time, to normalize the situation, it was being discussed that instead of focusing on 'controversial' Kalabagh dam and wasting time, work should be started on the 'uncontroversial' Bhasha dam.

"The work on Bhasha dam will start with its earth-breaking in the first week of February. We have not developed a complete consensus on Kalabagh dam as there are still reservations about its construction in the NWFP and Sindh," declared the president of Pakistan in his 80-minute address in January 2006. He revealed that there were 'misperceptions and reservations' about the Kalabagh dam and many people were not supportive of the project. Promising to address the reservations the president said 'I respect this public opinion.' Earlier speaking at the groundbreaking ceremony of the Mangla dam raising project in 'AJK' despite all protests on September 30, 2002, President Musharraf had said that both Kalabagh and Bhasha dam would have to be built to meet Pakistan's future hydro demands. He argued the debate in the country had revolved around only Kalabagh dam, but no previous government had given serious thought to building Bhasha dam. Interestingly, President Musharraf's boast that he respects public opinion on the Kalabagh dam took an ugly turn while addressing the concerns of Gilgit-Baltistan. The 'disputed' status of the area made it easier to ignore the local protest and build up national consensus since the people of the area do not constitute part of national public opinion of Pakistan. Lack of any political structure, representing the local people, further helped Pakistan president to build up a 'national consensus' on constructing an 'uncontroversial' dam in a 'controversial' area to cater the needs of Pakistan!

Discontent Galore

What remained unheard and unaddressed were the woes of the local people who opposed the dam construction. While the opposition political parties in Islamabad raised unprecedented hue and cry against Kalabagh dam, they were in total agreement on the need for the construction of Bhasha dam. The Bhasha power project was first studied by Montreal Engineering Company of Canada in their 1984 feasibility report. While Pakistan asserts that there is a consensus on building the dam, WAPDA has reported resistance to the project by the local people since beginning, causing disruption in investigation and survey works. The initial demands of the locals were: (a) settlement of the project boundary dispute between Gilgit-Baltistan and NWFP; (b) a share in the royalty accruing from the revenue of the project; (c) employment to locals on the project work; (d) compensation for lands and houses to be inundated by the reservoir; and (e) change in the name of the project from Bhasha to Diamir dam. Four high-level meetings were conducted by the ministry of KANA during the period 1990-1992 at Islamabad to reportedly address the popular demands. But, no local leaders were invited to participate in these meetings. None of these meetings yielded any concrete result. On September 12, 1995 a standing committee was constituted to look into the matter. The committee asked WAPDA to prepare package for compensation and rehabilitation of the affected. It also advised the administration to go ahead with the dam construction 'in a low profile' and 'camouflaged manner' to avoid local resistance. In October 1998 another meeting of officials of the Gilgit-Baltistan, the KANA and the Ministry of Water and Power failed to arrive at any decision to meet the demands.

Gradually the movement for resistance became more organized, vocal and widespread. To quote Ismail Khan from Gilgit-Baltistan, "In 2001, the Northern Areas Legislative Council came up with a joint resolution in favour of the construction of the dam on the condition that it be renamed Diamir dam, but the generous offer, as is usual, received no attention in Islamabad. Today the public mood in the region has changed dramatically. People in the Northern Areas, and particularly Diamir, strongly believe that they should have been consulted, taken into confidence about the blessings and blights of the dam. Their long-standing conflict over boundaries with the NWFP should have been settled, and they should have been extended assurances for a fair treatment before the political announcement was made regarding construction of the dam." The Bhasha dam is being opposed by people in Gilgit as they fear that it would affect social, economic, demographic and ecological balance in the region, besides the very right of Pakistan to build the dam in Gilgit-Baltistan too was questioned. Some experts studying the earthquake that affected the area in October 2005 are also apprehensive of the project. [2]

Political parties and the general public of Gilgit-Baltistan resented the announcement and launched an anti-Bhasha dam campaign. On January 20, 2006 elected representatives of Diamir district threatened to launch a protest campaign throughout the region against Islamabad's decision to construct the dam without taking local people into confidence. On January 26, 2006 APNA strongly condemned the decision to construct the dam. In late January, a unanimous resolution was passed by the NALC which criticized Pakistan's negligence of the local opinion as 'a disrespect of the region's highest elected body and people of the area.' On February 1, 2006 hundreds of people blocked Karakoram highway at four different points. Protests were also held across the Diamir district, including Gonar Farm, Chilas, Thore, Darel and Tangeer valleys. Protestors held banners and urged President Musharraf to withdraw the 'injudicious and illogical' decision. NALC member from Diamir, Fidaullah said that Bhasha dam was 'a conspiracy to destroy the area.' "The people of the area would not let others impose decisions on them or negotiate their rights over vital issues," he said. Addressing a rally in Chilas, local leaders condemned the decision to build the dam, saying that it would displace 30,000 people, and inundate 31,580 acres of barren land and 1,600 acres of arable land in the Diamir district. On February 3, protestors in Chilas district issued warnings to engineers and other staff of WAPDA to stop survey on the site of the proposed dam. On February 6 BNF, Karakoram National

Movement, Balawaristan Labour Party and JKLF organized anti Bhasha dam rally in Gilgit. This led to arrest of large number of people. On February 15, 2006 an all parties conference criticized Islamabad for 'not taking the people and political leadership of the area into confidence' before making a decision on the construction of the dam. The Gilgit-Baltistan Alliance organized the event that was attended by religious, political and nationalist leaders of 'AJK' and Gilgit-Baltistan. A joint communiqué issued and signed by local leaders opposed the construction of the dam, saying it would submerge the district of Diamir. It read: "People in the Northern Areas are upset over the Bhasha/Diamir dam controversy. .... They are unhappy because some vested interests have succeeded in naming it Bhasha dam, after a village in the neighbouring Kohistan district of the NWFP, when the entire reservoir is situated in the Diamir district of the Northern Areas. They are disappointed because ill-intentioned planners are creating an unnecessary dispute by choosing to set up the power station on the left bank of the Indus in Bhasha, rather than establishing the same on the right bank of the river in the Northern Areas. The proposed dam... will submerge 110 kilometres of the Karakoram Highway in Diamir.... Some 24,000 people will be displaced.... However... royalties will go to the province where the power station, not the reservoir, is located. So it is simple: the Northern Areas will foot the bill for all the social, economic and ecological costs of Bhasha dam while the NWFP will pocket the royalties. Very equitable."[3]

Earlier a grand *jirga* of Diamir district termed the plan for construction of the dam a conspiracy and threatened to stop work on the dam. JKLF Chairman, Amanullah Khan, Raja Mazhar Iqbal and others were arrested for holding a demonstration against the dam. Despite the arrests Maulana Muhammad Sadiq, head of anti-Bhasha dam movement indicated that they plan more protests and rallies against the construction of the dam by mobilizing the people throughout the region.[4] The participants of an all parties' conference, convened by the anti-dam grand *jirga* of Diamir district in March 2006, called upon the government to initiate a dialogue with the local people. Former Chairman of the Gilgit-Baltistan National Alliance, Inayatullah Shumali cautioned, 'If our problems are not resolved today it would create many problems in future.' Representing the views of the grand *jirga*, the NALC member, Fidaullah said that they were opposed to the construction of dams in any part of the region, and they would not allow anyone to force their decisions on the people of the region. He suggested that dams could be built in areas that were not controversial. Another NALC member from Diamir district, Abdul Quddus said that the proposed Diamir-Bhasha dam is the problem of the area and the people had been protesting against the dam since 1980 when a Canadian firm started the feasibility study. He called upon the government to constitute a high-level committee comprising the local people.[5] APNA called a round table conference on March 13, 2006 at Islamabad on the issue of concern and apprehensions of the people of Gilgit-Baltistan on the construction of the dam. The participants finally concluded a unanimously agreed declaration entitled 'No Dam At All.' The joint declaration spoke volumes about the discontent of the people. It argued that the announcement of dam construction by Islamabad was without thorough and extensive valuation of the commercial, environmental and social issues. The project failed to meet the most basic international standards with regard to geopolitical sensitivity, resettlement and environment. The dam will submerge a region with a huge population density and force thousands of people of Diamir to exile. The declaration also argued that the district headquarter of Diamir with more than five hundred thousand years of history and Aryan, Buddhist monuments, attracting thousands of tourists every year, will disappear for ever. There is a great fear that this dam will adversely affect downstream environment and exacerbate the potential for regional conflict over water and hydel power net profit between Gilgit-Baltistan and Pakistan.

This joint declaration attempted to explore some of these issues and draw some broad policy recommendations. 1. Environmental Impact Assessment: no environmental impact assessment has been done so far; which results in potential environment, human rights and cultural heritage impacts. Instead of introducing a set of clear, legally binding, ex-ante environmental, development and human rights standards, the announcement of the construction of Bhasha dam without the consent of the local people and other stakeholders is just another act of extension of authoritarian rule by Islamabad in the region. The International Union for Conservation of Nature and Natural Resources has opposed dam on environmental concern and has called it a 'recipe of disaster.' The announcement of the dam construction without any consultation with the people and denial of public access to environmental information is not a sine qua non of best international development practice. Moreover, non-disclosure runs counter to a number of conventions to which Pakistan is a signatory, including the International Convention of Human Rights and the UN Convention on Access to Information, Public Participation in Decision-Making and Access to Justice in Environmental Matter. The human rights violation in the Gilgit-Baltistan and the continuing denial of basic democratic governance rights is a serious concern. The declaration also noted with concern that continuing human rights violations in the region have led many to question whether international human rights and environmental standards can ever be met whilst the area remains under direct control of Pakistan.

The declaration recommended that Pakistan should adopt clear, ex-ante standards that apply to all its projects in the areas of the state of Kashmir under its control. Such standards should reflect best international practice, as exemplified, by the recommended guidelines of the World Commission on Dams, and should cover human rights, environment, cultural heritage, gender and development impacts. Pakistan should not construct the dam until an Environmental Impact Assessment is released to the public. Besides, institutional investors review their portfolios and assess whether the reputation and project risks of these institutions with investments in such a project is sufficiently contained. Given the urgent need for development, democracy and self-governance in the region, the declaration urged that the UN should intervene and ask Pakistan to fulfil its obligations under UNCIP resolutions to ensure the implementation of its agreed commitment to ensuring the language, cultural and political rights of the local people. Pakistan should restrain itself from changing the geo-political boundaries of Gilgit-Baltistan, as it is propagated that Bhasha is part of NWFP which is untrue, since Bhasha up till Sazeen was part of district Diamir until 1973, when then Pak Prime Minister Zulfiqar Ali Bhutto decided to hand over the administrative control of Shinaki Kohistan of district Diamir to NWFP. This temporary administrative control does not constitute constitutional suzerainty of Pakistan over these areas. It is proven by the land and revenue records that geographically and historically it is still part of district Diamir. Construction of any mega dam without consultation of all the stakeholders will be resisted by all means, the joint declaration emphasized.

The Concerns

Kashmir Liberation Front condemned the decision to construct dam in the area that is part of the erstwhile princely state of Jammu and Kashmir, which is for Pakistan a disputed territory. It is argued that territory being disputed cannot be used by any one party without the consensus of all other parties in the dispute. Hence, it is an 'unconstitutional, illegal and immoral step.' Related with this is the argument given by JKLF that Pakistan had no right to go ahead with the project without the final resolution of the Kashmir dispute. It is contended that 'if the government of Pakistan does not recognize the constitutional and democratic rights of the 'NA,' how can it take a decision on such a mega project without the consent of its people and political leaders?' It is also claimed that a great treasure in form of many ancient archeologically important monuments of Hinduism and Buddhism will be destroyed with the construction of the dam. According to the leader of the BNF, Nawaz Khan Nazi, "the Bhasha dam not only adversely affects a population of one and a half lakh but also demolishes mosques, dishonours graves and destroys the remnants of an ancient civilization." The local people also argue that the proposed construction is not meant to benefit the locals but for the benefit of the people of Pakistan. The people feel it is unfair and unjust to use their land to build a water reservoir that would benefit Pakistan when they are still waiting for a defined status. On January 22, 2006 talking to newspaper *Dawn* the chairman of the Bhasha Dam Naam Namanzoor Committee, Haji Ghandal Shah, alleged that the government named the dam after Bhasha that lies in NWFP to contrive a justification for paying the royalty to the frontier province. He accused the government of resorting to 'white lies' in providing the data about the dam. According to him, it was wrong for Islamabad to claim that the reservoir would submerge only 1,600 acres of agricultural land. The submerged area would be a sizable chunk in the mountainous area where agricultural land is already scarce.

Local people also challenge the argument, fostered by Islamabad, that the human displacement due to the dam construction will be comparatively less. First, the number of displacement will be much more that the official figures. The 1983 estimate of the population affected by reservoir inundation was 13,600. By the year 2000, estimate of the affected population had reached 22,000. The latest estimate put the number of the affected people at thousands. Second, the dam will flood Chilas in its entirety and displace the Shina-speaking inhabitants of this valley who belong to an ethnic minority. There is no space available for the relocation of these people who have a distinct and unique culture due to the region's mountainous terrain. They may be settled in different places thereby endangering their distinct identity. A study of Jammu

Kashmir National Liberation Front points out that Pakistan is planning to build five huge dams in Gilgit-Baltistan including Bhasha, Bonji, Yulbo, Yogo and Skardu or Katzara that would ultimately submerge the substantial land of the area into water. The Bonji dam will make the homeless at least 15,000 people, Yalbo dam 20,000, Yogo dam 30,000 and Katzara dam 30,000. Before 2025, one-third population of the area will become home less.[6] Though the environmental hazards have not been made a big issue yet it is apprehended that the dam would change weather of the area with long-term consequences.

As mentioned earlier, the local people objected over the name of the dam. They challenged the logic under which the dam was named Bhasha, a village that falls in NWFP, though it would be built in the Diamir district in Gilgit-Baltistan. They demanded renaming the dam as Diamir. Related with this was the issue of royalty wherein it was alleged that the dam was named Bhasha under a strategy so that the royalty could be exclusively given to the NWFP as per the constitution of Pakistan.[7] Article 161 (2) of the constitution of Pakistan stipulates that the royalty and the bulk of the net profits earned from a hydroelectric station shall go to the province where the station is situated. Most of the storage area of the proposed dam lies in the territorial jurisdiction of the Gilgit-Baltistan, but the powerhouse is planned to be built in the NWFP. The Bhasha village, which would house only one per cent of the dam, is shown to be in the NWFP, hence earnings from the dam would go to the frontier province. People questioned that 'the dam will be built at our site and we will be affected by it. Under what logic did the government name it after a region of the NWFP and decide to give royalty to the province?' To quote a leader of APNA, "President General Pervez Musharraf's announcement of construction of Bhasha and Skardu dam after failure to construct Kalabagh dam has exposed the mentality and intentions of Pakistani bureaucracy and government towards the people of Bolor (Gilgit-Baltistan). They are thinking that this territory and its inhabitants are their slaves and they are treating the area likewise. For last 58 years they similarly treated the Bolor people and kept them in dark away from even very basic rights and needs. Inspite of being the disputed territory they are bold enough to announce such mega projects even with out the consent of any single party of the dispute. They could not able to gather their own people for Kalabagh dam so to hide the shamefulness they announce the Bhasha dam as they think this is the territory they can play game with. The people of Bolor and Jammu Kashmir are the real owners of land to think about such projects. Pakistani authorities should clear their minds that they have signed UN resolution as one party of the dispute to withdraw its forces from the region within four weeks period and has agreed upon the will of the people to whom they will join. So till final decision how they dare to start such mega projects in a disputed territory? Instead of giving rights what they promised they are planning to change our geography and even they have changed our demography by settling non locals after abolition of state subject rule. The people of Bolor in some time will seek the details of misdeeds made by Pakistani authorities in last 58 years. One thing must be clear that Bolor people will never allow any country or party to submerge themselves and their motherland to facilitate and irrigate others."[8]

Had Islamabad addressed the initial demands of the people with a flexible hand, the discontent might not have assumed such an insurmountable proportion. The non-fulfilment of initial demands has awakened the revolutionary spirit of the people. As a result the initial demands of accommodation have been converted into assertion of basic rights of the people. Some of the later demands included:[9] 1. Ownership of Gilgit-Baltistan over River Indus as well as on the proposed dam to be accepted and recognized internationally. 2. Agreement between the representatives of the area and Pakistan to be reached in the presence and guarantee of the UNSC that representation from the area in dialogue with Pakistan would include the NALC members, Bhasha Dam

Naam Namanzoor Organization, tribal elders of Diamir district and one member from each local party. 3. Six billion Pakistani Rupees should be given to area annually as royalty in the current rate of inflation. It needs to be increased according to the inflation rate annually. 4. Income generated from the dam to be handled by both the parties (Gilgit-Baltistan and Pakistan) by joint account in any international bank. 5. Ten times more of the total submerged land should be given to the land owners of Diamir from Pakistani territory. 6. Full employment in the project to be given to the local people by open interview to be conducted by UN or any impartial body in the presence of the local representatives. 8. Equal post (in grade wise and number wise) should be given to both the parties, i.e. Gilgit-Baltistan and Pakistan in administration and finance. 9. The representatives and people of area to be informed about any foreign loan, aid and terms of conditions. Without the approval of the local representatives, foreign loans, aid etc. not to be given to the dam. 10. Compensation of land to be given according to the international standards. Compensation should be given in case of environmental or any other damages before, during or after completion of dam. 11. 1/4th of the total production of electricity should be given to the area free of charge. 12. Offices for power house and administration and residential quarters to be built in Diamir, not in NWFP. Offices would be controlled equally by both the parties but residential houses only by the local employees. 13. After completion of the dam, bills will be considered from the main meter consumption in the main powerhouse. The royalty from that bill first to be paid to Gilgit-Baltistan. 14. The main meter will be handled by both local authorities and Pakistan equally. 15. After the resolution of the Kashmir dispute, Pakistan will be bound to abide by all the terms and conditions, in case if Gilgit-Baltistan becomes part of Pakistan. The people of Balawaristan will reserve their rights to review this pact, if the area becomes free country or becomes a part of any free country. The Government of Pakistan did not pay attention to any of these demands that it perceived challenging its authority over the area.

The Pakistan government later accepted two demands partially. Prime Minister Shaukat Aziz in February 2006 announced that the dam would be renamed Diamir-Bhasha. It also decided to distribute the royalty between the NWFP and Gilgit-Baltistan on equal basis. The controversy, however, did not subside. On February 28, 2006 Amanullah Khan said that protest would continue till the dam is named Diamir dam.[10] The resolution of the issue does not seem to be in horizon as the people demand 100 per cent royalty. Speaker of NALC, Malik Muhammad Maskeen expressed his unwillingness to accept fifty per cent royalty.[11] At a stage KANA directed WAPDA to brief the NALC members on the dam initiative. This was the first time that Islamabad made an effort to put the public representatives of the region into the loop. However, WAPDA officials failed to satisfy the local leadership on various counts including rehabilitation, compensation and royalty.

The people also questioned the rationale behind calling the dam 'best project among all the proposed ones.' They argue that the Kalabagh dam was more feasible than Bhasha. An editorial published in a Pakistan newspaper *Daily Times* can be mentioned in this context. It quotes PML-Nawaz member, Hafiz Hafeezur Rehman saying that the Bhasha project will serve only the hydropower needs of the country whereas Kalabagh dam is a multi-purpose project that will also meet irrigation needs, besides having the more capacity of storing water.[12] Similarly, Sardar Ejaz Afzal, the JI Chief in 'AJK' pointed out that the Gilgit-Baltistan area is a non-monsoon area and the dam would receive only 30 per cent of water from glaciers. Kalabagh dam was more feasible because it would get 70 per cent of water from monsoon rains and 30 per cent from glaciers. The editorial in the *Daily Times* also pointed other concerns related to the Bhasha dam. It pointed, "Building the highest dam in the world, hence, comes with very high costs. To enumerate a few, in the case of a breach of the dam during an earthquake, a 500-foot high wave would flow down from its 920-foot height and destroy downriver dams and bridges and wash riverside cities into the Arabian Sea. With complete disregard for the greater risk, the height of the planned dam was actually increased by 33 feet to give it a larger water and power capacity than Kalabagh dam."[13] As per the editorial, experts had warned that the dam's capacity has been grossly overstated just to establish its superiority over Kalabagh.

Since October 8, 2005 earthquake, renewed concerns have been expressed about the location of the dam in a seismic zone where a powerful earthquake in December 1974 killed thousands of people. The dam is being built in Chilas which is quite close to the Bisham-Battagram fault-line where the recent quake has wreaked havoc. In this context, there are two major concerns. First, the dam may cause large-scale destruction if another earthquake struck. Second, this may lead to an earthquake since huge dams are supposed to cause earthquake. In an attempt to end the apprehensions, WAPDA issued a press release pointing that although the dam is located in a seismic zone, no earthquake has been recorded within the radius of 40 kilometres radius from the dam site.[14] The apprehensions, however, had not been subsided in the wake of the fact that earthquakes are highly unpredictable.

On March 9, 2006 India protested against construction of the dam on the ground that it would inundate considerable parts of Kashmir, which is an integral part of India. "The Government of India conveyed through diplomatic channels to the Government of Pakistan, its protest against the proposed construction of Bhasha dam in territory that is part of the State of Jammu and Kashmir, which is an integral part of India by virtue of its accession to it in 1947," an External Affairs Ministry spokesman said. Pakistan Foreign Ministry Spokesperson raked up the 'disputed status' of Kashmir in response to India's protest and also put forward that the dam is being constructed for the welfare of the people of the area. [15] Yet, the mass discontent in form of protests and demonstrations that became a part of everyday life in Gilgit-Baltistan is clear indicator of mismatch between words and actions of Pakistan. Despite Pakistan's lackadaisical response, India's objections showed its increasing assertiveness regarding issues of concern in Kashmir across the LOC.[16] It is the third issue with regard to Gilgit-Baltistan that India has officially expressed its concern. In October 2005, India had asked Pakistan to act with 'utmost restraint' and 'observe international human rights standards' in Gilgit-Baltistan and expressed concern over sectarian unrest in the area. Earlier the ceding of territory from the area to China by Pakistan too was objected by India. The World Bank, while linking its funding to the feasibility report and detailed engineering report, has pronounced since India is Pakistan's neighbour and a signatory to Indus Waters Treaty its objection to the dam should be given due consideration.

The dam issue was also raised in the Upper House of Indian Parliament. The unstarred question no. 2910 raised by Mangani Lal Mandal on August 24, 2006 raised the following issues:

(a) whether it is a fact that India has raised objection against the plan of constructing Diamir-Bhasha dam by Pakistan in the northern region of J&K;
(b) whether it is a fact that this year in the month of April, the above mentioned dam has been inaugurated by the President of Pakistan;
(c) whether it is a fact that Pakistan has ignored the objections by India; and
(d) if so, the details thereof ?

The answer by the Minister of State in the Ministry of External Affairs, E. Ahamed was:

(a) Yes. Government conveyed, through diplomatic channels to the Government of Pakistan, its protest against the proposed construction of Bhasha dam in territory that is part of the state of J&K, which is an integral part of India.
(b) Yes. On April 26, 2006, Pakistan President Musharraf took part in the ground-breaking ceremony of the proposed dam.

(c) (d) According to reports, Pakistan proposes to complete the construction of the Bhasha dam by 2016.

The Response

Knowing that people of Gilgit-Baltistan continue to remain deprived of fundamental rights and mobilization of a large movement against the dam was not easy, Pakistan used this deprivation for its own benefit. Since all decisions regarding the area could only be made by KANA with no real power in the hands of NALC, it was well known in Pakistan that any decision of Islamabad would be final irrespective of the local discontent. Brushing discontent aside, President Musharraf laid the foundation stone for the dam in April 2006 at Chilas amidst tight security to prevent any protests from the locals during the ceremony. It would not be out of context to mention that earlier the laying of the foundation stone had been put off thrice. In his address at the dam site Musharraf vowed to build other major reservoirs including the controversial Kalabagh dam by 2016 with 'national consensus.' In an attempt to pacify people he made a number of announcements such as the affected will be paid compensation before work is begun, model towns will be built for the affected people, the government will settle the delimitation issue between the NWFP and Gilgit-Baltistan, residents of Diamir district will be preferred in consideration for jobs in the project and a new portion of the Karakoram Highway will be constructed. The president announced royalties from the dam would go to both Gilgit-Baltistan and NWFP. One turbine would be built in the territorial limits of the former and the other at Bhasha village that territorially falls in the latter. It was also announced that the proposed height of the dam would be reduced by 10 metres to prevent the submersion of Chilas city. The height of Diamir-Bhasha dam will be 270 metres with the capacity to store 7.4 MAF of water, with a live storage capacity of more than 6.4 MAF.[17] The demand for further reduction in the height to save the Chilas city air strip was, however, not conceded. (See Tables 2 and 3)

Table 2
Environment and Resettlement*

(After Reducing Dam Height by 10m)	
No. of villages affected	30
No. of Houses Affected	2200
Population affected	22,000
Agricultural land submerged	1,500 acres
Area under reservoir	25,000 acres
Length of KKH submerged	100 km
Proposed new settlements	9
Infrastructure	Electricity, roads,water supply, schools, health centres etc.

*Subject to refinement during detailed design stage

Source: http://www.presidentofpakistan.gov.pk/bhasha%20dam.aspx

Table 3
Revised Salient Features

Location	40 km downstream of Chilas
Main dam	
Maximum Height	270 m
Type	Roller Compacted Concrete (RCC)
Diversion System	2 No. Diversion tunnels 1 No. Diversion canal Upstream and Downstream Cofferdams
Main Spillway	
No. of gates	9
Size of gate	16.5 × 15.0 m
Reservoir Level	1160 m
Gross capacity	7.3 MAF
Live capacity	6.4 MAF
Min. operation level	El. 1060 m

Outlets	
Intermediate level	8
Low level	4
Power Houses	2
Total installed capacity	4500 MW
Location and type	Toe of the Dam (one each on the right and left side)
No. of units	8, each of 560 MW
Average generation	16,500 Gwh/year
Estimated Cost (Year 2005)	US $ 6.5 Billion

Source: http://www.presidentofpakistan.gov.pk/bhasha%20dam.aspx

The Information Minister of Pakistan, Muhammad Ali Durrani described the launch of work on the Bhasha Dam as a landmark occasion, saying that this dam built by 'consensus would have far-reaching effects on economic development of all parts of the country (Pakistan) and also foster inter-provincial harmony.'[18] The postponement of the ceremony thrice and tight security measures at the time of the foundation stone lying ceremony, however, tells all is not well. Even after the foundation ceremony and some concessions by the Pak government the local people are not ready to give up. They do not consider it as a 'win-win' situation but as the zero sum game wherein everything is gained by Pakistan at the cost of the people of Gilgit-Baltistan who do not have any say at national, regional or international level. Ismail Khan observed, "they will protest, strike, grow violent, but in the end their demand for fairness and justice will most likely be ignored. Just as all their concerns about turning Gilgit-Baltistan into the faceless and ambiguous 'NA' have been ignored, just as their inalienable political and constitutional rights have been ignored for the last 58 years...." But, his hope that "when the president performs the ground-breaking ceremony at the dam site, he will break new grounds by providing justice to the unfairly wronged people" remained unfulfilled. Even the demands that have been conceded are not believed to be fulfilled. As JKLF argued, "Construction of dam on the disputed area against the wishes of the people is violation of the international law and principles. Example of Mangla dam is before us. On the Indian protest in the United Nations Pakistan assured that all the income of the dam will be handed over to the people of 'Azad Kashmir.' But after passing of 40 years not a single penny has been given. In case Pakistan Government changes the name of dam as Diamir dam and give royalty to the Gilgit-Baltistan who will trust on any guarantee of Pakistan? We request to the international community to help the people of Gilgit-Baltistan in the agitation against dam." The days ahead would determine how the situation turns up. Pakistan would in all probability construct the dam to meet its water demands but the apprehensions of the serious long term consequences of this decision could not be ignored keeping in view the fact that movement for independence in the area has already in the process of taking a concrete shape. Given the history of alienation and oppression, the people feel that the dam is yet another indicator showing Islamabad has no regard for their sentiments and concerns.

Mangla Dam

The Mangla dam is the twelfth largest dam in the world, third largest earth-filled and first one to be built as a part of Indus Basin project as per the Indus Waters Treaty. As per the Indus Waters Treaty signed in 1960, India gained rights for Ravi, Sutlej and Beas rivers, while Pakistan, in addition to waters of above three rivers in her area and some monetary compensation, got rights to develop Jhelum, Chenab and Indus river basins. Until 1967, the entire irrigation system of Pakistan was fully dependent on unregulated flows of the Indus and its major tributaries, the consequence being low agricultural yield. The project was designed primarily to facilitate easy availability of water for irrigation with a secondary function of generating electricity. The dam was constructed across the Jhelum River in 1967 in the district Mirpur in 'AJK' with the help of World Bank. It comprised 4 embankment dams, 2 spillways, 5 power-cum-irrigation tunnels and a power station. The main dam was 10,300 feet long and 454 feet high with a reservoir of 97.7 square miles. Since its construction 1.13 MAF sedimentation took place and gross storage capacity of 5.878 MAF has reduced to 4.68 MAF. In view of this fact it has been argued that the raising of the dam is important on account of the growing shortage of irrigation facilities in Pakistan. The Mangla dam raising project thus came into picture. (see Table 4)

Table 4
Salient Features

Dam Type:	Earthfill
Height:	380 ft. (above riverbed)
Length:	10,300 feet
Lake Area:	97.7 sq. miles
Catchment Area:	12,870 sq. miles
Gross Storage Capacity:	5.88 MAF
Live Storage Capacity:	5.34 MAF
Main Spillway Capacity:	1.01 million cusecs
Year of Completion:	1967
Hydropower Generation:	1,000 MW from 10 units of 100 MW each
No. of people to be displaced by raising of dam:	40,000

Source: http://www.descon.com.pk/Sectors/Infrastructure/manglaDamRaising.aspx

Raising of the Height

Just like Bhasha dam in Gilgit-Baltistan the military regime planned to increase the height of the Mangla dam in 'AJK' as consensus on the construction of Kalabagh dam in

Pakistan territory could not be evolved. In its Vision 2025 report, WAPDA has proposed raising the height of the dam with storage capacity of 5.7 MAF, and installed generation capacity of 3360 MW at a cost of Rs 400 billion ($ 6.60 billion) in a time span of around 10 years. The major objective of the project, as per WAPDA, is regaining the storage capacity of the reservoir lost to sedimentation. Other claimed benefits include power generation, flood control, recreation, fisheries etc. The WAPDA documents point that at the time of its construction in late 1960s the dam had a gross storage capacity of 5.88 MAF and live storage capacity of 5.34 MAF. With the passage of time the live storage capacity has come down to 4.64 MAF. It is argued that the raising of dam would increase the storage capacity as also the power generation capacity. An increased storage capacity shall reduce the intensity of high floods. It will also provide new avenues for fishing. Recreation facilities developed along the reservoir water would attract the tourists. (see Table 5)

Table 5
Facts about the Dam Raising Project

Client and Owner:	WAPDA
Consultant/Designer:	Mangla Joint Venture (MJV), NESPAK, ACE, Barqaab, Binnie Black, Veatch & Harza
Description of Works:	Mangla Dam raising project envisages its main crest level to be raised by 30 ft, from EI. 1234 ft. to EI. 1264 ft. The existing 454 ft. high dam is an earthfill structure with clay core and gravel and rolled sand stone shoulders. The main and emergency spillways will be modified for the raised conservation level.

Main Components:	Main Dam & Intake Embankment
	· Sukian Dyke
	· Jari Dam & Rimworks
	· Main Spillway
	· Emergency Spillway
	· Gate Equipment
	· Mirpur Bypass Road
Man-hours:	21.3 million
Expected Completion Date:	September 20, 2007

Source:http://www.descon.com.pk/Sectors/Infrastructure/manglaDamRaising.aspx

The compensation package in the WAPDA proposal included compensation for all categories of land at market price; compensation based on replacement cost of house; minimum compensation of Pakistani Rs 300,000; replacement cost of houses also for settlers on WAPDA land; free of cost 5 *marla* plot per family to refugee settlers on government land; permission to owners to cultivate land when reservoir level is low; resettlement in new city and other towns in close vicinity; infrastructure development at project cost; plot size 5 *marla* to 1 *kanal*, those affected with lesser holding to receive 5 *marla* plots; plots in new city and other towns on payment by affected; vocational training and job opportunities.

Interestingly, on this occasion Islamabad felt no need to consult the government of 'Azad' Kashmir.[19] The news of extension received widespread condemnation across 'AJK.' Anti-extension committee was set up in Mirpur in 2000 comprising of people from all walks of life. The members included lawyers, teachers, bankers, journalists, artists, poets, writers, labourers and transport workers. The committee rejected the extension proposal as being 'destructive and anti-people.' Arif Chaudhry, spokesperson for the Anti-Mangla Dam Extension Committee, said that they will use all possible means, including diplomacy, dialogue, protest, hunger strike and road closure, to stop the dam extension. Interestingly, Anti-Mangla Dam Extension Committee was also set up in Britain where over hundred thousand people from 'AJK' are currently settled following the construction of Mangla dam. Mohammed Younis Tiriyabi, one of the prominent leaders of the anti-dam committee, warned Islamabad in a huge public meeting in Birmingham that 'imposed extension' would give the locals 'right to dismantle the Mangla dam, an illegal construction.' Widespread opposition to the dam extension was based primarily on the following grounds:[20]

1. The rise in silt level is a result of WAPDA failure to clean the dam every year, which was part of the maintenance plan, and appropriate machinery was provided to carryout this task at the time of dam construction. WAPDA has not cleaned the dam even once.
2. The rise in silt level is also a result of deforestation in 'AJK' by the Pakistani authorities through their puppets in 'AJK.' A land with 40 per cent forests has become nearly barren due to this collaboration between the two who are once again collaborating to wipe out another large chunk of the Mirpur district and throw over 70,000 people out of their homes.
3. Even the Pakistani experts including the Director of the Metallurgical department have clearly and repeatedly stated that given the recent history of floods virtually no increase in the storage capacity can be achieved.
4. Land is already scarce in Mirpur. Even if Pakistani government delivers its promises of resettling displaced people in the nearby land, what will happen to the surplus population of the district in the near future?
5. While the dam is built on the Kashmiri land all the official Pakistani documents shows it in Pakistan.
6. Pakistan government must pay the entire amount due towards royalty (over 100 billion rupees) to 'AJK' government followed by a mutually agreed annual royalty.

Due to strong protests, Pakistan government had to defer the project. Yet, WAPDA continued its survey regarding the possible extension. The minister of KANA set up two committees to resolve issues of resettlement and compensation. In July 2002, the minister declared that the project would be launched only after resolving all pending issues. In a meeting attended by President Musharraf, the minister of KANA, high officials of WAPDA, the president and prime minister of 'AJK,' it was decided to evolve a consensus before beginning the project work. In the same year a seven member committee was formed by 'AJK' legislative assembly to evolve 'consensus' on the project. However, all these exercises proved to be futile. In September 2002 President Musharraf inaugurated the extension project by announcing a package for the affected and royalty for 'AJK' government.[21] The inauguration was expectedly done amidst mass protests by locals despite curfew and heavy presence of armed forces. This volcanic eruption of the people's anger forced Islamabad to sign a formal agreement with the 'AJK' government on the issues concerning the dam.

An agreement for the raising of Mangla dam was signed by the Ministry of Water and Power of Pakistan, WAPDA and 'AJK' government in Islamabad on June 27, 2003. The Chairman of WAPDA General (retd.) Zulfiqar Ali Khan, Secretary Water and Power Ministry Saeedullah Jan and Chief Secretary of 'AJK' Shahid Rafi signed the document. While the Pakistan authorities lauded the agreement, people of 'AJK' rejected it. They claimed that the agreement was between three Pakistani institutions, the Water and Power Ministry of Pakistan, WAPDA and non-native chief secretary of 'AJK' appointed by Pakistan. Nonetheless, the salient features of the agreement included a resettlement package; royalty and fishery rights to the 'AJK' government and a temporary reduction in the electricity tariff in 'AJK' from Pakistani Rs. 4.50 to 2.32. The then Prime Minister of 'AJK', Sardar Sikandar Hayat Khan and Minister for Water and Power in Pakistan, Aftab Ahmad Khan Sherpao, witnessed the signing episode that set the stage for beginning of work on the project. Talking to newsmen, the 'AJK' prime minister claimed that all the grievances were amicably settled. Giving an all going well impression he said more than 70 per cent people of 'AJK' have access to electricity and raising of the dam will benefit about three hundred fifty thousand families. Sherpao pointed that the agreement provided for billions of rupees resettlement package. Interestingly, describing the project as very important for the development of Pakistan and for 'AJK' Sherpao stated 'strong Pakistan means prosperous Kashmir' ('AJK').

The Discontent

There are manifold reasons for popular dissatisfaction. The promises made in 1960s had not been fulfilled yet. The promises included alternative residential plots; compensation for loss of business; alternative allotments for loss of irrigational land; free electricity; free water supply; a railway station and a railway line connecting Mirpur with rail network of Pakistan; 50 per cent quota for employment and royalty for the dam to 'AJK.' However, royalty was not paid, electricity available in the area is of poor quality and expensive, there is no railway line, and still there are many families who did not get their allotments.

Promise of free electricity to the area was never fulfilled. It is reported that the electricity that was promised free of charge to local people priced almost double the amount paid per unit by the Pakistanis across Jhelum. It is reported that the total electricity consumption in 'AJK' is even less than ten per cent of the total production from the dam. The high quality electricity generated in the Mangla dam is supplied to Pakistan provinces and for 'AJK' the low quality electricity comes from Warsak dam. The royalty was not given to 'AJK' till recently. The royalty was denied to the area on the pretext that it could be only paid to provinces of Pakistan as per the constitution. Interestingly, the constitution did not prohibit the construction of a dam on an occupied property. During the construction of the Mangla dam, thousands of acres of land was submerged and thousands were displaced. Some of the affected persons are still waiting for payment of compensation. Many of the displaced who were allotted land in Punjab and Sindh provinces of Pakistan as part of resettlement plan are still not able to get possession of their allotted land that is under the occupation of local mafias. Another section of affected people settled in the districts of Jhang and Khushab are still to get the ownership rights.[22]

The promised townships and new Mirpur city were left half way in construction. It is argued that the new Mirpur city was largely built with the remittances sent by the diaspora. The people of 'AJK' also contend that they have never been taken into confidence regarding the dam project. In the year 2000 the then speaker of the 'AJK' legislative assembly, Abdul Majeed Chaudhry demanded of the Pakistan government to take the Kashmiri leadership into confidence over raising of the height of the Mangla Dam, saying the issue should not 'strain cordial relations' between Pakistan and 'AJK.' Speaking at a public meeting held against the proposed expansion of the Mangla Dam Chaudhry, who himself belongs to the Mirpur district, urged Islamabad to abandon the proposed plan of the Mangla dam's extension. He said imposition of decisions on the Kashmiris and their suppression on the Mangla dam issue would produce dangerous results.

Pakistan military regime has planned to increase the height of the Mangla dam as national consensus on the construction of Kalabagh dam could not be evolved. It is beyond the comprehension of the people of 'AJK' as to why Pakistan is not able to construct dams on its own territory. Planning for Mangla dam and Kalabagh dam were made around same time. The Mangla dam was constructed in 1967 and thereafter it continues functioning till date providing water and electricity to provinces of Pakistan. The Kalabagh dam, plans for which were made in early 1950s and over the years millions of dollars have been spent on feasibility reports, each confirming it to be a viable, is yet to be constructed. People of 'AJK' feel that Islamabad has not built the Kalabagh dam to avoid annoying its 'own people.' Instead, uprooting the people of 'AJK' for the second time was considered a viable option to meet the growing demands of water and electricity in Pakistan since they are from an *azad* territory. Similar logic, as already mentioned, has been applied in constructing Diamir-Bhasha dam in Gilgit-Baltistan. The resentment is also widespread on the ground that the expansion of the dam would affect thousands of acres of land in Mirpur district, further displacing people. Many of these people would be forced to leave their places for the second time.

The anti-dam activists argued that upraising will devastate the economy,. environment and culture of Mirpur region. Economically, a significant part of the new Mirpur city will be submerged including the whole infrastructure, established businesses, schools, etc. Culturally, the mosques, playgrounds, graveyards, etc. will be eroded. This would put immense burden, the activists argue, on an already traumatized community that is yet to fully recover from dam construction in 1960s. Environmentally, it is argued that the dam extension would be catastrophic. In a 1991 article, Roger Ballard of the Manchester University argued: "To Pakistan Mangla is a vital asset which brings many benefits...Mangla is thus critical to the success of the Pakistani economy as a whole. Yet despite the great benefits which Mangla has brought to everyone in Pakistan proper, those unfortunate enough to live immediately upstream of the dam have had... to bear the brunt of its environmental costs."[23] Yet, Islamabad overlooked the popular resentment, or tried to crush it, or, interestingly, tried to convince people that any protests against Pakistan would 'jeopardize the movement for independence in Kashmir against India.' To quote Shabir Choudhry, "When I was President of the JKLF, I was cautioned by very high ranking Pakistani officer to abandon our plan of holding a demonstration outside Pakistani High Commission in London. I told him that we are holding this demonstration against closure of K2 newspaper, arrest of Kashmiri leaders in Rawalpindi and upraising of the Mangla dam. He tried to persuade me that it will divert attention from what is going on in... Kashmir, hence it will be an indirect help to India. When I refused to follow his instructions he warned me that I will have to pay a price for this."[24] At other place he pointed, "Pakistan government has not only money but has other means to silence the people of Mirpur, and if needed has power to crush their opposition, and complete the extension of Mangla dam. But what would be fall out of this? My fear is that it would provide a spark that might not be easy to extinguish; and this could create a situation where angry youths of Azad Kashmir might resort to violent struggle against Pakistan."[25]

Thousands of families, who were forced to migrate from POK in 1947 and currently living in J&K, have expressed serious concern over the decision of raising the height of the Mangla dam. Rajiv Chunni, President of SOS, an NGO working for the welfare of displaced from 'AJK,' told the authors[26] that the increase in the height of the dam would not only affect many families staying there but would also submerge a large chunk of land and the immovable property worth thousands of crores mainly belonging to those who left the area when Pakistan occupied it in 1947. These people who are living as displaced in J&K have not been compensated for the losses they suffered. Since they are not currently living in 'AJK,' Rajiv argued, they will be deprived of the compensation as their land would be submerged with the increase of the dam height.

The issue of Mangla dam cannot be overlooked because it has largely shaped the growing acrimony between the people of 'AJK' and Pakistan. The locals contend that their natural resources and particularly water is commandeered by Islamabad to their utter disadvantage. Considering themselves 'scapegoats' people in 'AJK' feel they have to bear all the brunt and the benefits of the dam being reaped by provinces of Pakistan.[27] A poem written on the dam by an 'AJK' native speaks volumes about the miseries that Mangla dam has created. It read:[28]

Sirkar (government) built the dam,
Drowning our ancestral land,
Arid and worthless,
Cultivated by our fathers, grandfather
Back to the beginning.

Sirkar built the dam,
Uprooted our community,
Destroyed our culture and language,
For water and power.

Sirkar built the dam,
And issued passports to the people of the *khet* (field),
The farmers, *maalis* (gardners), *baparyees* (traders), *ajaragys* (goat herders),
Who had never ventured far from Mirpur.

Sirkar built the dam,
Scattered the people like pollen
To Pakistan, America, Canada, *walayat* (foreign)
Every corner of the world.

The presentation titled, "Mangla Dam Upraising - Pakistan government another favour to people of Kashmir," made by Shabir Choudhry, Chairman Diplomatic Committee of JKLF, in a seminar held during the UN Sub Commission on Human Rights in Geneva, on August 6, 2003 is worth mentioning. The presentation pointed that Mangla dam construction was illegal and against wishes of the local people. It was fiercely opposed by the local people of Mirpur, but this opposition was ruthlessly put down. The project was completed on graves of the fore fathers of the locals and by destroying history and culture of the local area. Giving the details of unfulfilled promises Choudhry argued that the thousands of the affected were told that in order to meet water and energy need of Pakistan this dam has to be built; but they were promised generous compensation for their 'sacrifice.' But most of the promises were not honoured by respective Pakistani governments. Comparing this scenario with Tarbela dam in Pakistan, which was constructed after the Mangla dam, he argued that this construction too uprooted people, but they were properly compensated and resettled. The government of NWFP had a written agreement with WAPDA, and used its power and influence to implement it in letter and spirit. WAPDA has been regularly paying Net Hydel Profit to NWFP in spite of its financial problems. But, Islamabad owes millions of rupees to 'AJK.' Attacking the leaders in 'AJK' who favour Pakistan, Choudhry pointed that the puppets say that this is a trivial matter and people of Kashmir are ready to make more sacrifices; and are ready to uproot themselves to build more dams for Pakistan. Arguing that it is not sacrifice but exploitation of resources of 'AJK' and subjugation of local people, he dared the puppets to ask Islamabad to build dams inside its own territory.

There is also apprehension that the raising is done to misappropriate the large sum allocated for the dam extension. Rs. 300,000 has been allocated for each affected family of the original construction in 1967. But it would be virtually impossible to trace those people as many have died and others have dispersed to various places. Hence, there would be plenty of opportunities for some officials to make money and that is why they oppose the idea of de-silting and insist on upraising the dam, bigger the bounty better the dividends for them. Though it seems that Pakistan has 'won' the battle for the time being, in the long-term the battle may prove disastrous for it.

References

1. *Dawn*, November 14, 2004.
2. Seema Shekhawat, "The Bhasha Dam Controversy," *Across LOC*, January- March 2006, p. 6.
3. Quoted in M. Ismail Khan, "The Bhasha Dam Rip-off," *The News International*, February 2, 2006.
4. *Daily Times*, February 4, 2006.
5. *Dawn*, March 26, 2006
6. *http://www.krrc.org/content/view/957/32/*. Accessed on February 13, 2007.
7. *Daily Times*, January 30, 2006.
8. *htttp://www.balawaristan.net/BhashaDamAbbas.html*. Accessed on January 9, 2007.
9. *http://www.balawaristan.net/BhashaWhynotDiamar.html*. Accessed on January 17, 2007.
10. *Daily Times*, February 16, 2006.
11. *The Pakistan Tribune*, June 15, 2006.
12. "Is Bhasha Dam no Longer an Option?," *Daily Times*, November 13, 2005.
13. Ibid.
14. *Daily Times*, February 15, 2007.
15. *Daily Times*, March 9, 2006.
16. Seema Shekhawat, "The Bhasha Dam," *Daily Excelsior*, March 23, 2006.
17. *Daily Times*, April 7, 2006.
18. *Pakistan Observer*, April 27, 2006.
19. Debidatta Aurobinda Mahapatra, "Raising of the Mangla Dam Height: Issues and Concerns," *Across LOC*, vol. 2, no. 2, April-June 2006, pp. 3-5.
20. Shams Rehman, "Dam Extension in Pakistani Administrated Kashmir: General Musharraf Uses Army to Crush Kashmiris." *http://kashmir.ahrchk.net/mainfile.php/v2n1/265/*. Accessed on January 26, 2007.
21. *The Dawn*, August 4, 2002.
22. *The News*, January 25, 2001.

23. Roger Ballard, "The Kashmir Crisis: A View from Mirpur," *Economic and Political Weekly*, vol. 2, March 2-9, 1991, p. 516.
24. Shabir Choudhry "I am a Failed Man." *http://www.krrc.org/*. Accessed on February 2, 2007.
25. Shabir Choudhry, "De silting." *http://www.krrc.org/*. Accessed on February 2, 2007.
26. Personal Interview, October 15, 2006.
27. Personal Interview, with anonymous person from 'AJK.'
28. Khadim Hussain, "Mangla Dam." h*ttp://www.neukol.org.uk/teesblog/index.php/gfac/2006/09/07/mangla_dam*. Accessed on February 21, 2007.

7

Earthquake and its Implications

The October 2005 earthquake is significant from many ways. The devastating quake showed that the huge disaster both in terms of lives and properties surpassed bilateral animosities and rivalries. The disaster proved to be a double tragedy; besides the natural impact, the lacklustre attitude of concerned authorities and the lack of needed cooperation between India and Pakistan further exacerbated the impact of the catastrophe. Though the later events such as opening of roads between the J&K and 'AJK' indicated a mature handling of the disaster, much still remained vague.

From a broader perspective, the earthquake presented a two-fold scenario- at times contradictory. It provided opportunities to both India and Pakistan to cooperate in such an hour of devastation. On the other hand it laid the ground for renewal of terrorist strategy in 'AJK' by attempting to put a humanitarian mask. Reportedly, Pakistani army gave enough leeway to these organizations to lead relief and rescue work. This humanitarian face of these radical organizations, sworn in to play havoc in J&K and other parts of India, may lead to swelling of their ranks, thus making the peace process a difficult endeavour. The aftermath terrorist attacks corroborate this point of view. Besides this complex scenario, the earthquake also revealed the inefficiency of the administration in 'AJK' and Pakistan to handle the situation. The post-earthquake 'AJK,' termed graveyard of dead people, was chock-a-block by those who suffered from mental trauma, diseases, abjectly poor living conditions and harsh climate.

The Devastation

The Pakistani government's official earthquake related death toll was 87,350. Some reports put the estimation at 100,000. Most of the affected areas being in the mountainous terrain, access was impeded by landslides that blocked the roads. Hostile weather and terrain in hilly regions jeopardized the plans to carry out relief activities. Jan Egeland, the UN Emergency Relief Coordinator told journalists after visiting the earthquake affected region, 'tens of thousands of people's lives are at stake and they could die if we do not get to them in time.'

The UN reported that over 4 million people were directly affected. It has been estimated that damages incurred are over 5 billion US dollars.[1] The earthquake paralyzed the whole governance system in 'AJK.' Muzaffarabad city's only health facility, the 400-bed Combined Military Hospital, had crumbled, killing hundreds. Even the prime minister's secretariat, the supreme court, and the legislature building turned to rubble in the quake. Then Prime Minister of 'AJK,' Sikandar Hayat Khan, who himself shifted to a tent in the lawns of his damaged house described the capital city, Muzaffarabad, as 'graveyard.' Sardar Anwar Khan, then President of 'AJK' lamented: 'I am president of the cities of the dead.' According to then UN Secretary General, Kofi Annan, 'This (the earthquake) is a huge, huge disaster. It is a race against time to save the lives of these (affected) people.' Roads, bridges, local hydropower units, power, telephone links, urban water supply and sewerage facilities, etc. in cities of Muzaffarabad, Rawalakote, Bagh, Balakot and other towns were destroyed. The impact of the earthquake was felt over far regions such as Gilgit-Baltistan wherein, according to *newsinsight.com*, about 15 to 20 per cent damage occurred to Pakistani nuclear facilities and storage sites.

In the whole affected area, including Pakistan and 'AJK,' an estimated three million people were in need of shelter, while about 67,000 persons were seriously injured, according to a UN official. Aid organizations were alarmed at the potential for diseases in several camps that have sprung up in the quake zone, and the WHO had expressed fear that epidemics such as cholera could spread in the area. While there were no reports of outbreaks of epidemics, health workers feared acute respiratory infections such as diarrhoea, dysentery and tetanus, etc. spreading, especially in cramped tent settlements. In the second week of November 2005 WHO reported 300 cases of acute diarrhoea in just one of the tent settlements in Muzaffarabad. Ron Redmond, spokesman of the UN High Commissioner for Refugees stressed the urgency to get a good sanitation system into these camps as well as clean water.

As per the reports of the UNICEF more than half of the 3.3 million people displaced by the quake in the whole region of J&K, Pakistan and 'AJK' are 'severely affected.' According to UNICEF relief spokesman Michael Bociurkiw, 'half of them are 18 years old and under, and a fifth are five years and under that make the most vulnerable group.' There are already early signs of nutritional deficiencies in remote mountain areas hit by the quake and weakened people will fall prey to disease, observes the United Nations agency's emergency coordinator Michael Jones. According to him, 'In a month's time we will start to see malnutrition-related diseases and we will start to see people dying, they will say from hunger or starvation but it will be from weakened bodies.' The CNN has reported that there are tens of thousands of pregnant women among the earthquake survivors. The unborn would not have escaped the trauma their mothers suffered. Exposure, crowding, weak diets and bad sanitation further compounded the problems.

There were widespread reports of devastated people resorting to criminal activities to survive. *Outlook*'s correspondent in Muzaffarabad witnessed looting in several villages. On his way up into the mountains, in the week of the earthquake, masked youngsters accosted him, brandishing guns. He was not harmed only because he had an armed escort; and because he told the looters he was a local journalist. When asked why they had taken to crime, one of the youngsters replied, 'We are desperate. Had it not been for the quake, we wouldn't have been doing this.'

Sluggish Rehabilitation

The politics within Pakistan aftermath of the earthquake lacked the required coordination to carry the relief and rescue work effectively. Faulty relief distribution, administrative hiccups and the traffic chaos on roads leading to the calamity-hit areas were some of the features of the lack of coordination and mismanagement. These not only affected smooth operation, but also gave the impression of a country that looked and acted discriminately even in the hour of emergency.[2]

At October 19, 2005 donors' conference in Geneva, $ 580 million was promised to Pakistan for rehabilitation, of which US $16 million was for immediate relief and $ 564 million for long-term reconstruction. At the donors' conference in Islamabad on November 19, $ 6.5 billion was pledged ($ 2.5 billion in grants and $ 4 billion in loans). However, many European donors voiced concerns about transparency and accountability and demanded civilian participation and oversight, as did Musharraf's political opposition within and outside the parliament. The military government replied that donor funds would be used in an accountable and transparent manner but rejected civilian control and parliamentary oversight of the process.[3] Similarly, about opposition demand that a part of foreign exchange reserves, marked for defence expenditure, should be spent for post-earthquake reconstruction, Prime Minister Shaukat Aziz said that the defence budget could not be slashed as 'peace lies in power, not in weakness.' In a customary style, Pakistan went ahead with negotiating with US on plans to purchase F-16 fighter planes sidelining the popular concerns.

About 40 NGOs had been working in affected areas. Eighteen of them were Pakistani and the rest foreign based. In addition to them, a team of NATO military engineers and doctors were working in areas where no other relief parties would reach. Though international aid poured in and international forces such as NATO helped in relief and rescue operations, the major concerns like construction of buildings for rehabilitation of homeless, rehabilitation of orphans, provision of tents and medicine to prevent epidemics, rising mental disorder and re-establishment of educational institutions remained problematic. Proper sanitation system, keeping people well fed and warm really remains a colossal job, opined Chief United Nations Humanitarian Coordinator, Jan Vandemoortele. Fears were expressed of a 'second wave of death' for earthquake victims due to harsh winter. It has been reported that the tents provided to the homeless were not winterized, i.e. to prevent leaking so as to stand harsh winters that goes down many degrees below zero. The affected people have expressed dissatisfaction over the slow relief work and staged demonstrations. Yet, the resentment was dealt with baton. Analysts have already expressed fear that unless the reconstruction work is coordinated properly, the catastrophe may lead to 'slumification' of the entire region.

The Pakistani army kept itself in control of all the relief operations. Samina Ahmed, Islamabad-based director of the ICG, observes: "In recent years there has been a disproportionate build-up of the army and a neglect of civilian concerns. The military lacks professional management skills. They are trained to fight wars. They can get boots on the ground but that's it." General Musharraf said keeping all relief operations under army control was important because of the army's credibility. But the fact is that the quake dealt a severe blow to the credibility of the army. It was accused of the sluggishness, arrogance, unwillingness to help and above all of corruption. The affected alleged the Pakistan army men deployed in 'AJK' grabbed relief goods. For instance, it has been alleged by some quarters that the army has grabbed good quality blankets meant for the affected people and supplied them with poor ones. How low the army's credibility had fallen was reflected in the demand of a joint body of NGOs in Peshawar on October 22, 2005 that the army must be kept away from reconstruction work. The furious and ailing people in Balakot reportedly threw stones at army men for their refusal to help 200 children trapped under the debris of their school building. In another incident canes were used by the security forces to break up a peaceful demonstration in Muzaffarabad on November 11,2005, by approximately two hundred earthquake survivors protesting eviction from their makeshift camp, injuring many. It is also alleged that the military did not have sufficient equipment to rescue trapped people, let alone bury the dead. Many pin the blame for the high death toll on the apathy of the rulers (the Punjab establishment) towards non-Punjabi provinces. Critics say the Pakistan army is prone to treating 'AJK' as 'a garrison, erecting their zones of comfort in a land of abject poverty, indifferent to undertaking development work there.' This apathetic attitude apparently led to more killings since there were no roads or bridges to reach the affected. According to Syed Mohammad Ali, a developmental consultant in Pakistan, the earthquake did not just reveal the hazards of reckless and haphazard construction but also the consequence of the seemingly less serious negligence of environmental destruction.[4] The earthquake brought to the fore the ills plaguing the construction business. Public buildings, like schools and colleges, collapsed under the impact of the earthquake, instantaneously turning these into mounds of death. Akther Naeem of Peshawar's University of Engineering and Technology feels it wasn't the quake that killed people; ignorance and a careless attitude did. A post-earthquake report of HRW gave a dismal picture of Pak army's performance in the earthquake devastated 'AJK.' It read:

"In the first seventy-two hours after the earthquake, thousands of Pakistani troops stationed in Azad Kashmir prioritized the evacuation of their own personnel over providing relief to desperate civilians. The international media began converging on Muzaffarabad within twenty-four hours of the earthquake and fanned out to other towns in Azad Kashmir shortly thereafter. They filmed Pakistani troops standing by and refusing to help because they had 'no orders' to do so as locals attempted to dig out those still alive, sending a chilling message of indifference from Islamabad. Having filmed the refusal, journalists switched off their cameras and joined the rescue effort themselves; in one instance they shamed the soldiers into helping. But unlike the death and destruction, the media were not everywhere.... prior to the earthquake, the Pakistani military kept a close watch on the population to ensure political compliance and control; this was facilitated by the placement of military installations frequently in close proximity to populated areas. In the context of a military presence that was more abuser than protector, and domineering Pakistani political control, the failure of the authorities to respond quickly and more humanely to the after effects of the earthquake in Azad Kashmir came as little surprise. That failure generated massive public resentment against the Pakistani state, and it highlighted the need for an examination of the conduct of Pakistani authority in Azad Kashmir."

Similarly Jan McGirk, correspondent for the *The Independent*, reported, "Nearly a quarter of a million troops were already stationed in the area .... It took days before the army would reach any stricken areas beyond the towns; while it dallied, tens of thousands of loved ones were smothered under the rubble and the injuries of survivors went septic. Without any shelter, vulnerable infants and elders contracted pneumonia when intermittent downpours soaked their bedding. In grief, people could only cling to one another for body heat as hail pelted down and thunderclaps heralded more aftershocks. Villagers grumbled that the army must be tending to its own casualties first and had abandoned its hapless civilians to the elements."[5] The credibility of Islamabad received another jolt when an Oxfam report said the expenditure incurred on reconstruction work was inflated six times. It recommended more civilian involvement in the reconstruction work. This was also the opinion of many of the donor countries. The HRW has made following suggestions especially to donors and other international actors for a transparent and effective relief and rehabilitation operation in the earthquake affected area.[6]

- Use every available opportunity to press for an end to impunity for perpetrators of human rights abuses, including members of the military, intelligence agencies, police and militant groups. Urge respect for international due process and fair trial standards and press for impartial inquiries into, and accountability for, cases of arbitrary detention and torture and other ill-treatment in detention.
- Bilateral donors and international lending agencies, including the World Bank and Asian Development Bank, should insist that the government of Pakistan commit itself to providing training in human rights law and norms to all law enforcement personnel, particularly its military forces in Azad Kashmir.
- Donors should provide assistance, through government agencies and NGOs, to promote the administration of justice.
- Ensure contracts for earthquake reconstruction are handled through proper procurement procedures that allow bidding by private agencies, and not just military entities.
- Ensure independent auditing of relief funds and materials to ensure transparency and accountability.
- Ensure greater civilian oversight of relief, rehabilitation and reconstruction efforts. Aid should be handled through a process that involves the government, as well as local, national and international NGOs, and civil society groups, particularly those working in the field.

The bickering within political parties in Pakistan further created troubles for effective implementation of earthquake relief programmes. For instance, the PPP refused to join the National Disaster Management Council, established by the Islamabad for the rehabilitation of victims of the earthquake. Similarly, amongst conflicting reports, it has not become yet clear as regarding how far the affected have received compensation. Opposition leader in 'AJK' assembly, Sardar Qamar-u-Zaman charged that the 'AJK' government under

Sardar Attique has completely failed to give compensation money to earthquake affected people. In order to provide prompt help and assistance to the victims of any natural disaster or catastrophe, a Disaster Management Authority has been established in 'AJK.' It has also launched various public welfare programs in the quake-hit areas, including the Livelihood Support Cash Grant Programme. Yet, the things remained in poor shape. To quote Akbar Zaidi, "While there is quasi-civilian Government (in Pakistan), real power still rests with the President and the military institutions supporting him. The response to earthquake needs to be seen in this light.... The military is a key constituent of the government.... It was therefore the force expected to react immediately by providing relief and help, particularly medical support... The quake's aftermath has exposed a much-trumpeted 'success' story of Musharraf's regime.... Its obsession with its notion of 'security' continues to undermine real human security...."[7]

A Double Tragedy

Pakistan has yet to come out from its accustomed ways of thinking, even in the face of the enormity of the disaster confronting it. This was evident from the attitude shown by the Pak authorities regarding the help from India thereby delaying the rehabilitation work.[8] Immediately after the earthquake, on October 9, 2005, a proposal was made to send fortified biscuits for the immediate relief of the affected. These biscuits were produced in collaboration with the World Food Programme and one million students in Afghanistan receive a packet every day. New Delhi was ready to finance this. When the WFP contacted Islamabad, they were told it would be difficult to accept the offer. The reason: the biscuit packets had the flags of India and Afghanistan on it. When Pakistan finally accepted the biscuits, they could be sent only in the third consignment of aid, on October 17, 2005. In three lots, a total of 16,500 blankets, 620 tents, 15 tonnes of plastic sheets, 22 tonnes of medicines and 100 tonnes of biscuits were sent by India.

Although thousands of soldiers were stationed in 'AJK,' it took the Pakistan army three days to reach major towns and far longer to reach many remote villages that were close to the LOC and easily tractable from Indian side. Initially Pakistan expressed reluctance to accept offers of assistance from India, which had the capacity to provide timely help, particularly in the hardest hit and remote areas on Pakistan's side of the LOC. The events just aftermath of earthquake, reflecting mistrust, need further elaboration. India had offered its helicopter services for relief and rescue operations in 'AJK,' which Pakistan rejected.[9] Later, Islamabad told the Pakistani media about its willingness to accept helicopters from India but without pilots. Then Indian Foreign Secretary, Shyam Saran informed his Pakistani counterpart that New Delhi was willing to undertake relief work across the LOC, more accessible from India, which was rejected. Pakistan President, General Pervez Musharraf cited 'local sensitivities' as the reason for denial of Indian offer for joint relief and rescue operations in 'AJK.' In his interview to *Financial Times*, General Musharraf said, "the world should understand that we cannot allow Indian soldiers to operate in Kashmir ('AJK'). Our whole defence system is there, our whole military is there."[10] Pakistan's suggestion of allowing Indian helicopters without Indian pilots appears to have been caused by sense of fear and mistrust. To India's offer, Pakistan's Foreign Ministry Spokesperson, Tasleen Aslam replied that there is no possibility of joint relief and rescue operations on both sides of the LOC. Knowing well that India's offer could have proved helpful, Pakistan's rejection only accentuated the damage to the affected people. As per reports, Pakistan's army, after the earthquake, was busy guarding and closing the LOC.

To provide help to quake-victims India offered aid worth US $ 25 million on October 28, 2005 ahead of the official-level meeting to discuss opening of the LOC for relief coordination. India's offer was made at the meeting of UN Office of the Coordinator for Humanitarian Affairs at Geneva by Minister of State for Statistics and Programme Implementation, Oscar

Fernandes. India's External Affairs Ministry spokesman Navtej Sarna told reporters that 'the government of Pakistan would be welcome to use this contribution for rebuilding homes and rehabilitating people, reconstructing the infrastructure and restoring essential services.' Earlier on October 21, 2005 India offered to undertake specific projects in education and health sectors in the quake-hit areas of Pakistan. The Bharat Sanchar Nigam Limited, government of India owned Telecom Company, on October 19, 2005 commissioned free telephone services for the quake-hit for contacting their relatives across the LOC. The services were made available for fifteen days at four destinations in the state at the Srinagar police control room, the Central Telegraph Office, Jammu, Uri and Tangdhar police stations. Indian willingness to contribute to the people affected received lukewarm response from Islamabad. The Pakistan leadership preferred to make appeals to international community for help than accepting India's offer for cooperation.

The optimistic editorial of *The Hindu* of October 11, 2005 pointing "the terrible tragedy may have taken place in disputed territory but it has united the two parties that stake claim to it, India and Pakistan, in a common grief...It has opened up the possibility of bringing the two countries closer on an emotive issue, one that will strike an immediate chord with their peoples," did not seem to hold much ground as the events unfolded. While the nations of the world including India were concerned about the humanitarian aspects of the disaster, the Pakistani leadership appeared more interested in the political dimension of the Kashmir conflict. President Musharraf used the occasion of the International Donors' Conference at Islamabad on November 19, 2005 to raise the Kashmir issue. He pointed out that the earthquake has provided the opportunity to both the countries to resolve the Kashmir issue. It might appear from General Musharraf's initial words that he is serious for peace. But his later words were marked by ambiguity. He urged India to play a role to solve the Kashmir issue in a way as to 'India's donation to Kashmir.' The exact words were: 'Let success and happiness emerge from the ruins of this catastrophe, for the devastated people of Kashmir, let this be the Indian donation to Jammu and Kashmir.' The Indian External Affairs Minister of State, E. Ahmed responded by saying New Delhi was "prepared to resolve all issues, including Jammu and Kashmir through dialogue between our two countries in an atmosphere free of terrorism and violence."[11] Pakistan's attempt to utilize every opportunity to raise the issue of Kashmir is well known. The stated Indian position is that unless the flow of terror is not subdued by peaceful atmosphere, the Kashmir issue would remain a difficult task for a solution. Taking these developments into account *The Economist* called the disaster 'double tragedy' that not only wasted human life but also wasted a chance of reconciliation between the two neighbours.

Apparently, in order to stave off pressure and criticism, Pakistan proposed of opening the LOC at five points for the affected people to meet their brethrens and for relief operations. In spite of opposition from some quarters, the government of India undertook a bold step in opening the LOC at five points: Tangdhar-Teetwal, Uri-Chakothi, Uri-Hajipir, Poonch-Rawalakote and Mendhar-Tattapani. On November 7, 2005 Poonch-Rawalakote route was opened and India sent 25 truckloads of good including food, tents, tarpaulins and medicines. On this occasion, a signboard on the Indian side read, 'we have not opened the LOC, we have opened our hearts.' Hence, despite all the problems the earthquake in a way provided the occasion to convert the line of control into the line of contact.[12] On November 21, 2005 nine persons walked across the LOC in Poonch. Chakan-da-Bagh on the LOC became the second point to witness the movement of human beings, the first being the Kaman Bridge in Uri district. On November 7, 2005 when it was first opened for exchange of relief for victims of the earthquake a large crowd had gathered across the LOC in anticipation of crossing over. Reportedly, some of them had actually run towards the LOC and had to be deterred by the Pakistan security forces. After nearly two months of the earthquake, the *Karvaan-e-Aman* (Caravan of Peace) from

Srinagar to Muzaffarabad resumed service on December 2, 2005 from the Indian side up to the *Aman Setu* (peace bridge) on the LOC with 20 passengers on board. The last (14th) *Karvaan-e-Aman* had rolled out from Srinagar on October 6, 2005, two days before the earthquake. In June 2006, both the countries agreed to open Poonch-Rawalakote road for civilian traffic. Besides, it is also reported that India took a conciliatory approach and did not fire at Pak helicopters that came too close to the LOC while carrying rescue operations. According to Major Nasrullah Khan of Pakistan, "it has not happened since 1947. Before that choppers moving near LOC were used to be fired upon from across the border. But we are now flying freely over LOC without any fear."[13]

'Humane' Terrorists

Despite Musharraf's claims of banning terrorist outfits and dismantling their infrastructure, jehadi training camps and bases had remained intact in NWFP and 'AJK.'[14] The devastating earthquake brought forth this fact in an alarming way. Almost all major jehadi groups operating in J&K - LeT, JeM, HM, the Tehreek-ul-Mujahideen and Al-Badr - had a presence either in Muzaffarabad or the areas adjoining it in 'AJK.' According to a report, these camps were part of the 85 terrorist training centres being operated by ISI along the LOC. These camps were equipped with ultra modern gadgets and arms to train terrorists for J&K. The report further said that due to the earthquake the terrorist camps at Chakothi, Kahuta and Bagh were totally obliterated.[15] Their casualties vary anywhere between 2,000 -3,000. The highest ranking militant killed in earthquake was Muhammad Ishaq alias Hyder, Chief Commander of Tehreek-ul-Mujahideen.[16] As per Jan McGirk, "the quake killed a hundred militants in training camps established near the Line of Control... the government has never acknowledged that such camps exist, even though India has since 1989 accused Pakistan of arming and supporting Islamic guerrillas and demanded the camps' closure."[17]

The terrorist groups in 'AJK' demonstrated tremendous alacrity in undertaking rescue and relief operations. The United Jehad Council, a conglomerate of terrorist organizations based in Muzaffarabad, called for suspension of terrorist operations aftermath of the quake to facilitate relief operation. Long before the arrival of army regulars, international aid agencies, or emergency search and rescue teams, the jehadis swung into action. The efforts won accolades from the anguished survivors. In Muzaffarabad, a big banner was erected over a tarpaulin that identified the 'energetic do-gooders' as members of JuD, parent organization of LeT. This group is widely seen as the fundraising and recruiting wing for 'Islamist warriors' who cross into India.[18] It can be mentioned here that the LeT was banned by the Pakistan government in 2002 as a terrorist organization. The JuD claims to have severed its links with the LeT, but retains ostensibly at least its moral support for its actions in the Indian zone. [19] The 'humanitarian arm,' of JuD, Idara Khidmat-e-Khalq, maintained a field hospital complete with X-ray equipment, a makeshift operating theatre, and even a tent for visiting journalists. It also operated ambulance services and surgical camps, constructed 1,000 shelters and provided electricity through generators. The person heading this hospital was an orthopaedic surgeon Amir Aziz Khan, who abandoned his Lahore clinic to treat the quake-affected. He had been arrested on October 21, 2002, for allegedly assisting Al Qaeda in developing biochemical weapons. The jehadi groups openly operated relief camps, distributed relief goods and advertised their presence through banners and billboards at their camps and along the main streets of earthquake-affected areas. The JuD alone claimed to have mobilized 2,500 volunteers for the relief work.

These organizations were also prominent in camp management, running 37 out of the 73 organized camps in and around Muzaffarabad. The extremist groups had a presence in every affected district of 'AJK' in the Neelum and Jhelum valleys, including Muzaffarabad, Bagh, Hattian, Dhir Kot, Rawalakote, Haveli and Athmuqam. In their response to the earthquake, jehadi 'humanitarian' groups drew on their existing infrastructure in 'AJK' as also their knowledge of the local terrain. Besides, the widely reported close cooperation with the Pakistan army, which provided logistical support and other facilities including helicopters, too helped the extremists to carry out the rescue operations. Like the jehadi organizations which benefited from their regional networks and access to sophisticated technology during their activities aftermath of the earthquake, the religious parties, who are also supporters of jehad, made their presence felt through their subsidiaries, including their welfare, educational and militant wings. Using local mosques and madrasas to network and coordinate their activities, the parties like, JUI, mobilized professional volunteers, including doctors, students, lawyers, teachers and labour leaders, to expand their relief operations. Reportedly, local charitable donations, in cash and kind, as well as external assistance from the United Arab Emirates, Saudi Arabia and Malaysia, have benefited both the religious parties and their jehadi allies. Al-Rasheed Trust, for instance, claims to have received substantial support from the Saudi Relief Centre.[20] The JUI is an ardent supporter of the ousted Taliban regime in Afghanistan. Al Khair Trust, which is connected to JUI, has been heavily supported by the Pakistani military in its relief and reconstruction work, especially in 'AJK.' The Al Khidmat Foundation, set up by JI, was one of the main organizations coordinating, collecting and distributing goods in the earthquake-affected region. The Foundation's subsidiary organizations included the Pakistan Islamic Medical Association, the Pakistan Engineers Forum, the Ghazali Education Trust, and the JI's Islami Jamiat Talaba (student wing) and Tanzeem al-Asataza (teachers' wing).[21] Other prominent jehadi groups conducting relief work include the Al Rasheed Trust, Al Safa Trust, Al Akhtar Trust and Al Rehmat Trust. All this humanitarianism, of course, remained limited only to 'co-religionists of the Ummah' and not to non-believers, like Shias in Gilgit-Baltistan.

Pakistani Islamist organizations such as the JI claimed that carrying out of the relief operation aimed at countering 'Jewish and Indian relief operations.' Reportedly, the JuD is putting into place an Islamic-oriented infrastructure to deal with the education of the swelling population of orphans, thus giving rise the possibility of increased jehadi influence in the form of madrasa education. This has become increasingly a concern for the ongoing peace process as the terrorist organizations' role in relief work would likely provide them a kind of legitimacy amongst the affected people.

The Army-Terrorist Nexus

The post-earthquake role of the terrorist organizations underlines the continuity of the Pak army-terrorist relationship. The Pakistani military apparently saw the earthquake as an opportunity to 'create a new image for these groups rather than an opportunity to disband them.' Interestingly, Islamabad justified the contributions by the jehadi groups to relief as 'need of the hour,' forgetting their oft repeated statement that there are no terrorist camps in the area. It portrayed the jehadis as the prime contributors to relief work, and Pakistan's Interior Minister Aftab Ahmed Khan Sherpao, called them as 'the lifeline of our rescue and relief work in Azad Kashmir right now.' President Musharraf justified his government's inaction, saying, "... since they are there, certainly we would not like them to stop, why should we not allow our own people who are going there and assisting those people, whether they are 'Jehadis' or anybody." Yet, aware of Western, in particular the US, concerns about the jehadi presence in NWFP and Kashmir under Pak control he declared: "We have warned them that if we see any single activity of their involvement in anything other than welfare, we are not only going to ban them but we are far better equipped to reach earthquake-hit communities than their moderate political adversaries... going to get them out of that place."[22]

Thus, one of the interesting features of the Pakistan politics that came out in open during the earthquake was the close nexus between Pakistan military and the jehadi groups.

The jehadi groups benefited from military patronage. Having served Pakistan's interests in Kashmir and Afghanistan for more than two decades, they see themselves as extension of the army. Nearly all jehadis interviewed by ICG aftermath of the earthquake claimed a close working relationship with local military commanders. A senior army official admitted, "we have no written or verbal direction to stop these outfits' activities, which is why we are coordinating with them in relief work."[23] Fearing that the jehadis will become even more entrenched with the military's help, a Human Rights Commission of Pakistan official said, "the Jehadi outfits will have enough funds to sustain their relief efforts well into the later stages of reconstruction, while some other NGOs won't have this capacity. So in the end, what will we be left with? The (jehadi) NGOs, of course."[24]

Fertile Ground for Grooming Terrorists

A dangerous consequence of the jehadi involvement in the relief operations was on the educational system in the affected area. The sidelining of the educational reconstruction by the government would only help the jehadi madrasas to take over the education network. This would likely have serious long-term consequences. The Deobandi Wafaqul Madaris Al-Arabiya, Pakistan's largest union of madrasas, has established an earthquake relief fund to rebuild 1,500 mosques and 300 madrasas in 'AJK' and NWFP. While the members of the madrasa union have been given a target of US $ 4.16 million, Al-Rasheed Trust's media organs, Islam and Zarb-e-Momin, have run advertisements to raise additional funds. Alongside the Deobandis, JI's Al-Khidmat Foundation is building Islamic schools and mosques, which would help spread the influence of its subsidiary, the HM. Other religious organizations, such as Al-Huda Foundation and Iqra Foundation, are also focusing on the education sector. Thus, imparting extremist education would be a first step towards indoctrinating the young.

The quake has also orphaned many who are considered potential members by the extremist groups. Every religious organization has announced, through mosque loudspeakers, banners and pamphlets, that it will adopt children orphaned by the earthquake, rather than leave them at the mercy of Western NGOs. Although the government has banned the adoption of orphans, the jehadi groups are reportedly 'taking care of them.' Farhad Burney of the Ansar Burney Welfare Trust, a leading local humanitarian organization, said, "we have heard from very reliable sources and seen with our own eyes that orphaned and lost children are being taken by jehadi organizations in northern Pakistan to be trained."[25] During its family-tracing program, aimed at reuniting lost children with their families, an international NGO faced jehadi opposition. When it tried to persuade camp managers to reunite a child in a JuD facility in Muzaffarabad with his mother, it was initially denied access. It took the NGO weeks to negotiate the reunion of the child with his mother. Clearly, the area has become a fertile ground for jehadi production.

Both the Islamist political parties and their jehadi allies are understandably concerned about changed public perceptions of the West due to the relief work of NATO and Western NGOs. Survivors and the public at large favourably compared Western professionalism and efficiency to that of government agencies, particularly in the days following the earthquake when Pakistanis saw Western workers rescue survivors while their own military stood by. A counter-campaign by the Islamist organizations is now underway in the disguise of 'saving affected from Western values and culture propagated by the foreign NGOs under the cover of relief work.' Castigating Christian relief agencies such as World Vision, a coordinator of an Al-Rasheed Trust camp in Balakot said, "their camps provide less relief and stress more on schools. Every World Vision camp has a school. We welcome their relief programs but cannot tolerate promotion of Christianity among the trauma-stricken needy people. We will go wherever this NGO opens a camp and set up our own."[26] The extremist organization have warned the foreign NGOs to leave the area 'as soon as their work is finished' to save themselves from jehadi wrath.

Terrorism Uninterrupted

Alongside the 'humanitarian' work in 'AJK,' the terrorists also continued their pogrom in J&K and elsewhere in India. It is reported that 'several training camps have resurfaced after the earthquake,' and when the Indian security forces were involved in relief and rescue operations, several terrorist groups managed to sneak into J&K. The incidents of terrorist attacks have gone up after the earthquake. On October 9, a day after the earthquake, the terrorists carried out attacks in Rajouri district, killing ten Hindus and a Muslim. No organization claimed responsibility for the massacre, but suspicion was on HM's Pir Panjal Regiment and the LeT. The Indian army foiled an attempt by a group of terrorists to infiltrate into J&K on October 12, killing all the eight in Kupwara sector. A woman suicide bomber blew herself up on the Srinagar-Jammu national highway at Awantipora on October 13, 2005. The blast occurred at 11:30 am, but no casualties were reported. Pakistan based JeM, claimed that the woman was a suicide bomber of its women's wing - Banati Ayesha (daughter of Ayesha). In a major terrorist attack on the security forces, two soldiers were killed and seven others injured when LeT attacked the battalion headquarters of the 158 Territorial army at Kalibari in Kathua district of J&K on October 16. In another incident, a prominent CPI (M) leader, Ghulam Nabi Ganai, was shot dead by extremists in Anantnag district on October 17. He was shot outside a local mosque near his house at Seer-Hamdan village of Mattan. Two extremist groups, Al Mansoorian and Islamic Jehad Front, in separate telephone statements claimed responsibility for the attacks. India's capital, New Delhi too suffered the heat after twenty one days of the earthquake. The apogee of terrorist upsurge after the quake was felt in New Delhi on October 29, 2005 when serial bomb blasts planted by the LeT killed more than 60 and injured 210. Terrorist attacks in Mumbai in July 2006 again led to killing of hundreds of people. All these incidents are pointers that the terrorists remain active in their designs and operations. One can gauge two-fold intentions of the terrorists. First, they are interested to show that the killer quake has not been able to quell their instinct to kill the innocent civilians. Second, they intend to show that irrespective of all such calamities which call for better cooperation and coordination of activities, they are not going to give up their methods and aims fanned by religious hatred and extremist propaganda. It still remains to be seen whether the proposed Anti-Terrorist framework jointly agreed between India and Pakistan during the NAM Summit in Havana in September 2006 is going to produce desired results.

The analysts argue that the UN, Western donors and humanitarian organizations should reject government guidelines if they translate into assisting Islamist organizations and choose instead to work with secular political parties, local communities and secular NGOs in identifying the most appropriate reconstruction schemes. Focus on education could also help prevent the affected areas from turning into fertile grounds for the spread of religious extremism. Besides, micro-credit schemes, vocational training centres and other means of sustainable income generation too need urgent attention. Islamabad should also be pressurized to end the practice of allowing banned jehadi organizations to operate under changed names.

References

1. "Devastating Quake Strikes Northern Pakistan," *Cowasjee Earthquake Study Centre NED Newsletter*, Vol. 5, no. 2, 2005, p. 1.
2. Imtiaz Gul, "Apathy of the Civil Administration," *The News*, November 30, 2005. Also see, Imtiaz Alam, "Black Saturday Exposed the Rulers, Crowned the People." *www.satribune.com*, October 13, 2005; and Tarique Niazi, "Victims of the Deadly Quake should not become Cash Cows for Usurpers," *www.satribune.com*, October 11, 2005.
3. ICG Policy Briefing, Asia Briefing N°46, Islamabad/Brussels, March 15, 2006.

4. Syed Mohammad Ali, "In the Earthquake's Aftermath," *The Kashmir Times*, November 30, 2005.
5. Jan McGirk, "Kashmir: The Politics of an Earthquake." *http://www.opendemocracy.net/debates/article.jsp?id=2&debateId=43&articleId=2941*. Accessed on October 4, 2006.
6. "With Friends Like These...," *Human Rights Watch Report*, Vol. 18, no. 12 (C), September 2006.
7. S. Akbar Zaidi, "Emergency Relief in a Military State." *http://www.inwent.org/E+Z/content/archive-eng/12-2005/debate_art3.html*. Accessed on August 24, 2006.
8. Debidatta Aurobinda Mahapatra, "Politics in the Aftermath of the Earthquake," *Across LOC*, Vol. 1, no. 3, October-December 2005, pp. 4-5.
9. According to Kuldip Nayar, the noted journalist, "Earthquake exposes Pakistan's anti-India bias." For his views see, Kuldip Nayar, "Distant Neighbours," *The Tribune*, October 19, 2005.
10. *Daily Excelsior*, October 29, 2005.
11. *The Asian Age*, November 20, 2005.
12. Pranab Dhal Samanta, "LoC now Line of Contact," *Indian Express*, October 23, 2005.
13. Ashraf Javed, "Helis Move across LoC," *The Nation*, October 21, 2005.
14. See Debidatta Aurobinda Mahapatra, "Kashmir and Chechnya: Issues in Terrorism," *India Quarterly*, Vol. 62, no. 2, April-June 2006, pp. 228-268; Debidatta Aurobinda Mahapatra and Seema Shekhawat, *Conflict in Kashmir and Chechnya: Political and Humanitarian Dimensions* (New Delhi: Lancer's Books, 2007), pp. 35-36.
15. *The Pioneer*, October 11, 2005.
16. Tariq Bhat, "Terror Takes a Hit," *The Week*, October 23, 2003, p. 50.
17. Jan McGirk, n. 5.
18. For instance Haji Javed-ul Hassan, Chief of Jamaat-ud-Dawa's relief programme, said, "Naturally, politically, religiously, and even morally, Kashmir is a part of Pakistan." See *Greater Kashmir*, December 22, 2005.

19. Stephen Ulph, "Jehadists Respond to Earthquake Victims in Pakistan." *http://www.jamestown.org/terrorism/news/article.php?articleid=2369816*. Accessed on August 14, 2006.
20. ICG Policy Briefing, n. 3.
21. Ibid.
22. *Financial Times*, October 26, 2005.
23. Quoted in ICG Policy Briefing, n. 3.
24. Quoted in Ibid.
25. Ibid.
26. Ibid.

8

Intra-Kashmir Dialogue: Problems and Prospects

If there is any key achievement worth to be counted among many gains in the last decade long relations between India and Pakistan, including the much hyped peace process, the initiation of intra-Kashmir dialogue would be obviously one. This intra-Kashmir dialogue has its own niche, compulsions and distractions; nonetheless, it has roused consciousness in both parts of Kashmir that the parties are working for the resolution of the issue. The most crucial aspect, in this stream of developments, is the realization among all parties that people of Kashmir must be involved to reach at any amicable solution.

The ongoing peace process is multi-dimensional involving multiple actors. Earlier the dialogue process was one-tracked, almost confined to the official level, whether it was between New Delhi-Islamabad, India-J&K or Pakistan- 'AJK' and Gilgit-Baltistan. But as the recent developments would indicate, especially after the opening of the Srinagar-Muzaffarabad route in April 2005, the major focus in the whole scheme has gradually shifted to the people of the undivided J&K. Though there is awareness that the governments must back this dialogue process, there is an increasing realization that it is only the people who can better steer the process towards any possible solution. The opening of cross-border routes, the proposed email-linking of passport offices in Srinagar-Muzaffarabad to ease travel, the increasing realization to commonly fight disasters like earthquake, the prospects of joint mechanisms—are all indicative of a government backed people centric process.

The Changing Scenario

The 1990s towards its end witnessed many changes in international political scenario and its obvious impact on conflict scenario thus ensued. The cold war ended in this decade, ending or transforming the old patterns of inter-state relations. Besides, the forces of globalization and democracy added new dimensions to whole spectrum of relations. The conventional territorial boundaries and related disputes are challenged by increasing globalization, trans-border cultural exchanges and popular acceptance of democratic means for conflict resolution.[1] This trend is equally applicable to the Kashmir conflict which is far more complex owing to multiple players – Indian, Pakistani, Kashmiri and international, and myriad diversities in the region. In the year 1998 both the countries had gone nuclear and in the succeeding year the Kargil crisis amongst these two foremost rival nations in South Asia raised possibilities of nuclear confrontation, thus necessitating a process of dialogue with pressures from international community, especially the US.

The realities of hard experience of past have made the parties to Kashmir realize that in peace lies the future of the subcontinent, not in war. The last three years have set the trend that the people have chosen the path of peace and this bearing on political leaders have witnessed some remarkable developments. Developments such as the start of bus service in 1999 from Amritsar to Lahore, and the opening of the LOC, cooperation in the earthquake relief measures, are almost instructive about the future of the subcontinent. In October 2003, India proposed ten confidence-building measures for improving people-to-people contact and communication by road, rail and sea between the two countries, etc. It was followed by another positive development wherein a cease-fire came into effect on November 26, 2003 in the state along the India-Pakistan international border, the LOC and the Actual Ground Positioning Line. It is historic for two reasons. Firstly, it is the first formal truce between the two countries since the outbreak of militancy in the state. Secondly, it is for first time that firing on the border stopped almost completely, thus bringing a sigh of relief for people living near the LOC. The culmination of these developments was the agreement between the then Indian Prime Minister Atal Behari Vajpayee and Pakistani President Pervez Musharraf to initiate a peace process on the sidelines of the South Asian Association for Regional Cooperation Summit meeting in January 2004. In a joint statement, they proclaimed willingness to start a composite dialogue for peaceful settlement of all bilateral issues including Kashmir. In this context of evolving scenario the speech of Indian Prime Minister, Manmohan Singh at Strategic Studies Institute in Islamabad in February 7, 2007, needs quotation at length: "When minds open, old vistas expand, new ones appear and then things start moving. Searching minds go near the goal of understanding. Understanding itself is a destination. Unless one reaches it, one cannot win a victory. In diversity lie the gems of universality. Unresolved issues have an in-built explosive potential. It is everywhere in the world. The land of Kashmir is no exception to this norm. Therefore I would like to conclude that South Asian peace remains in the lockers of Kashmir. Only honest resolve can unlock the sixty years old stiffened lockers to usher in an era of peace."

In 2004, both the countries resumed talks that had been stalled after the attack on Indian parliament in 2001; in April 2005 bus rolled from Srinagar to Muzaffarabad, in October 2005 both the countries opened the LOC to facilitate relief operation and later for movement of the people. The earthquake in October 2005 in a way showed the necessity of joint cooperation to tackle many issues of common concern. It was a tragedy for both, but it was tragedy with lessons. Both the countries seemed to realize the necessity of peace than to indulge in political bickering. Pakistan giving up its insistence on the UN resolutions and India softening stand towards making the LOC 'irrelevant' are some of the remarkable developments that could have been hardly imagined a decade earlier. Though various formula have been floated and forwarded to resolve bilateral issues, the single most important achievement has become the 'irreversibility' of the peace process. Both India and Pakistan came to realize the value of living in peace, because the peace-dividends are more valuable than the results of war and violence. The meeting of divided families after opening of the LOC, the organization of 'heart-to-heart' talks in Indian and Pakistani cities in which the civil society members from both sides played active role, and the playing of cricket in each other's ground are some of the big achievements. The recently concluded fourth round of composite dialogue between India and Pakistan on March 14, 2007 in Islamabad ended with the signs of optimism. Pakistan's suggestions for conducting more sporting events at bilateral level and starting helicopter service and postal service between Srinagar and Muzaffarabad can further boost people to people interaction. After the end of the meeting, both agreed not to create new defence posts on their side of the LOC, to the launch of Kargil-Skardu bus service and an early meeting on the Siachen issue.

At the internal level, a major peace mission was launched to create conducive environment for negotiations. It was initiated by India by announcing a unilateral non-initiation of combat operations in J&K during the month of *ramzan* on November 19, 2000. The initiative was extended twice up to February 26, 2001. Another important step was broadening the democratic activity by holding the elections. Thus, J&K witnessed assembly elections in 2002 that have been widely recognized free and fair. These elections brought a change in one party dominant politics of the state wherein the government was formed by the PDP in coalition with Congress and other parties. The state under the leadership of Mufti Mohammad Sayeed played an active role to facilitate and drive the peace process under the healing touch policy. According to Sayeed, "be it the healing-touch policy, opening of the Srinagar-Muzaffarabad or the Pooch-Rawalakote roads, or allowing travel on permit and not passport basis, it all added up to a collective political engagement and consequent reduction in the structural and individual alienation."[2] This was followed by Panchayat elections after more than two decades. The attempt has been a major one despite the fact that the voter turnout remained low in both the elections.

After attempting at creating a conducive environment the government of India reiterated its readiness to initiate dialogue with every group in J&K that abjures violence. In this context three important attempts need specific mention. First, the ongoing talks with the APHC (M) wherein Indian prime minister has met them twice. The Hurriyat meeting with prime minister was first ever meeting the separatist faction could have with the highest political leader of the country. During the National Democratic Alliance government in New Delhi they had talks at the level of deputy prime minister. The Hurriyat emphasis on step-by-step approach, its demand for an honourable and durable solution, its appeal to separatist groups to give up violence are some of steps which should be lauded. Second, three round table conferences were held (first in February 2006 in New Delhi, second in May 2006 in Srinagar and third in April 2007 in New Delhi) to listen to varied voices within J&K. Third, setting up of five working groups to look into various contentious issues confronting the state. It needs to be noted that during the second round table conference in Srinagar in 24-25 May 2006, Indian prime minister had announced setting up of five working groups to address some of the grievances of the 'alienated'[3] people of J&K. While the first one focuses on CBMs, the second focuses on strengthening relations across the LOC, the third one deals with economic development, the fourth aims at providing good governance to people and the fifth one aims at strengthening centre-state relations. The setting of five working groups is an important step towards recognizing that peace and development has to go hand in hand. The attempts together with the external dimension of the peace process have created a historic environment wherein the hopes regarding the possibility of a resolution of the complex problem remain high.

During the third round table, held in New Delhi on April 24, 2007, Indian Prime Minister, Manmohan Singh, noted that he has a vision of new Jammu, Kashmir and Ladakh in which the full potentials of the region can be explored. Seeking to reach out to the 'hearts and minds' of the people, the prime minister expressed concerns over human rights violations and promised steps to minimize them. However, he made it clear that reduction of troops in the state would depend on the scale of terrorism. Reportedly the government of India has asked the security forces to carry out their 'difficult tasks in a humane manner.' India, as reflected in deliberations in the roundtable, has encompassed a broader vision for India and South Asia that is importantly linked to 'reconciliation with Pakistan.' Noting two dimensions to the problems of J&K- internal and external- which involves Indo-Pak relations, Manmohan Singh said "it is our intention and sincere desire to advance on both fronts towards resolving problems through a process of dialogue," further adding, "However these efforts will not be fruitful unless a peaceful environment is created through honouring of commitments made, in letter and spirit, to curb terrorist activities,"[4] apparently referring to Pakistan's promise in this regard made in 2004.

The recommendations made by the four working groups (the fifth one on centre-state relations has not yet submitted its report) came up for discussions during the third round table. It gave in principle endorsement to the approach suggested by the working group on CBMs across segments: strengthening human rights protection and improving relief and rehabilitation of widows, orphans and other victims of violence. The conference approved the suggestions of the group three on balanced economic development of J&K and asked the central and state governments to take steps to carry them forward. It also backed the recommendations of the group four on good governance and asked the state government to bring greater transparency, efficiency and accountability in the process of governance. Most importantly, the roundtable endorsed the recommendation of group two to promote people-to-people contact and trade between the two parts of Kashmir and to further streamline these processes. It also decided to expand these measures in tourism and other spheres of life. In fact, as already mentioned, besides engagement between India and Pakistan and between New Delhi and Srinagar the third important dimension of the ongoing peace process is that of engagement between both the parts of the undivided Kashmir.

Intra-Kashmir dialogue can lead to fruition as, among many things, both the Kashmirs possess enormous potentials for joint cooperation.[5] Two statements need special mention in this context. On December 31, 2006 the J&K Chief Minister Ghulam Nabi Azad said that some sort of 'joint management' with 'AJK' is possible in the fields of tourism, trade, culture and water resources, which could pave the way for a lasting solution to the Kashmir issue. On February 10, 2007 Sardar Attique Khan, Prime Minister of 'AJK' offered to supply gas and electricity to J&K and invited entrepreneurs from 'all regions and religions' to invest in 'AJK.' In his words, "The gas can be provided to the Kashmir valley through Chakothi and through Sialkot to Jammu at Suchetgarh if the authorities on the other side are willing." He further invited doctors and engineers from J&K and asked universities in J&K to admit students from his region. Needless to add, he could not have proposed all these measures without Islamabad's consent.[6] There are also enough trade potentials, besides tourism. Items which can be sent from J&K to 'AJK' include drugs, red beans, spices, basmati rice, coriander, fresh fruits, tamarind, handicrafts items, shawls from Basholi and Kashmiri carpets, green tea, saffron, Basholi paintings, cement, iron rods, paints, PVC pipes, willow cleft, walnuts and automobile spare parts. The items which can be brought to J&K include cotton suits for ladies, raw salt, pulses, herbal items, raisin, etc.[7]

Involvement of People

The involvement of people in the peace process gained momentum in the years 2005 and 2006. Both these years have not only witnessed bonhomie between India and Pakistan but also increasing level of people-to-people interactions.[8] Besides the bus service between Srinagar and Muzaffarabad, termed 'mother of all confidence building measures,'[9] the year 2005 has also witnessed visits of many delegations from both sides across the LOC. The bridge connecting both sides of Kashmir over river Neelum, known as *aman setu* (peace bridge), was not just symbolic of peace process but it sent a resonant message that 'the way forward is peace and democracy and not armed conflict.'[10] Easing of the visa process, exchanges through the bus, train and air services between Srinagar and Muzaffarabad, Lahore and Delhi have facilitated ever growing people-to-people interaction. Besides the meeting of the APHC leaders with Indian prime minister, their visit of to the Kashmir across the LOC and Pakistan in June 2005 and in January 2007 are some of the developments that indicate forward movement of peace in the region with the inclusion of the people of Kashmir. This is important despite the fact that doubts have raised by many quarters from both sides of the LOC regarding the representative character of the APHC.

The people-to-people talks have given a tremendous boost to optimism regarding the ongoing peace process. This can be called one grand achievement of the ongoing peace process with more than one positive implication. First, it provides opportunity to people from both sides of the LOC to know each other and to see the realities on the other side. Generally, people follow leaders and form their opinions accordingly. But these interactions, though limited in scale, bring into picture the divergence of opinions and plethora of views on the issues which were earlier closed for an open discussion. These interactions revived old sentiments of belongingness and fraternity among the people from both the sides and help shed years of hatred and animosity against each other. During a trip to twin districts of Rajouri-Poonch in J&K to study the impact of Poonch-Rawalakote bus service in April 2007 authors came across many interesting revelations. The local people told the authors that the visitors from other side are surprised to see freedom enjoyed by the people in this side. The guests from across the LOC told authors on the condition of anonymity that they are fed on the propaganda that there is least freedom in J&K for the people, especially for the Muslims and they are not even allowed to perform their religious duties. All such premonitions vanish when they come and see their brethrens enjoying freedom which can rival any other democracy in the world.[11]

In February 2007 there was a huge gathering in the Poonch city— about two hundred people from Sikh community raised religious slogans while receiving one of their relatives from across the LOC who happens to be a Maulavi in that region. It would not be out of context to mention that in Rajouri-Poonch districts there are hundreds of Hindu families with Muslim relatives across the LOC. It is no hidden truth that during the turmoil in Kashmir, many people fled their homes in POK and came to J&K. In this tragedy many people got separated from their families. The ceasefire led to not only the division of the state but also of the families. Most of the Hindus that remained in POK converted to Islam while their relatives who came to J&K remained Hindus. Giridhari Lal Saigal, currently a resident of Surankote (about 30 km from Pooch towards Jammu), narrated his heartrending story of fleeing his native place in Kotli in 1948 and reunion with his relatives during visit to 'AJK' recently. During his trip to the other side he was happy to see his deceased brother's son Maqbool and grandson Farooq who expressed eagerness to establish marital relations with his family. The story of Savitri Devi, now

Naseema, was further touching. Savitri, then 16 years old, was abducted during partition from Poonch and married in Kotli. Her elder brother, Surya Prakash visited her through the Poonch-Rawalakote bus service. The meeting of brother and sister not only brought back old memories but also tears, told Loknath, an advocate in Rajouri District Court who accompanied Surya Prakash. Mohammad Banu, a resident of Potha Billa village near Surankote, while narrating the story of the partition and separation from her elder brothers now living in Mirpur could not control her emotions. There are thousands of such people on both sides of LOC who have waited for more than six decades to meet their brethrens. The above narratives reveal that love transcends religious and territorial barriers. The change of religion has not been able to erase the relation of blood.

There are demands to open more routes. In this context the Kargil-Skardu road, the feasibility of opening of which was studied by the authors during a trip to Kargil in July 2006 and May 2007, needs special mention. Kargil-Skardu route, about 179 km from Kargil (169 km from the last Indian border check post) passes into the area of Gilgit-Baltistan along the side of Shingo river. After the partition of the Indian subcontinent the route has been closed. It came to lime light recently due to ongoing peace process in which both India and Pakistan agreed to open routes as parts of confidence building measures. Prime Minister Manmohan Singh during his visit to Kargil in June 2005, after assessing the popular sentiments, observed, 'I have been told that the people of Kargil are keen on having the links restored with Gilgit-Baltistan and opening of the Kargil-Skardu road is under consideration.' Despite official talks the route has not yet been opened.

The crucial importance the Kargil-Skardu route can be gauged from the following points. First, the utility of the road lies in its durability in winter months. During winter the whole Ladakh region (including Kargil) becomes cut off from the main land due to heavy snowfall on the Srinagar-Leh national highway. As a result, the Zojila pass remains intractable for about six months (October-March). The Kargil-Skardu route that lies in cold but arid region in the Himalayas remains in pliable conditions even in these harsh months. The local people argue to open this route as it can be used in winter to go to Skardu and other areas for marketing and for other necessary purposes. As it is clearly demarcated, the reconstruction of the route may not incur heavy expenditure on part of the governments. Second, the route can facilitate the meeting of the members of divided families on both sides of the LOC. The people of the border village, Badgam expressed keen desire to meet their kith and kin in Skardu. The 65 year old lady, Mariam expressed grief as she could not be able to meet her husband for the last 35 years. It so happened that the village came to Indian side after the 1971 war and her husband, away for marketing, remained back on the other side of the border. She exchanges occasional letters with her husband, but her heart pines for meeting the beloved. There are many like Mariam who have their near and dear ones on the other side, and they are interested to meet them. The old people are more interested to see the route open, as they, unlike the young, become nostalgic of their past when the whole region was a united one and there was no artificial border. Grief and sorrow marked their face as their repeated urges to open the route seem to have fallen on deaf ears. There are many other people who do not have any kith and kin in Gilgit-Baltistan yet are natives of the place. They crossed to Ladakh when Gilgit and Baltistan went under control of Pakistan. These people too are eager to see their birthplace. As Abdul Qadir pointed, "No one can ever forget his place of birth. I have spent my childhood in Skardu and am eager to see that place again. The permit system to visit the POK should be extended to the natives of that place also who do not have the relatives there. We do not have relatives there but we do have friends there and also our childhood memories keep haunting us."[12]

The route can be used for trade across the divide. The local people expressed the firm belief that the route would not only help divided families to meet but also accrue economic benefits to government and local business men. From Skardu, apricot (it is said the Skardu variety of apricot is the best one), raisin, and herbs can be imported, while from Kargil sugar, tea, garments and vegetables can be exported to the other side. Tourist resorts and stalls can be made on the road side in which local products can be displayed. This would not only provide employment to local people but also bring economic development to the region. Unfortunately, some of the apricot fields on the LOC have gradually become barren, ostensibly due to planting of mines, non-cultivation as well as negligence due to fear of war and military intervention. The artificial border has, therefore, not only kept people in a suffocated atmosphere but also hampered their economic growth.[13] The moot question then arises: why the route has not been opened yet? The Vice President of Islamia School, Sheikh Ahmed Mohammadi, a highly venerated Shia leader in the region, confided that Pakistan seems to be reluctant to open the route. In his words, "The people in Gilgit-Baltistan live in a much poorer condition than their fellow beings in Kargil. Also the kind of freedom being enjoyed by the people in Indian side is never granted to them.... Pakistan fears that the opening of route might open Pandora's Box in the occupied Kashmir, leading to explosion of years long pent up popular dissatisfaction and anger."[14]

The people-to-people contact also provided opportunity to the members of civil society to think 'out of box,' independent of the stances of their respective governments. Interactions with the civil rights activists and leaders from both the sides gives the impression that the people of region are fed up with violence and want to live in peace. K. D. Sethi, the veteran octogenarian journalist and one time general secretary in Sheikh Abdullah's NC (resident of Jammu city though originally belongs to Kashmir across the LOC) told the authors that the people of whole Kashmir want peace and brotherhood among themselves.[15] For this to happen, he suggested opening of all routes between POK and J&K. His opinion is shared by almost all the people that authors interacted during their visits to all three regions of J&K- Jammu, Kashmir and Ladakh. Besides, the people who came from across the LOC and interacted with the authors too argued in favour of more and more contacts. Justice Abdul Majeed Mallick, former Chief Justice of 'Azad' Kashmir High Court, who led a delegation from across the LOC to J&K in August 2005, expressed optimism that the current wave of people to people interaction would help resolving Kashmir issue as it is the people of the region who can better steer the peace process than the 'vested interests.'[16]

The interactions amongst people in form of 'heart-to-heart' talks in Jammu and New Delhi in September 2005 and New Delhi in April 2007 provided the occasion for the leaders and activists of different shades from both sides of the LOC to speak their hearts on a single platform. At the end of the talks in New Delhi in September 2005, the participants issued a 16-point document calling for opening up of all traditional routes across the border to facilitate more interactions among people, promoting trade and tourism, establishing an inter-parliamentary forum, developing mechanism for rehabilitation of displaced people, etc. Though the participants converged at some issues and diverged at others, the most successful outcome of the talks was that the participants across the region agreed that violence can not bring a solution to the vexed issue of Kashmir and it is peace that must be cultivated for the purpose.

The Hurriyat visit to 'AJK' and Pakistan in June 2-16, 2005[17] and January 18-27, 2007 can be described as steps in the right direction for peace in the region and for reaching at an 'honourable and durable solution' of the Kashmir issue. The Hurriyat delegation led by Mirwaiz Umar Farooq visited Pakistan and 'AJK' from January 18-27 and met with important leaders including the president of Pakistan and president and prime minister of 'AJK.' Mirwaiz and 'AJK' president Raja Zulqarnain Khan and Prime Minister Attique Ahmed Khan decided to form two working groups to unite the moderates on both sides of the LOC to drum up support for the peace process. The Hurriyat leader met several members of UJC, an amalgam of various terrorist groups and sought their cooperation for the peace process. "There are many groups and leaders from the UJC who are supportive of the process. In the UJC, there are about 18 parties. People have been coming individually and meeting us. There are groups and leaders. They are quite keen that this process should move further," Mirwaiz observed.[18] He further stated, "Militants should give peace a chance. We feel that time has come for all those who believe in the process has to come forward" and "strengthen the peace process and try to see how things can move on." Mirwaiz's desire to play a kind of bridge between moderates and hardliners including terrorists can become successful, depending on his persuasion to terrorists to give up arms.

The Limitations

The peace process in past few years undoubtedly has moved at a fast pace giving rise to high expectations of an early resolution of the Kashmir issue. But, the complexity of the issue not only leads to diversification of interpretations regarding the issue itself but also regarding any possible solution. The peace process is no exception in this context. The recent debate on demilitarization is a clear example how various actors interpret the peace process as per their suitability. The idea of demilitarization is no doubt a good one whether it comes from Pakistan President Pervez Musharraf, or any other person or forum. The heavy presence of army has caused inconvenience to the common people in the region. As the recent mood in the public is in favour of peace, it is understandable that the demand for troop reduction has support from certain segments of the local people. India has made it clear until there is violence and infiltration there is little scope for it. The Pakistan argues that there must be something on the ground to show that peace process is moving forward in substance. The motive behind

General Musharraf's insistence on troop withdrawal in J&K, and very specifically from the two districts of Baramulla and Kupwara is questionable. A deeper scrutiny of the trajectory of violence in the J&K indicates that the rationale goes beyond the simple fact that these are districts close to the LOC. More importantly, the two serve as a gateway to the Kashmir valley and have, for long, been crucial to the prospects of jehad in J&K. These two districts witness high levels of infiltration and terrorist activity and any lowering of guard there could allow the terrorists, who have been under pressure lately, to regroup and recover lost ground. Hence, troop withdrawal would likely cede the operational advantage to the terrorists.[19]

Any decision to withdraw forces must be taken with caution. For a start, Indian can withdraw some forces on a conditional and temporary basis. The demand for the repeal of laws such as Public Safety Act and Armed Forces (Special Powers) Act can be looked from the above point of view. Any complaints of human rights violation, misuse of powers, fake encounters and any unlawful activities by the armed forces must be dealt with an iron hand. Depending on the prevailing circumstances, these strict laws can be relaxed and gradually repealed. At this juncture, however, it also needs to be argued that Pakistan which is harping over the issue of demilitarization in J&K is not even partially ready to do the same in parts of Kashmir under its occupation. India has posted its army in the area in large number to counter the cross-border terrorism. Yet it remains beyond comprehension as to why Pak army in thousands of number is posted in 'AJK' and 'NA' besides presence of an array of various intelligence agencies. The heavy presence of army in Kashmir across the LOC could not be overlooked as merely to 'protect the LOC sanctity' as often harped by Pakistan. The atrocities committed by Pakistan agencies and army in 'AJK' and 'NA' are no longer under the iron veil and reports published by ICG, HRW and the EU provide insight to the continuing atrocities in the area.

On April 1, 2007, while speaking to CNBC TV before his departure from Islamabad to New Delhi to attend the 14th SAARC summit, the Pakistan Prime Minister, Shaukat Aziz, stated that "SAARC has a lot of potential. But dispute resolution, particularly the Kashmir issue and peace and harmony, was a must to realize this potential." He further observed if India wants to play a major role in international politics, Kashmir issue must be resolved. Recently the 'AJK' Prime Minister, Sardar Attique Khan, in his speech at Bradford, emphasized on the resolution of the Kashmir issue. He mentioned that if India wants to play an effective role outside the region then it should come forward and persuade in settling the issue once for all..." The statements of Shaukat Aziz and Attique Khan are laudable, but their exhortation to India to resolve the Kashmir issue does not seem to be supported by practical steps to address the issues of concern in 'AJK' and 'NA.'

It is a sign of optimism that Pakistan has welcomed the Hurriyat talks with Indian prime minister. It has also signalled that it would consider Indian proposal favourably for allowing divided Kashmiri families to meet at five places at the LOC including Mendhar, Poonch, Suchetgarh, Uri and Tangdhar. General Musharraf is reported to have said both India and Pakistan have 'demonstrated commitment to continue the peace process to resolve amicably the long standing Jammu and Kashmir issue.' But his comparison of Kashmir with Palestine at Interfaith Dialogue and Cooperation for Peace meet in New York in September 2005 seems to undermine his commitment. In fact, the ongoing peace process is a mixed baggage. Whether it would lead to ultimate success, thus resolving the issue amicably and bringing peace to the suffering people would depend on various factors. Two conditions must be fulfilled for the peace to have a lasting impact on the region. First, the leaders and the rights activists from both the sides of the border must rise above their establishments' thinking and condemn violence in all respect and work in unison to end infiltration across the border. Second, Pakistan must stop encouraging cross-border terrorism. It needs to make genuine efforts to 'convince the gun-wielding boys to give up arms in the largest interest of people.'

Pakistan on March 14, 2007 sought to keep the militant violence in Kashmir out of the ambit of the joint anti-terror mechanism, constituted after the common agreement on it by India and Pakistan at the sidelines of Havana Non-aligned Movement summit in November 2006. It can well be gauged the success of the mechanism without taking into account violent activities in J&K. Pakistan's argument that the region is disputed, hence it does not come under the purview of the joint mechanism seems to be a well calibrated tactic to have edge over India on this particular issue. The leaders from 'AJK' such as Sardar Abdul Qayuum Khan and Justice Mallick would deny any existence of terrorist groups in its territory. They say there are no terrorist groups in the region. Intelligence reports not only of India but also of the US confirm existence of terrorist groups that train the people to indulge in violent activities. Syed Salahuddin, the supreme commander of HM and the leader of the terrorist groups conglomerate, UJC is a known opponent of the peace process. He called the Hurriyat-Prime Minister talks 'futile and purposeless.' In an interview to *Friday Times* he even went on to ask for military help from Pakistan which, as per his version, is only providing moral support to militancy in the J&K.[20] According to him, "Those people who attend various dinners as well as lunches should keep this in mind that if they are invited for such a thing or invited for talks with Indian Prime Minister Manmohan Singh or Pakistan President General Pervez Musharraf it is all due to the gun and the people who are carrying the gun in their hand or who have died while taking part in various militant actions."[21] The preceding chapter has pointed out how the terror infrastructure across the LOC not only remains intact but also how it has got a boost in the post-earthquake period.

An alliance of Kashmiri militant groups with the backing from across the LOC has rejected the call of Mirwaiz Umar Farooq to give up armed struggle to pave the way for fruitful negotiations for a lasting settlement of Kashmir issue. "These unmatched sacrifices were not offered for self rule, internal autonomy or for that matter for an irrelevant ceasefire line (LOC) but for the Kashmiris' right to self-determination," a spokesperson of UJC said, adding, "those who have turned a blind eye towards these sacrifices and are showing signs of retreat have no right to lead the nation." "If Mirwaiz and other leaders of his like have become tired, disenchanted or hopeless about the future of freedom struggle due to adverse circumstances, we suggest them to sit back in their homes to lead a life of comfort. But they should not teach the lesson of cowardice and hopelessness to the caravan of freedom seekers," he said.[22] Similarly, the criticism of people-to-people contact in form heart-to-heart talks too has created hurdles in the path of peace. Barrister Sultan Mahmood, a recognizable face in Kashmir, refused to attend the heart-to-heart talks, saying 'it was not in the interest of the Kashmiri people.' He was a bitter critic of Sardar Qayuum, and termed his participation in the peace conference 'betrayal of the sacrifices of Kashmiri people.' It is difficult to understand how the participation in a peace conference, without any strings attached to it, can betray the cause of the Kashmiri people. If gun has failed to bring peace, then dialogue must be given a chance. The killing of people of minority community in Doda and Udhampur in 2006, and the killing of tourists show that the terrorists have not inculcated the culture of peace. This is another question as to who really controls the terrorist activities. General Pervez Musharraf's stand in this regard is apparently dubious. In his January 2002 speech he categorically stated that he would not allow terrorism to operate in Pak territory, but later he denied having any control on them. It becomes difficult to accept the veracity of his conflicting claims. In this crossfire of denial and non-denial, the common people of the region suffer the most.

The recent opening of routes has beckoned new hopes for divided families. However, there are many impediments which the authors discovered during the survey in Poonch. First, the frequency of bus service should be increased in view of large number of aspiring visitors. Currently, the bus service is fortnightly, thus keeping people waiting for months even after they get the permit. Second, there is a need to simplify travel procedures, which needs immediate attention for two reasons. One, there are many old aged people who want to see their relatives and that has become their last wish to be fulfilled. Two, the procedure is so complicated that most of the people have to seek professional help to complete the formalities thereby putting not only financial burden but also unwarranted harassment at the hands of authorities. To make the journey easier the government of India is planning to authorize the concerned Deputy Commissioners to issue the permits. "I feel that the present system of permit is very difficult and people face lot of problems while getting these permits issued by the Passport office," said the chief minister of J&K. But his statement should be complemented with effective policy measures. Third, not only the travel formalities have to be simplified but the clearance procedure of the permits should be given immediate attention. Seventy two year old Sakeena Bi has not met her sister living in Kotli for almost six decades when she along with her husband crossed the LOC during the 1948 war. She had almost lost the hope to meet her sister. The announcement of the bus service came as the biggest dream come true, however her hopes met with a traumatic experience. As her desire to meet the sister grew, also increased the hassles in preparing travel documents ranging from 'getting permission' from her husband to let her apply for a permit to going from pillar to post to complete all the formalities, from waiting patiently for a year to get the permit to the realization that the duration of permit was very short. Despite all odds, Sakeena Bi was lucky enough to make her dream fulfilled but there are many others whose patience is running out as the permit takes usually one year or even more. Late Armaan Ali left for the heavenly abode waiting for the permit. It becomes more difficult for people to restrain themselves from participating in any event in their families across the LOC after the bus service has started. To quote Ameena Begum, "Earlier we were dying to see our relatives across LOC but knew that it is almost impossible but now the times have changed. The bus service has enabled us to travel and when we meet our relation becomes stronger. We now want to participate in all the happenings of our relatives whether it is marriage or death, but alas it is not possible due to permit system that would take almost a year. Marriage is OK...it can be planned even before one year but what about death?"

The Hurriyat's shifting position on its place at the talks too has created confusion. While at the beginning of the talks, even during its visit to 'AJK' and Pakistan, the Hurriyat emphasized on triangular talks, implying the separatist faction would talk separately with the leadership of India and Pakistan. Now it seems the moderate faction of the Hurriyat has shifted its position and talked about tripartite talks, implying it would talk the leaders of both the countries at one place, with itself as a party with equal status. The Hurriyat leader, Mirwaiz Umar Farooq's insistence that Kashmir issue is no longer bilateral is contradictory to India's position that it is a bilateral issue and it must be resolved bilaterally and peacefully. Mirwaiz's demand for full membership of Organization of Islamic Countries (at present the Hurriyat enjoys observer status at the Islamic body) may be seen as a prelude to its desire to emerge as an organization of a separate and independent entity. The Hurriyat refusal to participate in the round table conferences not only need to be seen as a set back to the ongoing peace process but also raise suspicion on its commitment to peace. It can be noted here the conference is one of most viable forum for intra-Kashmir dialogue. The separatists' argument that there is no point in including the mainstream parties and leaders seem not to be consonant with their standpoint. First, primarily it is because of the separatists' demand that people of the region must be involved in the peace process India has undertaken such a measure. But, that may not be the whole scene. The government of India, especially after 2003, has taken a people-centric approach to the resolution of the Kashmir issue. Second, the separatists' demand that the mainstream parties do not have any special demand such as separation, hence there is no logic in convening such a huge and pompous gathering at the 7, Race Course Road. But, the separatists are not the sole voice of Kashmir. The influence of both the factions of the APHC is confined to the valley. There is no following of it in Jammu, Ladakh, 'AJK' and Gilgit-Baltistan despite its claim of representing all. The leaders of Jammu and Ladakh have clearly expressed their reservation on consideration of APHC as sole representative of the people. The Ladakhi leader and member of J&K Legislative Assembly, Pinto Narboo argues: "There is little chance of the Hurriyat Conference gaining a standing in Ladakh."[23] Even the leaders of 'AJK' and Gilgit-Baltistan have time and again raised doubts over claim of APHC as sole representative of Kashmir. Lack of a single voice of the region has further complicated the peace process. In J&K Muslims have to share political and social space with Hindus, Buddhists, Sikhs and Christians who have an equally strong claim on their homeland. Even the Muslim population of Kashmir can be distinguished as Kashmiri, Muzaffarabadi, Dogri, Gujjar, Bakerwal, Poonchi, Balti, Shina etc. because all these communities have their own distinct cultural identities, different compulsions and conflicting interests.

Any Kashmir-centric peace process must require the participation of all sections of people from across the region. Whether it is people from J&K or 'AJK' or 'NA,' all of them must be given due space and freedom to take part in the dialogue process. Though the steps of India in this matter are quite perceptible yet ironically Pakistan has not taken any significant step to listen to the voices of the people of Kashmir under its control. As mentioned in the earlier pages, the freedom and rights of the people in 'AJK' and the 'NA' are heavily restrained. When Pakistan talks about self-rule and self-determination of the people of Kashmir, it does not apply the same principle to the regions under its control. An EU report on Kashmir has disfavoured plebiscite in Kashmir, saying it would be 'meaningless' unless Pakistan withdraws all its troops from the parts under it, corrects the demographic changes and ensures return of territory under China. According to the report, "The constitution of AJK of 1974 would have to be altered if the people there are to be invited for plebiscite. The situation since 1947 has changed. The UN resolution on (undivided) J&K stipulated the condition that there should be complete withdrawal of troops from Pakistan from the occupied area and those who settled from outside Kashmir should also withdraw..... The Republic of India is the world's largest secular democracy and has evolved democratic structures at all levels, whereas the Islamic Republic of Pakistan still lacks full implementation of democracy in 'AJK' and has yet to start the process of democracy in Gilgit and Baltistan."[24]

References

1. This is one of the central arguments of the theory of Democratic Peace that is developed in the 1990s. Some of the basic assumptions of this theory are: democracy is the best form of government; democracies do not war with one another; and democratic government is peaceful. For a general view of this theory see, Griffith, Martin and Terry O'Callaghan, *International Relations: The Key Concepts* (London: Routledge, 2002), pp. 66-68.
2. Mufti Mohammad Sayeed, "Jammu & Kashmir Resolution: Context, Compulsions and Contours-I," *Kashmir Times*, December 7, 2006.
3. For some insight into the alienation in Kashmir valley see, Seema Shekhawat, "Addressing the Alienation," *Kashmir*

Times, April 28, 2007. For a more detailed account of internal dimension of the Kashmir conflict see Seema Shekhawat, *Conflict in Jammu and Kashmir: the Gender Dimension* (Jammu : Saksham Books International, 2006), pp. 51-56.

4. *Daily Excelsior*, April 25, 2007.
5. For details in this context see Debidatta Aurobinda Mahapatra, "Peace through Economic Reconstruction," *The Kashmir Times*, January 24, 2007.
6. A. G. Noorani, "Both Sides Now," *The Kashmir Times*, March 6, 2007.
7. Sanjeev Pargal, "Ahead of Visit, Import-Export Items Listed," *Daily Excelsior*, March 6, 2007.
8. Debidatta Aurobinda Mahapatra, "Involve People for Peace," *Kashmir Images*, July 29, 2006.
9. For details on the Srinagar-Muzaffarabad bus see Debidatta Aurobinda Mahapatra, "Bus Running for Reconciliation?," *Mainstream*, vol. 63, no. 20, May 7, 2005, pp. 27-29.
10. Ghazi Salahuddin, "Crossing a Bridge of Peace." *http://www.countercurrents.org/ipk-salahuddin100405.htm*. Accessed on January 7, 2007.
11. Debidatta Aurobinda Mahapatra, "Poonch for Peace," *Kashmir Times*, May 6, 2007.
12. Quoted in Seema Shekhawat, "Kargil-Skardu Route: The Humanitarian Dimension," *Kashmir Times*, May 17, 2007.
13. Debidatta Aurobinda Mahapatra, "Connecting Kargil-Skardu," *Kashmir Images*. August 12, 2006.
14. Personal Interview, July 25, 2006.
15. Personal Interview, August 10, 2005.
16. Personal Interview, August 6, 2005.
17. For a detailed account see, Debidatta Aurobinda Mahapatra, "Reflections on the Hurriyat Visit," *Mainstream*, Vol. 63, no. 33, August 6, 2005, pp. 6-8.
18. *The Daily Excelsior*, January 23, 2007.
19. Kanchan Laxman, "Deception at Every Step," *State Times*, March 6, 2006.
20. *Kashmir Times*, August 9, 2006.

21. *Kashmir Times*, February 8, 2007.
22. Tariq Naqash, "UJC Unimpressed," *Greater Kashmir*, January 21, 2007.
23. Victoria Schofield, *Kashmir in Conflict: India, Pakistan and the Unending War* (New Delhi: Viva Books Pvt. Ltd., 2004), p. 184.
24. *Daily Excelsior*, March 7, 2007.

Conclusion

The happenings across the LOC remained close for scrutiny for a long time. Starting from the accession of Kashmir to India to the bifurcation of the territory under Pakistan into two parts, from signing of the Karachi Agreement to investing one part of the occupied territories with semblance of democracy and keeping the other part deprived of even that comfort, from the promise of self-determination to the ideology of accession much remain untold about the Kashmir under the control of Pakistan.

The tribal invasion had taken place in Kashmir with collusion of Pakistan. As the letters of Maharaja reveal, it was Pakistan which violated the standstill agreement as a pressure tactic to grab the state. Interestingly, the Karachi Agreement of 1949 which put Pakistan in overlordship position in relation to 'AJK' and 'NA' had a mysterious origin. One of the main signatories to the agreement, Sardar Ibrahim, who happened to be then president of the provisional government of 'Azad Kashmir,' denied his involvement in the agreement in a 2003 interview. Even Pakistan denied the signing of any such agreement during the hearing of the Miskeen case though 'AJK' argued the signing of the agreement in the same case. The logic of two-nation theory and the role of Major Brown of the Gilgit Scouts were equally dubious. Brown's offer of the region to Pakistan in a platter was against popular sentiment as reflected in the movement by Mirza Hussain Khan.

The region never witnessed a genuine democratic set up till date. The UN calls 'AJK' a locally administered area. It is called free (*azad*) when it is mostly not-free. The Freedom House has declared the region one of the most 'not free' regions of the world. 'AJK' is invested with all kinds of democratic paraphernalia: president, prime minister, supreme court, high court, etc., but a closer study reveals that survival of these institutions depend how far they cater the interests of Pakistan. Pakistan often argues that the 'AJK' constitution is built by the local people, but the preamble brings forth the contradiction by saying that it has to be agreed by Islamabad for commencement. The text is replete with such contradictions.

The culture of dependency is incorporated into the very system of 'AJK,' which is subsequently perpetuated by Islamabad. Article 56 of the constitution gives Pakistan dominance over all affairs of the region. The composition of the Kashmir council chaired by Pak prime minister provides ample evidence of this culture of dependency. The preface to the constitution (1990 edition) commits 'AJK' to continue struggle for right to self-determination. It appears that the framers of the constitution had worked with an intention to bring self-rule to the people of the vast region, and the reading of the preface gives the impression that the region would likely emerge a free territory. However, this seemingly noble intention of effectuating self-determination of people ends in void as one goes deep into the provisions of the constitution. Sub section 7 of section 4 makes the ideology of accession supreme over the principle of self-determination. It is yet to be grappled with how can both the principles go together? Is it possible to have self-determination of the people of Kashmir by ceding the territory to Pakistan? The logical next follows: how can it be determined only on the behest of Pakistan that self-determination of Kashmir would lead to its accession to Pakistan?

The history of governance in 'AJK' and Gilgit-Baltistan is characterized by utter dominance and suppression. All the high officials are loaned from Islamabad. The legal constitutional status of 'NA' is more dubious than 'AJK.' In affairs of these entities it is KANA which rules the roost. As a former president of 'AJK' lamented, a clerk in KANA is more powerful than the leaders of 'AJK.' Even the limited rights were allowed to the inhabitants of these areas after much vacillation. While people of J&K exercised their right to adult franchise since 1950s to elect constituent assembly for its constitution, and then to elect representatives of the legislative assembly and the parliament, people of 'AJK' waited for around twenty years to exercise limited franchise under a Pak-introduced system called 'basic democracy.' Interestingly, the people's right to franchise was matched with frequent exercise of the same right, courtesy Islamabad's policy of pick and drop the office bearers at will. In a period of 25 years, 35 regime changes took place in 'AJK.' There are instances when the army commander in Muree summons the leaders to give directions. The fate of Mumtaz Rathore, ending up in a Rawalpindi prison in 1991, and the fate of Qayuum Khan who was denied presidentship despite support from the assembly in 2001, prove ominously that Pakistan is the ultimate arbiter of the destiny of the people. The Pak administration along with the ISI and the army works as the supreme trio in collusion to govern these areas. Sardar Attique Khan, who expressed disappointment with Pakistan's treatment of 'AJK' as a 'private estate' or a 'municipal committee,' is now ensconced in the office of prime minister because of his open support of Pak policies. The meeting of Sardar Attique with President Musharraf before one week of the 2006 elections brings to the fore the obvious blessings which Islamabad reserved for the MC. The blessings resulted in the massive support of government apparatus to the MC candidates. The refugee seats were given to the party in a platter. As the elections reveal, the exercise in democracy proves futile as those not subscribing to the ideology of accession were debarred from contesting. Putting it another way, the ideology of accession is the sole governing principle in 'AJK.' It would be pertinent to ask why after repeated assurances by the leaders of 'AJK' this principle has not been repealed from the 'AJK' constitution? Is Islamabad afraid lest this principle go the voice of the people would be an insurmountable force to contend with?

The situation in 'NA' is much worse since Pakistan consciously chose to keep this area under direct control. The strategic location in the crisscross of Central Asia, China, and Indian subcontinent has made Gilgit-Baltistan strategically important. Whether ceding territory to China, or construction of Karakoram highway, building dams or infusing Sunnis, the popular concerns have been totally neglected. People of Gilgit-Baltistan could get right of limited franchise only in mid 1990s. The powers of NALC are none, but recommendatory. The resolutions passed by the council are not 'even given a glance' by Islamabad. The NALC is headed by KANA minister who is neither native nor elected. Stark negligence of fundamental rights of the people is more clearly visible in this area than in 'AJK.'

An individual's political and economic destiny depends on how far he stoops to the rules of Pakistan. As already mentioned, no one can contest elections if he does not file affidavit conforming the ideology of Kashmir's accession to Pakistan. A number of political organizations like JKLF, APNA, etc. have strongly protested against this interference and they have questioned the machinations of Islamabad in the region. A person cannot be entitled to a government job unless he subscribes to the ideology of accession. The school text books are replete with phrases like 'Kashmir *banega* Pakistan.' The people are debarred to move freely in the whole region. To refrain the unified resistance Pakistan has consciously debarred free mingling of the people from 'AJK' with the people from 'NA' by denying any road links between the two and disallowing the political parties of one area to operate in other.

The impact of this trend is spurious, as it leads to the churning of a system which produces mass of fanatics, fundamentalists, and hence, stunts any possible growth of a modern, democratic society. It is no wonder then the region has become a hub of terrorism with complicity of Pakistan.

Pakistan continues to use the territory to train the terrorists for jehad in J&K and elsewhere. This facet of truth comes to the forefront more conclusively aftermath of the earthquake. The post-earthquake scenario also exposed massive corruption, mismanagement, and apathetic attitude of Pakistan towards the affected people. Pakistan army's vacillation in carrying out rescue and relief operations and its leaders' harping on an early resolution of the Kashmir issue left the affected people disillusioned. This disillusion was further exacerbated with the news of Indian army's commendable role in J&K to help the quake victims.

The rolling of buses between the two Kashmirs has exposed the people from across the LOC the ground realities in J&K, which are quite contradictory to the propaganda they are fed. It has also provided an opportunity to people from J&K to see the situation on the other side of the LOC. A person with the knowledge of ground realities of both sides of Kashmir can only imagine the veracity of lies that are propagated very often. One such lie that in J&K the Muslims are not allowed to perform their religious duties such as Namaz has burst in bubbles after visitors from across the LOC came to J&K and saw the reality. The complaints of human rights violations in J&K by Pak leaders can be seen in a comparative perspective. To start with, for instance, any complaint of excesses in J&K by Indian security forces must be accompanied by the knowledge of the role of Pak army in Kashmir across the LOC. The statement by a Srinagar-based separatist leader is quite revealing in this context. The leader avers 'if the kind of democracy prevailing in 'AJK' is the one that Pakistan reserves for us then we are better off with India.'

Sectarianism in the once Shia-dominated Gilgit-Baltistan needs special mention as it not only fuels mass discontent but also keeps the region boiling. The brunt of the radical Islamization policy of Zia by settling Sunnis in the area has fallen not only on the local people but also on Pakistan itself. Hence, when a sectarian carnage takes place in Gilgit, its echoes are felt in Islamabad. The policy of Islamization, the Afghan crisis in the 1980s, the revolution in Iran in 1979, have all cumulative effects on the sectarian turmoil and even after these events subsided and the Musharraf regime adopted the policy of enlightened moderation, nothing spectacular did happen so far to assuage the wounds of the people. In fact the sectarian monster has raised its ugly head more stridently. Besides oppression from above, factors such as illiteracy, poverty and lack of political organization have weakened any prospect of rising democratic voice in the region.

It is not difficult to say whether sectarianism was a natural growth on the soil of Gilgit-Baltistan or it was a calibrated policy on the part of Pakistan to keep the divergent people engaged in trivial issues and to promote Sunni variety of Islam in order to bring uniformity throughout the region. The text book controversy, the killing of a prominent Shia leader in 2005, and the refusal of the administration to a commonly agreed proposal are some of the indications that the region would likely undergo such turmoil for quite some time to come. Major parties like BNF, APNA, etc. have raised banners of dissent, and the movement for an independent Balawaristan has already gained ground.

The authors' interactions with the visitors from 'AJK' and 'NA' bring into light their utter dissatisfaction at the handling of affairs by Islamabad. Islamabad has adopted an ostrich like attitude to the demands of the local people. This has been clearly visible in recent years, when Pakistan, despite public protest decided to raise the height of the Mangla dam and construct the Bhasha dam. The Mangla dam, built in the 1960s, not only submerged huge chunk of area in Mirpur but displaced a large number of people. It may be understood that for the economic development dams are necessary, but the question can be rightly be asked- development for whom? The electricity produced by the dam went to Pakistan and till recently no royalty was given to 'AJK.' The displaced people have not been rehabilitated so far. The Bhasha dam construction in Gilgit-

Baltistan has raised almost similar issues. Environmentalists have raised the question of viability of the dam as it would not only submerge inhabitation but also many places of historical and architectural importance. Despite assurances by Musharraf regime, the local people's suspicion regarding the development of the region with the establishment of the dam is justifiable as their suspicion of Islamabad which has denied the basic rights, even after 60 years of its rule, is justified. The local people are led to believe themselves as pawns in the hands of Pakistan on its strategic and economic chessboard.

The 2005 earthquake not only devastated the region, it also brought forth the animosity between Pakistan and India to work together in such an hour of tragedy. Pakistan readily rejected Indian offer in the beginning and appealed for help from other countries. The earthquake proved to be a lost opportunity which could have brought two South Asian rivals together. However, the ongoing peace process raises expectations for peace in Kashmir. There seems to be a rising sense of sincerity among the leaders of both the regions and India and Pakistan. The start of bus service between the two Kashmirs, the holding of 'heart-to-heart' talks, and the movement of people across the LOC to meet members of divided families indicate the intra-Kashmir dialogue has taken the peace process forward. The trans-LOC linkages can also be used for promotion of trade, tourism and promotion of indigenous culture including matrimonial ties without any stringent government control. President Musharraf's rejection of violent elements in the peace process and Prime Minister Manmohan Singh's offer of treaty of peace and friendship are some of welcome developments in this regard. It is true that in Kashmir, and in Indo-Pak relations, the expected lines may be blurred with unexpected developments but the irreversibility of the peace process was never durable for such a long period. The engagement of the people in the process may pressure respective governments to work for a peaceful and amicable win-win solution of the Kashmir issue. In this direction,

Pakistan can make the status of 'AJK' and 'NA' clear devoid of ambiguity, grant them fundamental rights and shed the contradictions in its policies towards the areas.

Appendix

THE AZAD JAMMU AND KASHMIR INTERIM CONSTITUTION ACT, 1974

(ACT VIII OF 1974)

An Act to repeal and, with certain modifications, re-enact the Azad Jammu and Kashmir Government Act, 1970.

WHEREAS the future status of the State of Jammu and Kashmir is yet to be determined in accordance with the freely expressed will of the people of the State through the democratic method of free and fair plebiscite under the auspices of the United Nations as envisaged in the UNCJP Resolutions adopted from time to time;

AND WHEREAS a part of the territories of the State of Jammu and Kashmir already liberated by the people are known for the time being as Azad Jammu and Kashmir;

AND WHEREAS it is necessary to provide for the better Government and administration of Azad Jammu and Kashmir until such tine as the status of Jammu and Kashmir is determined as afore-said and for that purpose to repeal and re-enact the Azad Jammu and Kashmir Government Act, 1970, with certain modifications;

AND WHEREAS, in the discharge of its responsibilities under the UNCIP Resolutions, the Government of Pakistan has approved of the proposed repeal and re-enactment of the said the Azad Jammu and Kashmir Government Act, 1970, and authorized the President of Azad Jammu and Kashmir to introduce the Bill in the Legislative Assembly of Azad Jammu and Kashmir for consideration and passage;

It is hereby enacted as follows:-

1. Short title and commencement, etc.- (1) This Act may be called the Azad Jammu and Kashmir Interim Constitution Act, 1974. .

(2) It shall come into force on the day on which the Azad Jammu and Kashmir, Government Bill, 1974, is assented to, or is deemed to have been assented to, by the President.

(3) This Bill shall not be presented to the President for assent unless it has been passed by the votes of not less than two-thirds of the total number of members of the Assembly.

(4) The President shall assent to this Bill within three days after it has been presented to him for assent under sub-section (2); and, if the President fails to do so, he shall be deemed to have assented to this Bill at the expiration of the said period.

2. [Definitions- (1) In this Act, unless there is anything repugnant in the subject or context,-

'Agricultural income' means agricultural income as defined for the purposes of the law relating to income-tax;

'Assembly' means the Legislative Assembly of Azad Jammu and Kashmir;

'Azad Jammu and Kashmir' means the territories of the State of Jammu and Kashmir which have been liberated by the people of that State and are for the time being under the administration of Government and such other territories as may hereafter come under its administration.

'Corporation tax' means any tax on income that is payable by companies and in respect of which the following conditions apply:—

i) The tax is not chargeable in respect of agricultural income;

ii) no deduction in respect of the tax paid by companies is, by any law which may apply to the tax, authorised to be made from dividends payable by the companies to individuals;

iii) no provision exists for taking the tax so paid into account in computing for the purposes of income-tax the total income individuals receiving such dividends, or in computing the income-tax payable by, or refundable to, such individuals;

'Council' means the Azad Jammu and Kashmir Council constituted under this Act;

'financial year' means the year commencing on the first day of July and ending on the thirtieth day of June;

Government' means the Azad Government of the State of Jammu and Kashmir;

'Joint sitting' means a joint sitting of the Assembly, [the Federal Minister incharge of the Council Secretariat] and the elected members of the Council;

'Judge' in relation to the Supreme Court of Azad Jammu and Kashmir o the High Court, includes the Chief Justice of the Supreme Court of Azad Jammu and Kashmir or, as the case may be, High Court and also includes an Additional Judge of the High Court;

'Muslim' means a person who believes in the Unity and Oneness of Almighty Allah, His angels, the Books of Allah, the holy Quran being the last of them, His Prophets, the absolute finality of the Prophethood of Mohammad (peace be upon him), the day of Judgment, and all the requirements and teachings of the Holy Quran and Sunnah;

'Person' includes any body politic or corporate; -

'President' means the President of Azad Jammu and Kashmir and includes a person for the time being acting as, or performing the functions of, the President of Azad Jammu and Kashmir;

'prescribed' means prescribed by law or rules made there under;

'property' includes any right, title or interest in property, moveable or immovable, and any means and instruments of production;

'remuneration' includes salary and pension;

'service of Azad Jammu and Kashmir' means any service, post or office in connection with the affairs of Azad Jammu and Kashmir, including the Council, but does not include service as Chairman of the Council, President, Speaker, Deputy Speaker, Prime Minister, Minister, Federal Minister in charge of the

Council Secretariat or Advisor appointed under section 21, or a member of the Assembly or member of the Council;

'Speaker' means Speaker of the Assembly and includes any person acting as the Speaker of the Assembly;

'State Property' means any moveable or immovable property as belonged to the State of Jammu and Kashmir or its former Ruler or a Raja and is within the territories of Pakistan;

'State Subject' means a person for the time being residing in Azad Jammu and Kashmir or Pakistan who is a 'State Subject' as defined in the late Government of the State of Jammu and Kashmir Notification No. I-L/84, dated the 20th April, 1927, as amended from time to time;

'taxation' means the imposition of any tax or duty, whether general, local or special, and 'tax' shall be construed accordingly;

'tax on income', includes a tax in the nature an excess profits tax or a business profits tax.

(2) In this Act, 'Act of the Assembly' or 'Act of the Council' shall include an Ordinance promulgated by the President under sub-section (1) of Section 41, or as the case may be, under sub-section (4) of that section.

[(3) A person who does not believe in the absolute and unqualified finality of the Prophethood of Mohammad (peace be upon him) the last of the Prophets or claims to be a prophet, in any sense of the word or of any description whatsoever, after Mohammad (peace be upon him), or recognises such a claimant as a prophet or a religious reformer, is not a Muslim for the purposes of this Act or law.]

3. Islam to be State religion.- Islam shall be the State religion of Azad Jammu and Kashmir.

4. Fundamental Rights.- (1) Any law or any custom or usage having the force of law, in so far as it is inconsistent with the rights conferred by this section, shall, to the extent of such inconsistency, be void.

[(2) No law shall be made which takes away or abridges the rights so conferred and any law made in contravention of this sub-section shall, to the extent of such contravention, be void.]

(3) The provisions of this section shall not apply to any law relating to the members of the defence services or of the forces charged with the maintenance of public order for the purpose of ensuring proper discharge of their duties or the maintenance of discipline among them.

(4) The Rights

1. Security of person.- No person shall be deprived of liberty save in accordance with law.

2. Safeguard as to arrest and detention.- (1) No person who is arrested shall be detained in custody without being informed, as soon as may be, of the grounds for such arrest, nor shall he be denied the right to consult and be defended by a legal practitioner of his choice.

(2) Every person who is arrested and detained in custody shall be produced before the nearest Magistrate within a period of twenty-four hours of such arrest excluding the time necessary for the journey from the place of arrest to the Court of the Magistrate, and no such person shall be detained in custody beyond the said period without the authority of a Magistrate.

(3) Nothing in sub-paragraphs (1) and (2) shall apply to any person -

(a) who for the time being is an enemy alien, or

(b) who is arrested or detained under any law providing for preventive detention.

(4) No law providing for preventive detention shall authorise the detention of a person for a period exceeding three months unless the review board set up by the Government has reported before the expiration of the said period of three months that there is, in its opinion, sufficient cause for such detention.

(5) When any person is detained in pursuance of an order made under any law providing for preventive detention, the authority making the order shall as soon as may be, communicate to such person the grounds on which the order has been made, and shall afford him the earliest opportunity of making a representation against the order:

Provided that the authority making any such order may refuse to disclose facts which such authority considers it to be against the public interest to disclose.

3. Slavery and forced labour prohibited- (1) No person shall be held in slavery and no law shall permit or in anyway facilitate the introduction into Azad Jammu and Kashmir of slavery in any form.

(2) All forms of forced labour are prohibited.

(3) Nothing in this paragraph shall be deemed to affect compulsory service -

(a) by persons undergoing punishment for offences against any law; or

(b) required by any law for a. public purpose.

4. Protection against retrospective punishment.- No law shall authorise the punishment of a person - (a) for an act or ommission that was not punishable by law at the time of the act or ommission; or

(b) for an offence by a penalty greater than, or of a kind different from, the penalty prescribed by law for that offence at the time the offence was committed.

5. Freedom of movement.- Subject to any reasonable restrictions imposed by law in the public interest, every State Subject shall have the right to move freely throughout Azad Jammu and Kashmir territory and to reside and settle in any part thereof.

6. Freedom of assembly.- Every State Subject shall have the right to assemble peacefully and without arms, subject to any reasonable restrictions imposed by law in the interest of public order.

7. Freedom of association.- (1) Subject to this Act, every State - Subject shall have the right to form association or unions, subject to any reasonable restrictions imposed by law in the interest of morality or public order.

(2) No person or political party in Azad Jammu and Kashmir shall be permitted to propagate against, or take part in activities prejudicial or detrimental to, the ideology the State's accession to Pakistan.

8.Freedom of trade, business or profession.- Every State Subject possessing such qualifications, if any, as may be prescribed by law in relation to his profession or occupation shall have the right to enter upon any lawful profession or occupation and to conduct any lawful trade or business:

Provided that nothing in this paragraph shall prevent -

(a) the regulation of any trade or profession by a licensing system; or

(b) the regulation of trade, commerce or industry in the interest of free competition therein; or

[(c) the carrying on, by Government or the Council, or by a corporation controlled by Government or the Council, of any trade, business, industry or service, to the exclusion, complete or partial, or other persons.]

9.Freedom of speech.-Every State Subject shall have the right to freedom of speech and expression, subject to any reasonable restrictions imposed by law in the interest of the security of Azad Jammu and Kashmir, friendly relations with Pakistan, public order, decency or morality, or in relation to contempt of Court, defamation or incitement to an offence.

10. Freedom of religion- Subject to law, public order and morality-

(a) every State Subject has the right to profess and practise his religion; and

(b) every religious denomination and every sect thereof has the right to establish, maintain and manage its places of worship:

Provided that nothing contained in sub-paragraphs (a) and (b) shall be so construed as to abridge the authority to promulgate laws which may prescribe prohibition or penalty for conversion from Islam or the act of converting or the attempt of converting a Muslim to some other religion.

11. Safeguard against taxation for purposes of any particular religion.- No person shall be compelled to pay any special tax the proceeds of which are to be spent on the propagation or maintenance of any religion other than his own.

12. Safeguard as to educational institutions in respect of religion etc.- (1) No person attending any educational institution shall be required to receive religious instructions or take part in any religious ceremony, or attend religious worship, if such instruction, ceremony or worship relates to a religion other than his own.

(2) No religious community or denomination shall be prevented from providing religious instruction for pupils of that community or denomination in any educational institution maintained wholly by that community or denomination.

(3) No State Subject shall be denied admission to any educational institution receiving aid from public revenues on the ground only of race, religion, caste or place of birth.

(4) In respect of any religious institution, there shall be no discrimination against any community in the granting of exemption or concession in relation to taxation.

(5) Every religious community or denomination shall have the right to establish and maintain educational institutions of its own choice, and the Government shall not deny recognition to any such, institution on the ground only that the management of such institution vests in that community or denomination.

(6) Nothing in this paragraph shall prevent any public authority from making provision for the advancement of any society or educationally backward class of State Subjects.

13. Provision as to property- Subject to any reasonable restrictions imposed by law in the public interest, every State Subject shall have the right to acquire, hold and dispose of property.

14. Protection of property.- (1) No person shall be deprived of his property save in accordance with law.

(2) No property shall be compulsorily acquired or taken possession of save for a public purpose, and save by the authority of law which provides for compensation therefore and either fixes the amount of compensation or specifies the principles on which and the manner in which compensation is to be determined and given.

(3) Nothing in this paragraph shall, affect the validity of-

(a) any law permitting the compulsory acquisition or taking possession of any property for preventing danger to life, property or public health; or

(b) any law relating to the acquisition, administration or disposal of any property which is or is deemed to be evacuee' property under any law; or

[(c) any law permitting the taking over of any property which has been acquired by, or come into the possession of, any person by any unfair means, or in any manner, contrary to law; or

(d) any law providing for the taking over of the management of any property by the Government for a limited period, either in the public interest or in order to secure the proper management of the property, or for the benefit of its owner; or

(e) any law providing for the acquisition of any class of property for the purpose of-

(i) providing education and medical aid to all or any specified class of State Subjects; or

(ii) providing housing and public facilities and services such as roads, water supply, sewerage, gas and electric power to all or any specified class of State subjects; or

(iii) providing maintenance to those who, on account of unemployment, sickness, infirmity or old age, are unable to maintain themselves; or

(f) any law in force immediately before the coming into force of this Act.

Explanation.- In sub-paragraphs (2) and (3), 'property' shall mean immovable property, or any commercial or industrial undertaking, or any interest in any undertaking.

15. Equality of State Subjects.- All State Subjects are equal before law and are entitled to equal protection of law.

16. Non-discrimination in respect of access to public places.- In respect of access to places of public entertainment or resort not intended for religious purposes only, there shall be no

discrimination against any State Subject, on the ground only of race, religion, caste, sex or place of birth, but nothing herein shall be deemed to prevent the making of any special provision for women.

17. Safeguard against discrimination in services.- No State Subject otherwise qualified for appointment in the services of Azad Jammu and Kashmir shall be discriminated against in respect of any such appointment on the ground only of race, religion, caste or sex:

Provided that, in the interest of the said service, specified posts or services may be reserved for members of either sex.

18. Abolition of untouchability.- Untouchability is abolished, and its practice in any form is forbidden and shall be declared by law to be an offence.

5. President-[(1). There shall be a President of Azad Jammu and Kashmir, who shall be elected by the members of the joint sitting by the votes of majority of the total membership of the Joint sitting in such manner as may prescribed:

Provided that, if no person secures such majority in the first poll, a second poll shall be held between the persons who secure the two highest numbers of votes in the first poll and the person who secures a majority of votes of the members present and voting shall be declared to have been elected as President:

Provided further that, if the number of votes secured by two or more persons securing the highest number of votes is equal, further, poll shall be held between them until one of them secures a majority of votes of the members present and voting.]

(2) The election to the office of President shall be conducted under the control and supervision of the Chief Election Commissioner.

(3) The election of the President under sub-section (2) shall not be called in question in any Court or before any Tribunal or other authority.

[(3-A) Election to the office of President shall be held not earlier than sixty days and not later than thirty days before the expiration of the term of the President in office or, if the election cannot be held within that period because the Assembly is dissolved, within thirty days of the general election to the Assembly.]

(4) No person shall be qualified for election as President unless:

(a) he is a Muslim;

(b) he has attained the age of thirty-five years;

(c) his name appears on the electoral roll prepared for election of the members of the Assembly; and

(d) he is qualified to be elected as a member of the Assembly.

(5) Subject to the provisions of this Act, the President shall hold office for a period of five yeas from the date on which he enters upon his office and shall, notwithstanding, the expiration of his term, continue to hold office until his successor enters upon his office.

(6) Before he enters upon his office, the President shall make before the Chief Justice of [Azad Jammu and Kashmir] an oath in the form set out in the First Schedule:

Provided that this provision will not apply to a person acting as President:

Provided further that the oath made or deemed to have been made under the provisions, of the Azad Jammu and Kashmir Government Act, 1970, shall be deemed to have been made under this Act.

(7) The President may resign his office by writing under his hand addressed to the Speaker of the Assembly.

[(8) The President shall not be a member, or a candidate for election as a member, of the assembly and if a member of the Assembly is elected as President his seat in the Assembly shall become vacant on the day he enters upon his office.]

6. Removal of President.- (1) if one-third of the total number of members of the [Joint Sitting] give a notice in writing to the Speaker of the Assembly of their intention to move a resolution of no confidence against the President, the Speaker shall convene a meeting of the [Joint-Sitting] not later than two weeks from the date of receipt of the notice.

(2) The President shall have the right to appear before the [Joint-Sitting] during the consideration of the resolution under sub-section (1) and to make a statement if he so desires.

(3) If the resolution under sub-section (1) is passed by the [Joint- Sitting] by the votes of not less than two-thirds of the total number of members of the [Joint-Sitting], the President shall forthwith cease to hold office.

7. President to act on advice, etc.- [(1) Subject to an express provision to the contrary in this Act, in the performance of his functions, the President shall act] on and in accordance with the advice of the Prime Minister and such advice shall be binding on him.

(2) The question whether any, and if so what, advice was tendered to the President by the Prime Minister shall not be enquired into any Court.

8. Acting President.- At any time when the President is unable to perform the functions of his office due to absence, illness or any other cause, the Speaker of the Assembly [shall act as President and shall perform the functions of President.]

9. Casual vacancy in the office 'of President.- Where the office of President falls vacant due to death, resignation of any other cause, the Speaker of the Assembly [shall -].

(a) perform the functions of President till such time as a new President is elected; and

(b) cause an election to the office of President to be held within a period of thirty days from the date on which the office falls vacant or, if the election cannot be held within that period because the Assembly is dissolved, within thirty days of the general elections to the Assembly.

10. President's power of pardon and reprieve- The President has power to grant pardons, reprieves and respites and to remit, suspend or commute any sentence passed by any Court, tribunal or other authority.

11. Plebiscite Adviser- The President may appoint a Plebiscite Adviser to advise the Government in relation to the holding of a plebiscite in the State of Jammu and Kashmir in terms of the UNCIP Resolutions.

12. The Government- (1) Subject to this Act, the executive authority of Azad Jammu and Kashmir shall be exercised in the name of the President by the Government, consisting of the Prime Minister and the Ministers, which shall act through the Prime Minister who shall be the Chief executive of Azad Jammu and Kashmir.

(2) In the performance of his functions under this Act, the Prime Minister may act either directly or through the Ministers.

(3) The Prime Minister and the Ministers shall be collectively responsible to the Assembly.

[(4) Orders and other instruments made and executed in the name of the President shall be authenticated in such manner as may be specified in rules to be made by the Government, and the validity of an order or instrument which is so authenticated shall not be called in question on the ground that it is not an order or instrument made or executed by the President..

(5) The Government may regulate the allocation and transaction of its business and may for the convenient transaction of that business delegate any of its functions to officers or authorities subordinate to it.]

13. The Prime Minister- (1) The Assembly shall meet on the thirtieth day following the day on which a general election to the Assembly is held, unless sooner summoned by the President.

(2) After the election of the Speaker, the Assembly shall, to the exclusion of any other business, proceed to elect, without debate one of its Muslim members to be the Prime Minister.

(3) The Prime Minister shall be elected the votes of the majority of the total membership of the Assembly:

Provided that, if no member secures such majority in the first poll, a second poll shall be held between the members who secure the two highest numbers of votes in the first poll and the member who secures a majority of votes of the members present and voting shall be declared to have been elected as Prime Minister:

Provided further that, if the number of votes secured by two or more members securing the highest number of votes is equal, further poll shall be held between them until one of them secures a majority of the members present and voting.

(4) The member elected under sub-section (3) shall be called upon by the President to assume the office of Prime Minister and he shall, before entering upon the office make before the President oath in the form set out in the First Schedule.

14. Ministers.- (1) The Prime Minister shall appoint Ministers from amongst the members of the Assembly.

(2) Before entering upon office, a Minister shall make before the President oath in the form set out in the First Schedule.

(3) A Minister may, by writing under his hand addressed to the Prime Minister, resign his office or may be removed from office by the Prime Minister.

15. Prime Minister continuing in office.- (1) The Prime Minister shall continue to hold office until his successor enters upon the office of Prime Minister.

(2) Nothing in Section 13 or Section 14 shall be construed to disqualify the Prime Minister or a Minister from continuing in office during the period the Assembly stands dissolved.

16. Resignation of Prime Minister.- (1) Subject to sub-section (2) the Prime Minister may, by writing under his hand addressed to the President, resign his office and, when the Prime Minister resigns, the Ministers shall cease to hold office.

(2) The Prime Minister, and at the request of the Prime Minister, a Minister shall continue to perform the functions of the office of Prime Minister or, as the case may be, Minister until a new Prime Minister has been elected and has entered upon his office.

(3) If the Assembly is in session at the time when the Prime Minister resigns his office, the Assembly shall forthwith proceed to elect a Prime Minister, and if the Assembly is not in session the President shall for that purpose summon it to meet within fourteen days of the resignation.

17. Minister performing functions of Prime Minister.- (i) In the event of the death of the Prime Minister or the office of

the Prime Minister becoming vacant by reason of his ceasing to be a member of the Assembly the most senior Minister for the time being shall be called upon by the President to perform the functions of that office and the Ministers shall continue in office until a new Prime Minister has been elected and has entered upon his office.

(2) If the Assembly is in session at the time when the Prime Minister dies or the office of the Prime Minister becomes vacant the Assembly shall forthwith proceed to elect a Prime Minister, and if the Assembly is not in session the President shall for that purpose summon it to meet within fourteen days of the death of the Prime Minister or, as the case may be, of the office becoming vacant.

(3) When, for any reason, the Prime Minister is unable to perform his functions, the most senior Minister for the time being shall perform the functions of Prime Minister until the Prime Minister resumes his functions.

(4) In this section, 'most senior Minister' means the Minister for the time being designated as such by the Prime Minister.

18. Vote of no-confidence again Prime Minister.- (1) A resolution for a vote of no-confidence (hereinafter in this section referred to as the resolution) may be passed against the Prime Minister by the Assembly.

(2) A resolution shall not be moved, in the Assembly unless, by the same resolution the name of another member of the Assembly is put forward as the successor.

(3) A resolution shall not be moved in the Assembly while the Assembly is considering demands for grants submitted to it in the Annual Budget.

(4) A resolution shall not be voted upon before the expiration of three days, or later than seven days, from the date on which it is moved in the Assembly.

(5) If the resolution is passed by majority of the total membership of the Assembly, the President shall call upon the person named in the resolution as the successor to assume office

and, on his entering upon office his predecessor and the Minister appointed by him shall cease to hold office.

(6) If a resolution is not passed another such resolution shall not be moved until a period of six months has elapsed.

19. Extent of executive authority of Government.- (1) Subject to this Act, the executive authority of the Government shall extend to the matters with respect to which the Assembly has power to make laws.

(2) The executive authority of the Government shall be so exercised as:-

(a) not to impede or prejudice the responsibilities of the Government of Pakistan [in relation to the matters specified in sub-section (3) of section 31;] and

(b) to secure compliance with the Laws made by the Council.

(3) Notwithstanding anything contained in this Act, the Government may, with the consent of the Council, entrust, either conditionally or unconditionally, to the Council, or to its officers functions in relation to any matter to which the executive authority of the Government extends.

20. Advocate-General.- (1) The President shall appoint a person, being a person qualified to be appointed a Judge of the High Court to be the Advocate-General for Azad Jammu and Kashmir.

(2) It shall be the duty of the Advocate-General to give advice to Government upon such legal matters, and to perform such other duties of a legal character, as may be referred or assigned to him by the Government.

(3) The Advocate-General shall hold office during the pleasure of the President.

(4) The Advocate-General may, by writing under his hand addressed to the President resign his office.

(5) The person holding the office as Advocate-General immediately before the commencement of this Act shall be deemed to be the Advocate-General, appointed under this Act.

21. Azad Jammu and Kashmir Council (1) There shall be an Azad Jammu and Kashmir Council consisting of-

(a) The Prime Minister of Pakistan;
(b) the President;
(c) five members to be nominated by the Prime Minister of Pakistan from time to time from amongst Federal Ministers and members of Parliament;
(d) The Prime Minister of Azad Jammu and Kashmir or a person nominated by him; and
(e) six members to be elected by the Assembly from amongst State Subjects in accordance with the system of proportional representation by means of the single transferable vote.

(2) The Prime Minister of Pakistan shall be the Chairman of the Council.

(3) The President shall be the Vice-Chairman of the Council.

[(3-A) The Federal minister of State for Kashmir Affairs and Northern Affairs shall be an ex-officio member of the Council.]

(4) The qualifications and disqualifications for being elected, as, and for being, a member of the Council shall, in the case of a member referred to in clause (e) of sub-section (1), be the same as these for being elected as, and for being a member of the Assembly.

[(4-A) The seat of a member of the Council elected by the Assembly, hereinafter referred to as an elected member, shall become vacant if,-
(a) he resigns his seat by notice in writing under his hand addressed to the Chairman or, in his absence, to the Secretary of the Council;
(b) if he is absent, without the leave of the Chairman, from thirty consecutive sittings of the Council;
(c) he fails to make the oath referred to in sub-section (6) within a period of ninety days after the date of his election, unless the Chairman, for good cause shown, extends the period; or
(d) he ceases to be qualified for being a member under any provision of this Act or any other law.

(4-B) If any question arises whether a member has, after his election, become disqualified from being a member of the Council, the Chairman shall refer the question to the Chief Election Commissioner and, if the Chief Election Commissioner is of the opinion that the member has become disqualified, the member shall cease to be a member and his seal shall become vacant.

(4-C) An election to fill a vacancy in the office of an elected member shall be held not later than thirty days from the occurrence of the vacancy or, if the election cannot be held within that period because the Assembly is dissolved, within thirty days of the general election to the Assembly.

(4-D) The manner of election of elected members and filling of a casual vacancy in the office of an elected member shall be such as may be prescribed.]

(5) [An elected member shall hold office for a term of five years from the day he enters upon his office:

Provided that an elected member shall, notwithstanding the expiration of his term, continue to hold office until his successor enters upon his office.]

(6) [An elected member shall, before entering upon office, make before the Chairman oath in the form set out in the First Schedule.]

(7) [The executive authority of the Council shall extend to all matters with respect to which the council has power to make laws and shall be exercised, in the name of the Council, by the Chairman who may act either directly or through the Secretariat of the Council of which a Federal Minister nominated by the Chairman from amongst the members of the Council and not more than three Advisors appointed by the Chairman shall be incharge:

Provided that the Council may direct that, in respect of such matters as it may specify, its authority shall be exercisable by the Vice-Chairman of the Council, subject to such conditions, if any, as the Council may specify.

(8) An Advisor may be appointed from amongst the elected members or the members of the Assembly.

(9) An Advisor shall, before entering upon office, make before the Chairman oath in the form set out in the First Schedule.

(10) An Advisor who is a member of the Assembly [and the Federal Minister of the state for Kashmir Affairs and Northern Affairs] shall have the right to speak in, and otherwise take part in the proceedings of the Council, but shall not by virtue of this sub-section be entitled to vote.

(11) The Council may make rules for regulating its procedure and the conduct of its business, and shall have power to act notwithstanding any vacancy in the membership thereof, and any proceedings of the Council shall not be invalid on the ground that a person who was not entitled to do so sat, voted or otherwise took part in the proceedings.

(12) Orders and other instruments made and executed in the name of the Council shall be authenticated in such manner as may be specified in rules to be made by the Council and the validity of an order or instrument which is so authenticated shall not be called in question on the ground that it is not an order or instrument made or executed by the Council.

(13) The Chairman may regulate the allocation and transaction of the business of the Council and may, for the convenient transaction of that business, delegate any of its functions to officers and authorities subordinate to it.

Explanation: In this section, 'Chairman' means Chairman of the Council.

[(14) The words 'The Prime Minister of Pakistan' wherever occurring in this Section shall be deemed to include the person for the time being exercising the powers and performing the functions of the Chief Executive of Pakistan.

22. The Legislature of Azad Jammu and Kashmir shall consist of a Legislative Assembly consisting of [forty-eight] members of whom -

(a) forty shall be elected directly on the basis of adult franchise ; and

(b) [Five, who shall be women, shall be elected by the directly members;]

[(c) one, who shall be from amongst the Ulema-e-Din or Mushaikh and well-versed with the teachings of Islam, shall be elected by the directly elected members;

(d) one who shall be from amongst the Jammu and Kashmir State Subject residing abroad shall be elected by the directly elected members; and

(e) One, who shall be from amongst the technocrats and other professionals, shall also be elected by the directly elected members.

(2) The manner of election of the members of the-Assembly and the manner of filling casual vacancies shall be such as may be prescribed.

(3) Every Assembly, unless sooner dissolved, shall continue for five years from the date of appointment for their first meeting and no longer, and the expiration of the said period of five years shall operate as a dissolution of the Assembly.

[(4) A general election to the Assembly shall be held within a period of sixty days immediately preceding the day on which the term of the Assembly is due to expire unless the Assembly has been sooner dissolved, and the result of the election shall be declared not later than fourteen days before that day.]

23. Oath of members of the Assembly.- (1) A person elected as a member of the Assembly shall not take his seat in the Assembly until he makes before such person as is prescribed by rules of the Assembly an oath in the form set out in the First Schedule.

(2) The oath may be made at any time whether or not the Assembly is in session.

(3) If any person sits or votes in the Assembly knowing that he is not qualified to be, or is disqualified from being, a member of the Assembly he shall be liable in respect of every day on which he so sits or votes to a penalty of two hundred rupees a day which may be recovered from him as a debt to the Government recoverable as arrears of land revenue.

24. Qualification of members of the Assembly.- (1) A person shall be qualified to be elected as, and to be, a member of the Assembly if-

(a) he is a State Subject;

(b) he is not less than twenty-five years of age; and

(c) his name appears on the electoral roll of any constituency in Azad Jammu and Kashmir or Pakistan.

(2) A person shall be disqualified from being so-elected if-

(a) he is of unsound mind and stands so declared by competent court; or

(b) he is an undischarged insolvent unless a period of ten years has elapsed since his being adjudged as insolvent; or

(c) he has been on conviction for any offence sentenced to transportation for any term or imprisonment for a term of not less than two years unless a period of five years has elapsed since his release;

(d) he holds any office of profit in the service of Azad Jammu and Kashmir or in the service of Pakistan other than an office which is not a whole time office remunerated either by salary or by fee other than an office specified in the Second Schedule; or;

(e) he has been dismissed for misconduct from the service of Azad Jammu and Kashmir or the service of Pakistan unless a period of five years has elapsed since his dismissal: or

(f) he is otherwise disqualified from being a member of the Assembly by this Act or by or under any other law.

25. Seat in Assembly becomes vacant under certain circumstances. (1) The seat of a member of the Assembly shall become vacant if -

(a) he resigns his seat by notice in writing under his hand addressed to the Speaker, in his absence, to the Secretary of the Assembly; or

(b) he is absent from the Assembly without the leave of the Assembly for thirty consecutive sitting days of the Assembly; or

c) he fails to make the oath referred to in section [23,] within a period of ninety days after the date of his election unless the Speaker for good cause shown extends the period; or

(d) he is elected as a member of the Council; or

(e) he ceases to be qualified for being a member under any provision of this Act or any other law.

[(1-A) If a member of the Assembly is elected to more than one seat, he shall. within .a period of thirty days after the declaration of the result for the last such seat, resign all but one of his seats, and if he does not so resign, all the seats to which he has been elected shall become vacant at the expiration of the said period of thirty days except the seat to which he has been last elected or if he has been elected to more than one seat on the same day, the seat for election to which his nomination was filed last.

(2) If any question arises whether a. member of the Assembly has after his election become disqualified from being a member of the Assembly, the Speaker shall refer the question to the Chief Election Commissioner and, if the Chief Election Commissioner is of the opinion that the member has become disqualified, the member shall cease to be a member and his seat shall become vacant.

[(3) When, except by dissolution of the Assembly, a seat in the Assembly has become vacant not later than one hundred and twenty days before the term of the Assembly is due to expire, an election to fill the seat, shall be held within sixty days from the occurrence of the vacancy.]

26. Right to address and take part in Assembly proceedings - (1) The President may address the Assembly and send messages to the Assembly.

(2) The Advocate-General shall have the right to speak, and otherwise take part in the proceedings of, the Assembly or of any of its committees, but shall not by virtue of this section have the right to vote.

27. Meeting of the Assembly.- (1) The Assembly shall assemble at such time and such places as the President may appoint; and the President may prorogue a session of the Assembly except when the Assembly has been summoned by the Speaker.

(2) Any meeting of the Assembly may be adjourned by the Speaker or other person presiding thereat.

(3) There shall be at least two sessions of the Assembly every year and months shall not intervene between the first sitting of the Assembly in one session; and its first sitting in the next session.

[(4) On a requisition signed by not less than one-fourth of the total membership of the Assembly, the Speaker shall summon the Assembly to meet, at such time and place as he thinks fit within fourteen days of the receipt of the requisition, and when the Speaker has summoned the Assembly, only he may prorogue it.]

28. Dissolution of Assembly.- [(1) The President shall dissolve the Assembly if so advised by the Prime Minister, and the Assembly shall, unless sooner dissolved, stand dissolved at the expiration of forty eight hours after the Prime Minister has so advised.

Explanation.- Reference in this section to Prime Minister shall not be construed to include reference to a Prime Minister against whom a resolution for a vote of no confidence has been moved in the Assembly but has not been voted upon or against whom such a resolution has been passed or who is continuing in office after his resignation or after the dissolution of the Assembly or a Minister performing the functions of Prime Minister under sub-section (1) or sub-section (3) of section 17.

(2) When the Assembly is dissolved a general election to the Assembly shall be held within a period of ninety days after the dissolution, and the results shall be declared not later than fourteen days after conclusion of the polls.

29. Speaker of the Assembly.- (1) The Assembly shall, at its first meeting or as soon thereafter as may be, elect from amongst its members a Speaker [and a Deputy Speaker] of the Assembly.

(2) Before entering upon office, a member of the Assembly elected as Speaker [or Deputy Speaker] shall make before the Assembly an oath in the form set out in the First Schedule.

(3) All proceedings of the Assembly shall be conducted in accordance with Rules of Procedure made by the Assembly and approved by the President.

(4) The Speaker shall preside at the meetings of the Assembly and, when the office of the Speaker is vacant or the Speaker is absent or is unable to perform his functions due to any cause the Deputy Speaker shall act as Speaker, and if at that time the Deputy Speaker is also absent or is unable to act as Speaker due to any cause, such member of the Assembly present as may be determined by the Rules of Procedure of the Assembly shall preside at the meeting of the Assembly.

(5) So often as the office of Speaker or Deputy Speaker becomes vacant, the Assembly shall elect one of its members to fill the office.

(6) The Speaker may resign his office by writing under his hand addressed to the President.

[(6-A) The Deputy Speaker may resign his office by writing under his hand addressed to the Speaker.]

(7) The office of the Speaker [or Deputy Speaker] shall become vacant if-

(a) Except as provided in sub-section (8) he ceases to be a member of the Assembly; or

(b) he is removed from office by a resolution of the Assembly, of which not less than seven day's notice by not less than eleven members has been given and which is passed by a majority of total membership of the Assembly.

(8) When the Assembly is dissolved, the Speaker shall continue in his office till the person elected to fill the office by the next Assembly enters upon his office.

30. [Voting in Assembly and quorum.] (1) Subject to this Act,-

(a) a decision in the Assembly shall be taken by a majority of the votes of the members present and voting but the Speaker or the person presiding in his absence shall not vote except when there is an equality of votes in which case he shall exercise his casting vote;

(b) the Assembly may act notwithstanding any vacancy in its membership; and

(c) any proceedings in the Assembly shall not be invalid on the ground that some person who was not entitled to do so sat, voted or otherwise took part in the proceedings.

(2) If at any time during a meeting of the Assembly the attention of the person presiding at the meeting is drawn to the fact that less than [fourteen] members are present, it shall be the duty of the person presiding either to adjourn the meeting or to suspend the meeting until [fourteen] members are present.

30 A. Restriction on discussion in Assembly, etc.- No discussion shall take place in the Assembly or the council or the joint sitting with respect to the conduct of any Judge of the Supreme court of Azad Jammu and Kashmir or the High Court in the discharge of his duties.

30 B. Finance Committee.- (1) The expenditure of the Assembly within authorised appropriation shall be controlled by the Assembly acting on the advice of the Finance committee.

(2) The Finance Committee shall consist of the Speaker, the Finance Minister and such other members as may be elected thereto by the Assembly.

(3) The Finance Committee may make rules for regulating its procedure.

30 C. Secretariat of Assembly. (1) The Assembly shall have a separate Secretariat.

(2) The Assembly may by laws regulate the recruitment and conditions of service of persons appointed to the secretarial staff of the Assembly.

(3) Until provision is made by the Assembly under sub-section (2), the persons appointed to the Secretarial staff of the Assembly shall continue to be governed by the conditions of service for the time being applicable to them.

31. Legislative Powers.- (1) Subject to the succeeding provisions of this section, both the Council and the Assembly shall have the power to make laws -

(a) for the territories of Azad Jammu and Kashmir.

(b) for all State subjects wherever they may be; and for all officers of the Council or as the case may be, the Government, wherever they may be.

(2) Subject to sub-section (3).-

(a) The Council shall have exclusive power to make laws with respect to any matter in the Council Legislative List set out in the Third Schedule, hereinafter referred to as the Council Legislative list; and

(b) the Assembly shall, and the Council shall not, have power to make laws with respect to any matter not enumerated in the Council Legislative list.

(3) Neither the Council nor the Assembly shall have the power to make any law concerning.-

(a) the responsibilities of the Government of Pakistan under the UNCIP Resolutions;

(b) the defence and security of Azad Jammu and Kashmir;

(c) the current coin or the issue of any bills, notes or other paper currency; or

(d) the external affairs of Azad Jammu and Kashmir including foreign trade and foreign aid.

(4) No law shall be levied for the purposes of the territories of Azad Jammu and Kashmir except by or under the authority of an Act of the Council or the Assembly.

(5) No law shall be repugnant to the teaching and requirements of Islam as set out in the Holy Quran and Sunnah and all existing laws shall be brought in conformity with the Holy Quran and Sunnah.

32. Reference to Council of Islamic ideology.- (1) If one-third of the total number of members of the Assembly [or, as the case may be, the Council] so requires, the Assembly [or as the case may be the Council] shall refer to the Council of Islamic ideology constituted under the Constitution of the Islamic Republic of Pakistan (hereinafter referred to the Islamic Council) for advice on any question as to whether a proposed law is or is not repugnant to the Injunctions of Islam.

(2) When a question is referred by the Assembly [or, as the case may be, the Council] to the Islamic Council, the Islamic

Council shall, within fifteen days thereof, inform the Assembly [or, as the case may be, the Council] of the period within which the Council expects to be able to furnish that advice.

(3) Where the Assembly [or, as the case may be, the council] considers that, in the public interest, the making of the proposed law in relation to which the question arose should not be postponed until the advice of the Islamic Council is furnished, the law may be made before the advice is furnished:

Provided that, where a law is referred for advice to the Islamic Council and the Council advises that the law is repugnant to the Injunctions of Islam, the Assembly [or, as the case may be, the Council] shall reconsider the law so made.

33. Amendment of this Act. [(1) The provisions of this Act maybe amended in accordance with the following provisions:

Provided that no amendment shall be made in section 31, this section or section 56 save with the prior approval of the Government of Pakistan.]

(2) A bill to amend this Act may originate either in the Council or in the Assembly.

(3) Within ‘fourteen days of the day on which a Bill to amend this Act is introduced in the Council or the Assembly, the President shall summon a joint [sitting and if the Bill is passed in the joint sitting,] with or without amendment, by the votes of the majority [of the total membership of the joint sitting,] the Bill shall be presented to the President for assent.

33-A. [Procedure at joint sitting- (1) The President may, after consultation with the Chairman of the Council and the Speaker make rules as to the procedure with respect to the joint sittings.

(2) At a joint sitting, the Speaker or, in his absence, such person as may be determined by the rules made under sub-section (1) preside.

(3) The President may address a joint sitting and send message in a joint sitting.

(4) The Advocate-General shall have the right to speak in, and otherwise take part in the proceedings of, a joint sitting

or any of its committees, but shall not by virtue of this section have the right to vote.]

34. General provisions regarding Council, etc.- (1) The validity of any proceedings in the Council, the Assembly or a joint sitting shall not be questioned in any court

(2) An officer or member or an authority in whom powers are vested for the regulation of proceedings, conduct of business, maintain order in the Council, the Assembly, or a joint sitting shall not, in relation to the exercise by him of any of those powers, be subject to the jurisdiction of any court.

(3) A member of, or a person entitled to speak in, the Council, the Assembly or a joint sitting shall not be liable to any proceedings in any court in respect of anything said by him or any vote given by him in the Council, the Assembly or a joint sitting or in any Committee there of.

(4) A person shall not be liable to any proceedings in any court in respect of publication by or under the authority of the Council, the Assembly or a joint sitting of any report, paper, vote or proceedings.

(5) No process issued by a court or other authority shall except with the leave of the Chairman of the Council or the Speaker be served or executed within the precincts of the place where a meeting of the Council or, as the case may be, the Assembly is being held.

(6) Subject to this section, the privileges of the Council, the Assembly, the Committees and members of the Council or the Assembly and of the persons entitled to speak in the Council or the Assembly may be determined by law.

35. Authentication of Bills passed by the Council- A Bill passed by the Council shall not require the assent of the President and shall, upon its authentication by the Chairman of the Council, become law and be called an Act of the Council.

36. President's assent to Bills.- (1) Subject to this Act, when a Bill has been passed by the Assembly or a joint sitting it shall be presented to the President for assent.

(2) The President shall assent to a Bill within seven days after it has been presented to him for assent under sub-section (1) or under section 33; and if the President fails to do so he shall be deemed to have assented to the Bill at the expiration of the said period.

(3) When the President has assented or is deemed to have assented to a Bill, it shall become law and be called.-

(a) in the case of Bill to amend this Act, an Act of Azad Jammu and Kashmir; and

(b) in the case of a Bill with respect to any other matter, an Act of the Assembly.

37. Council Consolidated Fund.- (1) All revenues received by the Council, all loans raised by the Council and all moneys received by it in repayment of any loan shall form part of a consolidated fund, to be known as the Council consolidated Fund.

[(2) All other moneys-

(a) received by or on behalf of the Council; or

(b) received by or deposited with the Supreme Court of Azad Jammu and Kashmir or any other court established under the authority of the Council shall be credited to the Public Account of the Council;

(2-A) The custody of the Council Consolidated Fund, the Payment of moneys into that Fund, the withdrawal of money therefrom, the custody of other moneys received by or on behalf of the Council their payment into, and withdrawal from, the Public Account of the Council, and all matters connected with or ancillary to the matters aforesaid, shall be regulated by Act of the Council or, until provision in that behalf is so made, by rules made by the Chairman of the Council.]

(3) The Council shall, in respect of every financial year, cause to be prepared, and approve, a statement of the estimated receipts and expenditure of the Council for that year.

(4) The Chairman of the Council shall authenticate by his signature the statement approved by the Council under sub-section (3); and no expenditure from the Council Consolidated Fund shall be deemed to be duly authorised unless it is specified in the statement so authenticated.

[(5) If in respect of any financial year it is found-

(a) that the amount authorised to be expended for a particular service for the current financial year is insufficient, or that a need has arisen for expenditure upon some new service not included in the statement referred to in sub-section (3) for that year; or

(b) that any money has been spent on any service during a financial year in excess of the amount granted for that service for that year;

the Chairman of the Council shall have power to authorise, expenditure Consolidated Fund and shall cause to be laid before the Council a supplementary statement or, as the case may be, an excess statement, setting out the amount of that expenditure; and the provisions of sub-sections (3) and (4) shall apply to those statements as they apply to the statement referred to in sub-section (3).

(6) Notwithstanding anything contained, in the foregoing provisions of this section, the Council shall have power to make any grant in advance in respect of the estimated expenditure for a part of any financial year, not exceeding four months, pending completion of the procedure prescribed in sub-section (3) and (4).]

[37-A. Azad Jammu and Kashmir Consolidated Fund- (1) All revenue received by Government, all loans raised by the Government, and all moneys received by it in repayment of any loan, shall form part of a consolidated fund, to be known as the Azad Jammu and Kashmir Consolidated Fund.

(2) All other moneys-

(a) received by or on behalf of the Government; or

(b) received by or deposited with the High Court or any other court established under the authority of the Government;

shall be credited to the Public Account of the Government

(3) The custody of the Azad Jammu and Kashmir Consolidated Fund, the payment of moneys into that Fund, the withdrawal of moneys therefrom, the custody of other moneys received by or on behalf of the Government, their payment into,

and withdrawal from the Public Account of the Government, and all matters connected with or ancillary to the matters aforesaid, shall be regulated by Act of the Assembly or, until provision in that behalf is so made, by rules made by the President.]

38. (1) The [Government] shall, in respect of every financial year, cause to be laid before the Assembly a statement of the estimated receipts and expenditure for that year, to be called the Annual Budget.

(2) The Annual Budget shall be submitted to the Assembly in the form of demands for and the Assembly shall have power to assent to, or to refuse to assent to any demand, or to assent to any demand subject to a reduction of the amount specified therein:

Provided that, for a period of ten years from the commencement of this Act or the holding of the second general election to the Assembly after such commencement, whichever occurs later, a demand shall be deemed to have been assented to without any reduction of the amount specified therein, unless, by the votes of a majority of the total membership of the Assembly it is refused or assented to subject to a reduction of the amount specified therein.

(3) No demand for a grant shall be made except on the recommendation of the [Government] -

(4) The Annul Budget as passed by the Assembly shall be placed before the President who shall authenticate it by his signature.

[(5) If in respect of any financial year it is found -

(a) that the amount authorised to be expended for a particular service for the current financial year is insufficient, or that need has arisen for expenditure upon some new service not included in the Annual Budget for that year; or

(b) that any money has been spent on any service during a financial year .in excess of the amount granted for that service for that year; the Government shall have power to authorise expenditure from the Azad Jammu and Kashmir Consolidated Fund and shall cause to be laid before the Assembly a Supplementary Budget or, as the case may be, an Excess Budget, setting the amount of that expenditure, and the provisions of this section shall apply to those budgets as they apply to the Annual Budget.

(6) Notwithstanding anything, contained in the foregoing provisions of this section, the Assembly shall have power to make any grant in advance in respect of the estimated expenditure for a part of any financial year, not exceeding four months, pending completion of the procedure prescribed in sub-section (2) for the voting of such grant and the authentication of the Budget as passed by the Assembly in accordance with the provisions of sub-section (4) in relation to the expenditure.]

39. [Special provisions regarding Budget, etc.-] (1) Where the Annual Budget for any financial year cannot be passed by the Assembly by reason of its having been earlier dissolved, the [Prime Minister] shall cause to be prepared an Annual Budget for that year and by his signature, authenticate the Budget.

(2) The Annual Budget for any financial year authenticated by the [Prime Minister] under sub-section (1) shall, for the purpose of this Act, be deemed to have been passed by the Assembly.

40. Restriction on expenditure.- No expenditure shall be incurred by the Government except as authorised by the Annual or Supplementary Budget as passed or deemed to have been passed by the Assembly.

41. Power to make Ordinance.- (1) The President may, except when the Assembly is in session, if satisfied that circumstances exist which render it necessary to take immediate action, make and promulgate an Ordinance as the circumstances may require.

(2) An Ordinance promulgated under this section shall have the same force and effect as an Act of the Assembly and shall be subject to like restrictions as the power of the Assembly to make law, but every such Ordinance -

(a) shall be laid before the Assembly and shall stand repealed at the expiration of four months from its promulgation or, if before the expiration of that period a resolution disapproving it is passed by the Assembly, upon the passing of that resolution; and

(b) may be withdrawn at any time by the President.

(3) Without prejudice to the provisions of sub-section (2), an Ordinance laid before the Assembly shall be deemed to be a Bill introduced in the Assembly.

(4) The President [shall] likewise, except when the Council is in session, if so advised by the Chairman of the Council make, [promulgate and withdraw] an Ordinance as the circumstances may require; and the provisions of sub-section (2) and sub-section (3) shall apply to an Ordinance so made as if references therein to 'Act of the Assembly' and 'Assembly' were references respectively to 'Act of the Council' and 'Council'.

[42. Supreme Court of Azad Jammu and Kashmir.- (1) There shall be constituted a Supreme Court of Azad Jammu and Kashmir to be the highest Court of appeal.

(2) Subject to the provisions of this Act, the Supreme Court of Azad Jammu and Kashmir shall have such jurisdiction as is or may be conferred on it by this Act or by or under any law.]

[(3) The Supreme Court shall consist of a Chief Justice, to be known as Chief Justice of Azad Jammu and Kashmir, and one other Judge.]

(4) The Chief Justice of Azad Jammu and Kashmir shall be appointed by the President on the advice of the Council and each of the other Judges of the Supreme Court Azad Jammu and Kashmir shall be appointed by the President on the advice of the Council after consultation with the said Chief Justice.

(5) A person shall not be appointed a judge of the Supreme Court of Azad Jammu and Kashmir unless he has -

(a) for a period of, or for periods aggregating, not less than five years been a Judge of a High Court ; or

(b) for a period of, or for periods aggregating, not less than fifteen years, been an advocate or pleader of a High Court.

Explanation.- In this sub-section, 'High Court' includes —

(a) the High Court of Azad Jammu and Kashmir and a High Court or an equivalent Court that existed in Azad Jammu and Kashmir before the fourteenth day of August, 1947, and

(b) a High Court in Pakistan, including a High Court that existed in Pakistan at any time before the fourteenth day of August, 1973.

(6) Before entering upon office, the Chief Justice of Azad Jammu and Kashmir shall make before the President and any other Judge of the Supreme Court of Azad Jammu and Kashmir shall make before the Chief Justice, oath in the form set out in the First Schedule.

(7) A Judge of the Supreme Court of Azad Jammu and Kashmir shall hold office until he attains the age of sixty-five years, unless he sooner resigns or is removed from office in accordance with law.

(8) At any time when the office of Chief Justice of Azad Jammu and Kashmir is vacant, or the Chief Justice, is absent or unable to perform the functions of his office due to any other cause, the President shall appoint the most senior of the other Judges of the Supreme Court of Azad Jammu and Kashmir to act as Chief Justice of Azad Jammu and Kashmir.

[(8-A) If at any time it is not possible for want of quorum of Judges of the Supreme Court to hold or continue any sitting of the Court, or for any other reason it is necessary to increase temporarily the number of Judges of the Supreme Court, the Chief Justice of Azad Jammu and Kashmir may, in writing,-

(a) with the approval of the President, request a person who has held the office of a Judge of that Court, the Supreme Court of Pakistan or the Judicial Board or has held the office of Judge of the High Court for a minimum period of three years and since whose ceasing to hold that office three years have not elapsed; or

(b) with the approval of the President and except in the case of Chief Justice, with the consent of the Chief Justice of

High Court, require a Judge of that Court who has held office as such judge for a minimum period of three years; or

(c) with the approval of the President, request any person qualified for appointment as Judge of the Supreme Court, to attend sittings of the Supreme Court as an adhoc Judge for such period as may be necessary and while so attending an adhoc Judge shall have the same power and jurisdiction as a Judge of the Supreme Court.]

(9) The remuneration and other terms and conditions of service of a Judge of the Supreme Court of Azad Jammu and Kashmir shall be as provided in the Fourth Schedule.

(10) Subject to the succeeding provisions of this section, the Supreme Court of Azad Jammu and Kashmir shall have jurisdiction to hear and determine appeals from judgments, decrees, final orders or sentences of the High Court of Azad Jammu and Kashmir.

(11) An appeal shall lie to the Supreme Court of Azad Jammu and Kashmir from any judgment, decree, final order or sentence of the High Court of Azad Jammu and Kashmir.-

(a) if the High Court has on appeal reversed an order of acquittal of an accused person and sentenced him to death or to imprisonment for life; or, on revision, has enhanced a sentence to a sentence as aforesaid; or

(b) if the High Court has withdrawn for trial before itself any case from any court subordinate to it and has in such trial convicted the accused person and sentenced him as aforesaid; or

(c) if the High Court has imposed any punishment on any person for contempt of the High Court; or

(d) if the amount or value of the subject-matter of the dispute in the court of first instance was, and also in dispute in appeal is, not less. than fifty thousand rupees or such other sum as may be specified in that behalf by Act of the Council and the judgment, decree or final order appealed from has varied or set aside the judgment, decree or final order of the court immediately below; or

(e) if the judgment, decree or final order involves directly or indirectly some claim or question respecting property of the like amount or value and the judgment, decree or final order appealed from has varied or set aside the judgment, decree or final order of the court immediately below; or

(f) if the High Court certifies that the case involves a substantial question of law as to the interpretation of this Act.

(12) An appeal to the Supreme Court of Azad Jammu and Kashmir from a judgment, decree, order or sentence of the High Court in a case to which subsection (11) does not apply shall lie only if the Supreme Court of Azad Jammu and Kashmir grants leave to appeal.

[(13) If there is a difference of opinion between the two Judges of the Supreme Court, the judgment, decree, order or sentence of the High Court appealed from shall be deemed to be the judgment, decree order or sentence, as the case may be, of the Supreme Court:

Provided that if such difference of opinion is only in respect of the nature, quantum or extent of the relief, liability, penalty or punishment to be granted or imposed, the decision of the Supreme Court shall be expressed in terms of opinion of the senior of the two Judges.

(14) The person holding office as Chief Justice of the State of Azad Jammu and Kashmir immediately before the commencement of the Azad Jammu and Kashmir Interim Constitution (First Amendment) Act, 1975, shall as from such commencement hold office as Chief Justice of Supreme Court under this Act on the same terms and conditions of service as were applicable to him immediately before such commencement.

(15) All legal proceedings pending in the judicial Board, immediately before the commencement of the Azad Jammu and Kashmir Interim Constitution (first Amendment) Act, 1975, shall, on such commencement, stand transferred to, and be deemed to be pending before the Supreme Court for

determination and any judgment or order of the Judicial Board delivered or made before such commencement shall have the same force and effect as if it had been delivered or made by the Supreme Court.]

42-A. Issue and execution of processes of Supreme Court.- (1) The Supreme Court shall have powers to issue such directions, orders or decrees as may be necessary for doing complete justice in any case or matter pending before it including an order for the purpose of securing the attendance of any person or the discovery or production of any document.

(2) Any such direction, order or decree shall be enforceable throughout Azad Jammu and Kashmir as if it has been issued by the High Court.

(3) All executive and judicial authorities throughout Azad Jammu and Kashmir shall act in aid of the Supreme Court.

(4) Subject to this Act and law, the Supreme Court may, in consultation with the Council, make rule regulating the practice and procedure of the Court:

Provided that till the new rules are framed the rules framed by the Judicial Board shall, so far as they are not inconsistent with this Act and any other law, be deemed to have been made by the Supreme Court until altered or amended and references to the Judicial Board in these rules shall be construed to be references to the Supreme Court.

42-B. Decisions of Supreme Court binding on other Courts.- Any decision of the Supreme Court shall, to the extent that it decides a question of law or is based upon or enunciates a principle of law, be binding on all other Courts in Azad Jammu and Kashmir.

43. High Court.- (1) There shall be a High Court for Azad Jammu and Kashmir, hereinafter called the High Court, which shall consist of a Chief Justice and such number of other Judges as may be prescribed by an Act of the Assembly.

(2) The person holding office as Chief Justice or other Judge of the High Court immediately before the commencement of this Act shall be deemed to be the Chief Justice or other Judge as the case may be appointed under this Act.

(2-A) A Judge of the High Court shall be appointed by the President on the advice of the Council and after consultation -

(a) with the Chief Justice of Azad Jammu and Kashmir ; and

(b) except where the appointment is that of Chief Justice, with the Chief Justice of the High Court.

(3) (A person shall not be appointed) as a Judge of the High Court or Advocate-General unless —

(a) he has for a period, or for periods aggregating, not less than ten years, been an Advocate of Pleader of the High Court of Azad Jammu and Kashmir or a High Court in Pakistan;

Provided that the term 'High Court' herein shall include a High Court or an equivalent Court that existed at any time before the 14th day of August, 1947;or -

(b) he has for a period of not less than ten years held a Judicial Office out of which not less than three years shall have been as District and Sessions Judge.

(4) Before he enters upon his office, the Chief Justice of the High Court shall make before the President, and an other Judge of the High Court shall make before the Chief Justice, an oath in the form set out in the First Schedule.

(5) The Chief Justice or a Judge of the High Court shall hold office until he attains the age of sixty-two years unless he sooner resigns or is removed from office in accordance with Law:

Provided that the President may appoint a Retired Judge of any High Court of Pakistan to be the Chief Justice or a Judge of the High Court for a period not exceeding three years and such person shall hold office till he attains the age of sixty-five years.

(6) If at any time any Judge of the High Court is absent or is unable to perform his functions due to illness or some other cause, the President may appoint a person qualified for appointment as a Judge of the High Court to be an Additional Judge of the High Court for the period for which the Judge is absent or unable to perform his functions.

(7) A Judge of the High Court shall not-

(a) hold any other office of profit in the service of Azad Jammu and Kashmir if his remuneration is thereby increased; or

(b) occupy any other position carrying the right to remuneration for the rendering of services, but this sub-section shall not be construed as preventing a Judge from holding or managing private property.

(8) A person who has held office as a Judge of the High Court shall not hold office of profit in the service of Azad Jammu and Kashmir, not being a Judicial or quasi-judicial office or the office of Chief Election Commissioner or of Chairman or member of the Public Service Commission, before the expiration of two years after he ceased to hold that office.

(9) The remuneration and other terms and conditions of Service of Judge of High Court shall be as provided in the [Fifth Schedule.]

44. Jurisdiction of High Court.- (1) The High Court shall have such jurisdiction as is conferred on it by this Act or by any other law.

(2) Subject to this Act, the High Court may if it is satisfied that no other adequate remedy is provided by law -

(a) on the application of any aggrieved party, make an order -

(i) directing a person performing functions in connection with the affairs of Azad Jammu and Kashmir or a local authority to refrain from doing that which he is not permitted by law to do, or to do that which he is required by law to do; or

(ii) declaring that any act done or proceedings taken by a person performing functions in connection with the affairs of the State or a local authority has been done or taken without lawful authority, and is of no legal effect; or

(b) on the application of any person, make an order, -

(i) directing that a person in custody in Azad Jammu and Kashmir be brought before the High Court so that the Court may satisfy itself that he is not being held in custody without lawful authority or in an unlawful manner; or

(ii) requiring a person holding or purporting to hold a public office [in connection with the affairs of Azad Jammu and Kashmir to show under what authority of law he claims to hold that office;] or

(c) on the application of any aggrieved person, make an order giving such directions to the person or authority, including the Council and the Government, exercising any power or performing any function in, or in relation to, Azad Jammu and Kashmir as may be appropriate for the enforcement of any of the fundamental rights conferred by this Act.

(3) An order shall not be made under sub-section (2) of this section on application made by or in relation to a person in the Defence Services in respect of his terms and conditions of service, in respect of any matter rising out of his service or in respect of any action in relation to him as a member of the Defence Services.

(4) Where-

(a) application is made to the High Court for an order under clause (a) or clause (c) of sub-section (2); and

(b) The court has reason to believe that the making of an interim order would have the effect of prejudicing or interfering with the carrying out of a public work or otherwise being harmful to the public interest, the Court shall not make an interim order unless the Advocate General has been given notice of the application and the Court, after the Advocate-General or any officer authorised by him in this behalf has been given an opportunity of being heard, is satisfied that the making of the interim order would not have the effect referred to in clause (b) of this sub-section.

(5) In this section, unless the context otherwise requires, 'Person' includes any body politic or corporate, any authority of or under control of the Council or the Government and any court or tribunal other than the [Supreme Court of Azad Jammu and Kashmir,] the High Court or a Court or Tribunal established under a law relating to the Defence Services.

44-A. Rules of Procedure.- Subject to this Act and law, the High Court may in consultation with the Government, make rules regulating the practice and procedure of the Courts subordinate to it.

44-B. Decision of High Court binding on subordinate Courts.- Subject to section 42-B, any decision of the High Court shall to the extent that it decides a question of law or is based upon or enunciates a principle of law, be binding on all courts subordinate to it.

45. Contempt of Court.- (1) In this section 'Court' means the [Supreme Court of Azad Jammu and Kashmir] or the High Court.

(2) A Court shall have power to punish any person who-

(a) abuses, interferes with or obstructs the process of the Court in any way or disobeys any order of the Court.

(b) scandalizes the court or otherwise does anything which tends to bring the Court or a Judge of the Court into hatred, ridicule or contempt;

(c) does anything which tends to prejudice the determination of a matter pending before the Court; or

(d) does any other thing which, by law, constitutes contempt of the Court..

(3) The exercise of the power conferred on a Court by this section may be regulated by law and, subject to law by rules made by the Court.

46. High Court to superintend and control all Courts subordinate to it, etc.- (1) The High Court shall superintend and control all other courts that are subordinate to it.

(2) There shall, in addition to the [Supreme Court of Azad Jammu and Kashmir] and the High Court, be such other Courts as are established by law.

(3) A Court so established shall have such jurisdiction as conferred on it by law.

(4) No Court shall have any jurisdiction which is not conferred on it by this Act or by or under any other law.

[46-A. Advisory Jurisdiction.- (1) If, at any time, the Chairman of the Council or the President desires to obtain the opinion of the Supreme Court of Azad Jammu and Kashmir on any question of law which he considers of public importance, he may refer the question to the Supreme Court of Azad Jammu and Kashmir for consideration.

(2) The Supreme Court of Azad Jammu and Kashmir shall consider a question so referred and report its opinion on the question to the Chairman of the Council or, as the case may be, the President.]

47. Administrative Courts and Tribunals.- (1) Notwithstanding anything herein- before contained, the [Council in respect of matters to which its executive authority extends, and the Assembly in respect of matters to which the executive authority of the Government extends,] may by Act provide for the establishment of one or more Administrative Courts or Tribunals to exercise exclusive jurisdiction in respect of-

(a) Matters relating to the terms and conditions of persons who are or have been in the service of [Azad Jammu and Kashmir] including disciplinary matters;

(b) matters relating to claims arising from tortious acts of [the Council or the] Government or any person in the service of Azad Jammu and Kashmir]or of any local or other authority empowered by law to levy any tax or cess and any servant of such authority acting in the discharge of his duties such servant; or

(c) matters relating to acquisition, administration and disposal of any property which is deemed to be enemy property under any law.

(2) Notwithstanding anything hereinbefore contained, where any Administrative Court or Tribunal is established under sub-section (1), no other Court shall grant an injunction, make any order or entertain any proceeding in respect of any matter, to which the jurisdiction of such Administrative Court or Tribunal extends and all proceedings in respect of any such matter which may be pending before such other court immediately before the establishment of the Administrative Court or Tribunal shall abate on Such establishment..

3) An appeal to the [Supreme Court of Azad Jammu and Kashmir] from a judgment, decree, order or sentence of an Administrative Court or Tribunal shall lie only if the [Supreme Court of Azad Jammu and Kashmir] being satisfied, that the case involves a substantial question of law of public importance, grants leave to appeal.

48. Public Service Commission- (1) There shall be a Public Service Commission for Azad Jammu and Kashmir which shall consist of such number of members, including a Chairman, and perform such function as may be prescribed.

(2) The Public Service Commission existing immediately before the commencement of this Act and the persons holding office as Chairman and other members of that Commission immediately before such commencement shall be deemed to have been constituted and appointed under this Act

49. The Services.- (1) Subject to this Act, the appointment of persons to, and the terms and conditions of service of persons in, the service of Azad Jammu and Kashmir may be regulated by law.

[(2) Until an Act of the Council in respect of persons in the service of Azad Jammu and Kashmir employed in connection with the affairs of the Council, or an Act of the Assembly in respect of such persons employed in connection with the affairs of the Government, makes provision for the matters referred to in sub-section (1), all rules and orders in force immediately before the commencement of this Act, shall continue in force and may be, amended from time to time by the Council or, as the case may be, the Government.]

50. Chief Election Commissioner.- (1) There shall be a Chief Election Commissioner appointed by the President [on the advice of the Council] on such terms and be prescribed.

(2) The person appointed as Chief Election Commissioner under the Azad Jammu and Kashmir Government Act, 1970, or deemed to have been so appointed and functioning as such immediately before the commencement of this Act shall be deemed to have been appointed as Chief Election Commissioner

under sub-section (1) on the same terms and conditions of service as are applicable to him immediately before such commencement.

[50-A. Auditor General. - (1) There shall be an Auditor General of Azad Jammu and Kashmir who shall be appointed by the President on the advice of the Council

(2) Before entering upon office, the Auditor-General shall make before the Chief Justice of Azad Jammu and Kashmir oath in the form set out in the First Schedule.

(3) The terms and conditions of service, including the terms of office, of the Auditor-General shall be determined by Act of the Council and, until so determined, by rules made by the Council.

(4) The Auditor-General shall, in relation to -

(a) the accounts of the Council and any authority or body established by the Council; and

(b) the accounts of the Government and any authority or body established by the Government; perform such functions and exercise such powers as may be determined by or under Act of the Council and, until so determined, by rules made by the Council.

(5) The accounts of the Council and of the Government shall be kept in such form and in accordance with such principles and methods as may be determined by the Auditor-General with the approval of the Council.

(6) The reports of the Auditor-General relating to the accounts of the Council shall be submitted to the Chairman of the Council, who shall cause them to be laid before the Council; and the reports of the Auditor-General relating to the accounts of the Government shall be submitted to the President, who shall cause them to be laid before the Assembly.]

51. Continuance of existing laws.- Subject to the provisions of this Act, all laws which, immediately before the commencement of this Act, were in force in Azad Jammu and Kashmir shall continue in force until altered, repealed or amended by an Act of the appropriate authority.

[Explanation.- In this section, -

(a) 'laws' includes Ordinances, orders, rules, bye-laws, regulations and any notifications and other legal instruments having the force of law; and

(b) 'in force', in relation to any law, means having effect as whether or not the law has been brought into operation.]

52. General provisions regarding President and Ministers.- (1) [The President, the Prime Minister, a Minister or An Advisor shall not -

(a) hold any other office of profit in the service of Azad Jammu and Kashmir or any other country.

(b) occupy any other position carrying the right to remuneration for the rendering of service; but this action shall not be construed as preventing the President, [the Prime Minister, a Minister or an Advisor] from holding or managing his private property.

(2) No criminal proceedings whatsoever shall be instituted or continued against the President [or the Chairman of the Council] while he is in office.

(3) No civil proceedings in which relief is claimed against the President [or the Chairman of the Council] shall be instituted while he is in office in respect of anything done or not done, or purporting to have been done or not done, by him in his personal capacity, whether before or after he enters upon his office unless at least sixty days before the proceedings are instituted, notice in writing has been delivered to him, or sent to him, stating the nature of the proceeding, the cause of the action, the name, description and place of residence of the party by whom the proceedings are to be instituted and the relief which he claims.

(4) Except in relation to proceedings referred to in sub-section (3), no process whatsoever shall be issued from any Court, or Tribunal against the President [or the Chairman of the Council,] whether in a personal capacity or otherwise, while he is in office.

(5) Subject to this Act, [the President, the Prime Minister, the Chairman of the Council, the Federal Minister who is a

member of the Council,] a Minister or an Advisor shall not except in respect of anything done or not done by him in contravention of law, be answerable to any Court or Tribunal for the exercise of the powers, or the performance of the duties, of his office or for any act done or purporting to be done by him in the exercise of those powers or in the performance of those duties:

Provided that nothing in this sub-section shall be construed as restricting the right of any person to bring appropriate proceedings against the [Council or] as the case may be, the Government.

[52-A. Power to acquire property and to make contracts, etc.- (1) The executive authority of the Government and of the Council shall extend, subject to any Act of the appropriate authority to the grant, sale, disposition or mortgage of any property vested in, and to the purchase or acquisition of property on behalf of, the Government or, as the case may be, the Council, and to the making of contracts.

(2) All property acquired for the purposes of the Government or of the Council shall vest in the President or, as the case may be, in the Council.

(3) All contracts made in the exercise of the executive authority of the Government or of the Council shall be expressed to be made in the name of the President or, as the case may be, the Council and all such contracts and all assurances of property made in the exercise of that authority shall be executed on behalf of the President or the Council by such persons and in such manner as the President or, as the case may be, the Council may direct or authorise.

(4) Neither the President, nor the Chairman of the Council, shall be personally liable in respect of any contract or assurance made or executed in the exercise of the executive authority of the Government or, as the case may be, the Council, nor shall any person making or executing any such contract or assurance on behalf of any of them be personally liable in respect thereof.

(5) Transfer of land by the Government or the Council shall be regulated by law.]

53. Power to issue Proclamation.- (1) [The President, if so advised by the chairman of the Council that a grave emergency exists in which the security of Azad Jammu and Kashmir is threatened by war or external aggression or by internal disturbances, the President [shall] issue a proclamation of Emergency, hereinafter referred to as the Proclamation.

(2) A Proclamation shall be laid before a joint sitting which shall be summoned by the President to meet within thirty days of the Proclamation being issued and-

(a) shall cease to be in force at the expiration, of two months unless before the expiration of that period it has been approved by a resolution of the joint sitting; and

(b) shall, subject to the provisions of clause (a), cease to be in force upon a resolution disapproving the resolution being passed by the votes of the majority of the total membership of the joint sitting.

(2-A) Notwithstanding anything contained in sub-section (2), if the Assembly stands dissolved at the time when the Proclamation is issued, the Proclamation shall continue in force for a period of four months but, if a general election to the Assembly is not held before the expiration of that period, it shall cease to be in force at the expiration of that period unless it has earlier been approved by a resolution of the Council.]

(3) A Proclamation may be made before the actual occurrence of war or external aggression if the President is satisfied that there is imminent danger thereof.

53-A. [Deleted].

54. Power to suspend fundamental rights.- (1) While a Proclamation is in operation, the President may, by order, declare that right to move any Court for the enforcement of such of the rights conferred by section 4 as may be specified in the order, and all proceedings pending in any Court for the enforcement of the rights so specified, shall remain suspended for the period during which the Proclamation is in force.

(2) Every order made under sub-section (1), shall, as soon as may be, laid before the Assembly.

55. Power to vary or rescind Proclamation.- (1) A Proclamation issued under section 53 may be varied or revoked by a subsequent proclamation.

(2) The validity of any Proclamation issued or order made under section 53 or section 54 shall not be questioned in any Court.

56. Act not to derogate from responsibilities of Pakistan.- Nothing in this Act shall derogate from the responsibilities of the Government of Pakistan in relation to the [matters specified in sub-section (3) of section 31] or prevent the Government of Pakistan from taking such actions as it may consider necessary or expedient for the effective discharge of those responsibilities.

[56-A. **Failure to comply with requirement as to time does not render an act invalid.**- When any act or thing is required by this Act to be done within a particular period and it is not done within that period, the doing of the act or thing shall not be invalid or otherwise ineffective by reason only that it was not done within that period.

56-B. **Oath of Office.**- (1) An oath required to be made by a person under this Act shall be made in a language that is understood by that person.

(2) Where, under this Act, an oath is required to be made before a specified person and for any reason, it is impracticable for the oath to be made before that person, it may be made before such other person as may be nominated by that person.

(3) Where, under this Act, a person is required to make an oath before he enters upon an office, he shall be deemed to have entered upon the office on the day on which he makes the oath.

56-C. **Effect of repeal of laws.**- Where a law is repealed, or is deemed to have been repealed, by under, or by virtue of this Act, the repeal shall not, except as otherwise provided in this Act,-

(a) revive anything not in force or existing at the time at which the repeal takes effect;

(b) affect the previous operation of the law or anything duly done or suffered under the law;

(c) affect any right, privilege, obligation or liability acquired, accrued or incurred under the law;

(d) affect any penalty, forfeiture or punishment incurred in respect of any offence committed against the law; or

(e) affect any investigation, legal proceeding or remedy in respect of any such right, privilege, obligation, liability, penalty, forfeiture or punishment; and any such (investigation, legal proceedings or remedy may be instituted, continued or enforced, and any such penalty, forfeiture or punishment may be imposed, as if the law had not been repealed.]

57. Act to override other laws, etc.- (1) The provisions of this Act shall over-ride and have effect notwithstanding the provisions of any law for the time being in force.

No Court, including the [Supreme Court of Azad Jammu and Kashmir and] the High Court, shall call into question or permit to be called into question, the validity of this Act [or an Act to amend it.]

58. Power to make rules.- The President may make rules for carrying out the purposes of this Act.

59. Repeal and savings.- (1) The Azad Jammu and Kashmir Government Act, 1970, hereinafter referred to as the said Act, together with the Acts amending it, and the rules made thereunder are hereby repealed.

THE FIRST SCHEDULE
OATH OF OFFICE
PRESIDENT

(See Section 5 (6))

I,............. do solemnly swear that I am a Muslim and believe in the Unity and Oneness of Almighty Allah, His angels, the Books of Allah, the Holy Quran being the last of them, his Prophets, the absolute finality of the Prophethood of Mohammad (peace be upon him), the day of Judgment, and all the requirements and teachings of the Holy Quran and Sunnah:

That, as President of Azad Jammu and Kashmir I will remain loyal to the country and to the cause of accession of the State of Jammu and Kashmir to Pakistan.

That I will perform my functions as President honestly and faithfully; and

That I will not directly or indirectly communicate or reveal to any person any official secret which may come to my knowledge as President:

So help me Allah.

PRIME MINISTER
(See Section 13 (4))

I, ... do solemnly swear that I am a Muslim and believe in the Unity and Oneness of Almighty Allah, His angels, the Books of Allah, the Holy Quran being the last of them, His Prophets, the absolute finality of the Prophethood of Mohammad (peace be upon him), the day of Judgment, and all the requirements and teachings of the Holy Quran and Sunnah:

That, I will remain loyal to the country and to the cause of accession of the State of Jammu and Kashmir to Pakistan.

That I will perform my functions as Prime Minster honestly and faithfully; and

That I will not directly or indirectly communicate or reveal to any person any official secret which may come to my knowledge as Prime Minster of Azad Jammu and Kashmir:

So help me Allah.

MINISTER
(See Section 14 (2))

I, ... do hereby solemnly swear in the name of Allah;

That, I will remain loyal to the country and to the cause of accession of the State of Jammu and Kashmir to Pakistan.

That I will perform my functions as Minster honestly and faithfully; and

That I will not directly or indirectly communicate or reveal to any person any official secret which may come to my knowledge as Minster:

So help me Allah.

SPEAKER [OR DEPUTY SPEAKER] OF LEGISLATIVE ASSEMBLY

(See Section 29 (2))

I,............. having been elected as Speaker [or Deputy Speaker] of Azad Jammu and Kashmir Legislative Assembly do hereby solemnly swear in the name of Allah;

That 1 will remain loyal to the country and the cause of accession of the State of Jammu and Kashmir to Pakistan;

That I will perform my functions as Speaker [or Deputy Speaker] of the Legislative Assembly honestly and faithfully; and

That 1 will not directly or indirectly communicate or reveal to any person any official secret which may come to my knowledge as Speaker [or Deputy Speaker] of the Assembly;

So help me Allah.

MEMBER OF' LEGISLATIVE ASSEMBLY OR COUNCIL

(See section 21(6) and 23(1))

I..................... having been elected as Member of the Legislative Assembly (or Council) do hereby solemnly swear in the name of Allah;

That I will remain loyal to the country and the cause of accession of the State of Jammu and Kashmir to Pakistan;

That I will perform my functions as Member of the Legislative Assembly (or Council) honestly and faithfully;

That I will not directly or indirectly communicate or reveal to any person official secret which may come to my knowledge as Member of the Legislative Assembly (or Council);

So help me Allah.

CHIEF JUSTICE OF AZAD JAMMU AND KASHMIR JUDGE OF SUPREME COURT OF AZAD JAMMU AND KASHMIR

(See section 42 (6))

I............. having been appointed Chief Justice Azad Jammu and Kashmir (or Judge of the Supreme Court of Azad

Jammu and Kashmir) do solemnly swear that I owe allegiance to Allah and that I will faithfully perform the duties of my office to the best of my ability, knowledge and judgment and will administer justice according to the law in force in Azad Jammu and Kashmir without fear or favour, affection or ill-will.

OATH OF CHIEF JUSTICE-JUDGE HIGH COURT

(See section 43 (5))

I,............. having been appointed Chief Justice (or Judge) of the High Court of Judicature, Azad Jammu and Kashmir State do, solemnly swear that I owe allegiance to Allah and that I will faithfully perform the duties of my office to the best of my ability, knowledge and judgment and will administer justice according to the law in force in Azad Jammu and Kashmir without fear or favour, affection or ill will.

OATH OF ADVISOR

(See section 21(9))

I,............ do hereby solemnly swear in the name of Allah;

That I will remain loyal to the country and the cause of accession of the State of Jammu and Kashmir to Pakistan;

That I will perform my functions as Advisor honestly and faithfully; and

That I will not directly or indirectly communicate or reveal to any person any official secret which may come to my knowledge as Advisor;

So help me Allah.

AUDITOR-GENERAL

(See section 51(2))

1,................ do hereby solemnly swear in the name of Allah;

That, as Auditor-General of Azad Jammu and Kashmir, I will perform my functions honestly, faithfully, in accordance with the Azad Jammu and Kashmir Interim Constitution Act, 1974, and the law and to the best of my knowledge, ability and judgment, without fear or favour, affection or ill-will.

SECOND SCHEDULE

(See section 24 (2) (d))

1. An office which is not a whole time office remunerated either by salary or by fee.
2. The office of Lamberdar, Inamdar, Sufedposh and Zaildar, whether called by this or any other title.
3. The offices of the Chairman of the Union Council, Union Committee and Town Committee and of the Vice Chairman of the Municipal Committee and the District council.
4. Reserve of the Armed Forces.
5. Any other office which is declared by an Act of the Assembly not to disqualify its holder from being elected as, or from being a member of the Assembly.

THIRD SCHEDULE

(See section 31(2))

COUNCIL LEGISLATIVE LIST

1. Subject to the responsibilities of the Government of Pakistan under the UNCIP Resolutions, nationality, citizenship and naturalisation, migration from or into Azad Jammu and Kashmir, admission into, and emigration and expulsion from, Azad Jammu and Kashmir, including in relation thereto the regulation of the movements in Azad Jammu and Kashmir of persons not domiciled an Azad Jammu and Kashmir.
2. Post and Telegraphs, including Telephones, Wireless Broad-casting and other like forms of communications; Post Office Saving Bank.
3. Public debt of the Council; including the borrowing of money on the security of the Council Consolidated Fund.
4. Council public services and Council Public Service Commission.
5. Council pensions, that is say, pensions payable by the Council or out of the Council Consolidated Fund.
6. Administrative courts for Council subjects.

7. Council agencies and institutions for the following purposes, that is to say, for research, for professional or technical training, or for the promotion of special studies.
8. Nuclear energy, including-
   (a) mineral resources necessary for the generation of nuclear energy;
   (b) the production of nuclear fuels and the generation and use of nuclear energy; and
   (c) ionising radiations.
9. Aircraft and air navigation; the provision of aerodromes; regulation and Organization of air traffic and of aerodromes.
10. Beacons and other provisions for safety of aircraft.
11. Carriage of passengers and goods by air.
12. Copyright, inventions, designs, trade marks and merchandise marks.
13. Opium so far as regards sale for export.
14. Banking, that is to say, the co-ordination with the Government or Pakistan of the conduct of banking business.
15. The law of insurance and the regulation of the conduct of insurance business.
16. Stock-exchange and future markets with objects and business not confined to Azad Jammu and Kashmir.
17. Corporations, that is to say, the incorporation, regulation and winding up of trading corporations including banking, insurance and financial corporations, but not including corporations owned or controlled by Azad Jammu and Kashmir and carrying on business only within Azad Jammu and Kashmir, or, co-operative societies, and of corporations whether trading or not, with objects not confined to Azad Jammu and Kashmir, but not including universities.
18. Planning for economic coordination, including planning and coordination of scientific and technological research.
19. Highways, continuing beyond the territory of Azad Jammu and Kashmir, excluding roads declared by the Government of Pakistan to be of strategic importance.

20. Council surveys including geological surveys and Council meteorological organizations.
21. Works, lands and buildings vested in, or in the possession of, the Council for the purposes of the Council not being Military, naval or air force works but, as regards property situate in Azad Jammu and Kashmir, subject always to law made by the Legislative Assembly, save in so far as law made by the Council otherwise provides.
22. Census.
23. Establishment of standards of weights and measures.
24. Extension of the powers and jurisdiction of members of a police force belonging to Azad Jammu and Kashmir or any province of Pakistan to any area in such Province or Azad Jammu and Kashmir, but so as to enable the police of Azad Jammu and Kashmir or such Province to exercise Powers and jurisdiction in such Province or Azad Jammu and Kashmir without the consent of the Government of that Province or Azad Jammu and Kashmir; extension of the powers jurisdictions of members of a police force belonging the Azad Jammu and Kashmir or a Province of Pakistan to railways outside Azad Jammu and Kashmir or that Province.
25. Election to the Council.
26. The salaries, allowances and privileges of the members of the Council and [Advisors.]
27. Railways.
28. Mineral oil and natural gas; liquids and substances declared by law made by the Council to be dangerously inflammable.
29. Development of industries, where development under Council control is declared by law made by the Council to be expedient in the public interest.
30. Removal of prisoners and accused persons from Azad Jammu and Kashmir to Pakistan or from Pakistan to Azad Jammu and Kashmir.

31. Measures to combat certain offences committed in connection with matters concerning and the Government and the establishment of a police force for that purpose [or the extension to Azad Jammu and Kashmir of the jurisdiction of a police force established in Pakistan for the investigation of offences committed in connection with matters concerning the Government of Pakistan.]
32. Prevention of the extension from Azad Jammu and Kashmir to Pakistan or from Pakistan to Azad Jammu and Kashmir of infectious or contagious diseases or pests affecting men, animals or plants.
33. Population planning and social welfare.
34. Boilers.
35. Electricity.
36. Newspapers, books and printing presses.
37. State Property.
38. Curriculum, syllabus, planning, policy, centres of excellence and standards of education.
39. Sanctioning of cinematograph films for exhibition.
40. Tourism.
41. Duties of customs, including export duties.
42. Taxes on income other than agricultural income.
43. Taxes on corporations.
44. Taxes on the capital value of the assets, not including taxes on capital gains on immovable property.
45. Taxes and duties on the production capacity of any plant, machinery, undertaking, establishment or installation in lieu pf the taxes and duties specified in entries 42 and 43 or in lieu of either or both of them.
46. Terminal taxes on goods or passengers carried away by railway or air; taxes on their fares and freights.
47. Fees in respect of any of the matters enumerated in this list but not including fees taken in any court
48. Jurisdiction and powers of all courts with respect to any of the matters enumerated in this List.
49. Offences against laws with respect to any of the matters enumerated in this list.

50. Inquiries and statistics for the purposes of any of the matters enumerated in this List.
51. Matters which under the Act are within the Legislative competence of the Council or relates to the Council.
52. Matters incidental or ancillary to any of the matters enumerated in this List.

FOURTH SCHEDULE

(See Section 42 (9))

1. There shall be paid to the Chief Justice and every other Judge of the Supreme

Court of Azad Jammu and Kashmir a salary at the following rates:-

(i) Chief Justice: Rs. 6,500/- per mensem w.e.f 1-7-1981
Rs. 7,900/- per mensem w.e.f 1-7-1983

(ii) Judge: Rs. 6,000/- per mensem w.e.f 1-7-1981
Rs. 7,400/- per mensem w.e.f 1-7-1983

2. Every Judge of the Supreme Court shall be entitled to such privileges, allowances and to such rights in respect of leave absence as may be determined by the Council.

3. The pension payable to every Judge of the Supreme Court who retires after having put in not less than five years service as such, shall be at the following rates, depending on the length of his service as Judge and total service, if any in the service of Azad Jammu and Kashmir :-

Min. Max.

Pension per mensem Rs. 3,000/- 4,000/-w.e.f 1-7-1981
Rs. 3,600/- -4,600- w.e.f 1-7-1983

4. (i) The widow or widows or a Judge of the Supreme Court shall he entitled to a pension at the following rates, namely:-

(a) if the Judge dies after retirement – 50 % of the net pension payable to him; or

(b) if the Judge dies after having rendered not less than 3 years service as Judge and while still serving as such 50 % of the pension that would have been admissible to him at the minimum rate.

(ii) The pension shall be payable to the widow for life, or, if she remarries, until re-marriage.

(iii) if the widow dies, the pension, shall be payable-

(a) to the sons of the judge who are less than 21 years of age, until they attain that age; and

(b) to the unmarried daughters of the Judge who are less than 21 years of age, until they attain that age or are married, whichever first occurs.

Bibliography

Documents and Reports

'Azad Jammu and Kashmir' Interim Constitution Act, 1974 (Muzafarrabad: Azad Government of the State of J&K, 1990).

"A Strong Yearning for Autonomy," *Human Rights Commission of Pakistan*, 2006.

"Devastating Quake Strikes Northern Pakistan," *Cowasjee Earthquake Study Centre NED Newsletter*, vol. 5, no. 2, 2005.

"Discord in Pakistan's Northern Areas," *ICG Asia Report No. 131*, Brussels/Islamabad, April 2, 2007.

"HRCP mission to the Northern Areas," *Report of Fact Finding Mission of Human Rights Commission of Pakistan*, August-September 2005.

ICG Policy Briefing, *Asia Briefing N°46*, Islamabad/Brussels, March 15, 2006.

Rahman, Khalid and Ershad Mahmud, "Northern Areas of Pakistan – Facts, Problems and Recommendations," *IPS Task Force Report.*

Status of the Northern Areas, *Selected Clippings from the Pak Media (1990-94).*

"The Decision of Supreme Court of Pakistan," May 28, 1999, *Supreme Court Monthly Review*, vol. 32.

"With Friends Like These...," *HRW Report*, vol. 18, no. 12 (C), September 2006.

Books

Bazaz, Prem Nath, *The History of Struggle for Freedom in Kashmir* (Srinagar: Gulshan Publishers and Exporters, 2003).

Bose, Sumantra, *Kashmir: Roots of Conflict, Paths to Peace* (New Delhi: Vistaar Publications, 2003).

Cohen, Maurice, *Thunder over Kashmir* (Hyderabad: Orient Longman Ltd., 1995).

Cohen, Stephen Philip, *The Idea of Pakistan* (New Delhi: Oxford University Press, 2005).

Dani, Ahmad Hasan, *History of Northern Areas of Pakistan* (Islamabad: National Institute of Historical and Cultural Research, 1991).

Dasgupta, C., *War and Diplomacy in Kashmir: 1947-48* (New Delhi: Sage Publications, 2002).

Ganguly, Sumit, *Conflict Unending: India-Pakistan Tensions Since 1947* (New Delhi: Oxford University Press, 2002).

Ganguly, Sumit, *The Crisis in Kashmir: Portents of War, Hopes of Peace* (New Delhi: Foundation Books, 1997).

Gupta, Sisir, *Kashmir: A Study in India-Pakistan Relations* (New Delhi: Asia Publishing House, 1966).

Hassnain, F. M., *British Policy Towards Kashmir: 1846-1921* (New Delhi: Sterling Publishers, 1974).

Jagmohan, *My Frozen Turbulence in Kashmir* (New Delhi: Allied Publishers, 2000).

Khan, Amanullah, *Jehde Musalsal* (Rawalpindi: S.S. Combined, 1992)

Khan, F. M., *The History of Gilgit, Baltistan and Chitral: A Short History of two Millennia* (Gilgit: Eejaz Publishers, 2002)

Mahapatra, Debidatta Aurobinda and Seema Shekhawat, *Conflict in Kashmir and Chechnya: Political and Humanitarian Dimensions* (New Delhi: Lancer's Books, 2007).

Menon, V. P., *Integration of the Indian States* (Mumbai: Orient Longman Ltd., 1999).

Qureshi, Hashim, *Kashmir: The Unveiling of Truth* (Lahore: Jeddajudh Publications, 1999).

Raina, N. N., *Kashmir Politics and Imperialist Manoeuvres: 1846-1980* (New Delhi: Patriot Publishers, 1988).

Schofield, Victoria, *Kashmir in the Crossfire: India, Pakistan and the Unending War* (New Delhi: Viva Books Pvt. Ltd., 2004).

Shekhawat, Seema, *Conflict in Jammu and Kashmir: The Gender Dimension* (Saksham Books International, Jammu, 2006).

Singh, Jasjit, ed., *Pakistan Occupied Kashmir Under the Jackboot* (New Delhi: Siddhi Books, 1995).

Tariq, M. Sharif, *Kashmir in Strangulation* (Mirpur: Mohd. Sharif Tariq, 2003).

Articles

Ali, Farman, "Studied Silence," *The Herald*, February 2006.

Ali, Syed Mohammad, "In the Earthquake's Aftermath," *The Kashmir Times*, November 30, 2005.

"Another Sectarian Atrocity," *Dawn*, February 11, 2006.

Baid, Samuel, "Politics in "Azad Kashmir,"" in Jasjit Singh, ed., *Pakistan Occupied Kashmir Under the Jackboot* (New Delhi: Siddhi Books, 1995).

Baid, Samuel. "Political Crisis in PoK," *Daily Excelsior*, April 1, 2004.

Ballard, Roger, "The Kashmir Crisis: A View from Mirpur," *Economic and Political Weekly*, vol. 2, March 2-9, 1991.

Bhat, Tariq, "Terror Takes a Hit," *The Week*, October 23, 2003.

Bilal, Gulmina, "While Gilgit Burns," *The News*, November 22, 2005.

"Failure to Tackle Gilgit Violence is Unforgivable," *Daily Times*, December 7, 2005.

Gul, Imtiaz, "Apathy of the Civil Administration," *The News*, November 30, 2005.

Hayyat, Liaquat, "Politics of 'Azad' Kashmir: Behind the Scene Facts," *The Kashmir Times*, June 23, 2006.

"Is Bhasha Dam no Longer an Option?," *Daily Times*, November 13, 2005.

Javed, Ashraf, "Helis Move across LoC," *The Nation*, October 21, 2005.

Khan, Ahsan Wali, "Gilgit's Continuing Tension," *The News International*, August 7, 2005.

Khan, M. Ismail, "Justice Needed with or without Chief," *The Kashmir Times*, March 14, 2007.

Khan, M. Ismail, "The Bhasha Dam Rip-off," *The News International*, February 2, 2006.

Khan, Safdar, "Gilgit's Sectarian Conundrum," *Dawn*, October 30, 2005.

Khan, Zaigham, "Gilgit on Fire," *The International News*, January 15, 2005.

Laxman, Kanchan, "Deception at Every Step," *State Times*, March 6, 2006.

Mahapatra, Debidatta Aurobinda, "Bus Running for Reconciliation?," *Mainstream*, vol. 63, no. 20, May 7, 2005.

Mahapatra, Debidatta Aurobinda, "Connecting Kargil-Skardu," *Kashmir Images*, August 12, 2006.

Mahapatra, Debidatta Aurobinda, "Electoral Politics in AJK," *Across LOC*, vol. 2, no. 1, January-March 2006.

Mahapatra, Debidatta Aurobinda, "Involve People for Peace," *Kashmir Images*, July 29, 2006.

Mahapatra, Debidatta Aurobinda, "J&K and POK: A Comparison," *Across LOC*, vol. 2, no. 3, July-September 2006.

Mahapatra, Debidatta Aurobinda, "Kashmir and Chechnya: Issues in Terrorism," *India Quarterly*, vol. 62, no. 2, April-June 2006, pp. 228-268.

Mahapatra, Debidatta Aurobinda, "Other Kashmir Elections," *Kashmir Images*, July 22, 2006.

Mahapatra, Debidatta Aurobinda, "Pakistan-Occupied Kashmir: Myth vs. Reality," *Across LOC*, vol. 1, no.1, April-June 2005.

Mahapatra, Debidatta Aurobinda, "Peace through Economic Reconstruction," *The Kashmir Times*, January 24, 2007.

Mahapatra, Debidatta Aurobinda, "Politics in the Aftermath of the Earthquake," *Across LOC*, vol. 1, no. 3, October-December 2005.

Mahapatra, Debidatta Aurobinda, "Poonch for Peace," *The Kashmir Times*, May 6, 2007.

Mahapatra, Debidatta Aurobinda, "Raising of the Mangla Dam Height: Issues and Concerns," *Across LOC*, vol. 2, no. 2, April-June 2006.

Mahapatra, Debidatta Aurobinda, "Reflections on the Hurriyat Visit," *Mainstream*, vol. 63, no. 33, August 6, 2005.

Mahapatra, Debidatta Aurobinda, "Some Reflections on AJK Constitution," *Across LOC*, vol. 1, no.2, July-September 2005.

Mahmud, Ershad, "Azad Kashmir's struggle for Fair Polls," *The News International*, May 15, 2005.

Mahmud, Ershad, "Challenges before the New Government in NAs," *The International News*, December 11, 2004.

Mahmud, Ershad, "New Dispensation in Azad Kashmir," *The Kashmir Times*, August 3, 2006.

Naqash, Tariq , "UJC Unimpressed," *Greater Kashmir*, January 21, 2007.

Nayar, Kuldip, "Distant Neighbours," *The Tribune*, October 19, 2005.

Noorani, A. G., "Both Sides Now," *The Kashmir Times*, March 6, 2007.

Pargal, Sanjeev, "Ahead of Visit, Import-Export Items Listed," *Daily Excelsior*, March 6, 2007.

Puri, Balraj, "Kashmiriyat: The Vitality of Kashmir Identity," *Contemporary South Asia*, vol. 4, no. 1, March 1995.

Rose, Leo, "The Politics of Azad Kashmir," in Raju G. C. Thomas, ed., *Perspectives on Kashmir: The Roots of Conflict in South Asia* (Oxford: Westview Press, 1992).

Salik, Bahadur Ali, "Northern Areas Package a Joke with People," *The Nation*, June 15, 2000.

Samanta, Pranab Dhal "LoC now Line of Contact," *Indian Express*, October 23, 2005.

Sayeed, Mufti Mohammad, "Jammu & Kashmir Resolution: Context, Compulsions and Contours-I," *The Kashmir Times*, December 7, 2006.

Shahin, Sultan, "Across the Divide: Gilgit Valley Searches for Identity," *Asia Times*, December 18, 2004.

Shekhawat, Seema, "Addressing the Alienation," *The Kashmir Times*, April 28, 2007.

Shekhawat, Seema, "Elections in AJK: A Balance Sheet," *Across LOC*, July-September 2006.

Shekhawat, Seema, "Kargil-Skardu Route: The Humanitarian Dimension," *The Kashmir Times*, May 17, 2007.

Shekhawat, Seema, "Movement for Independence in Northern Areas," *Across LOC*, October-December 2005.

Shekhawat, Seema, "Sectarian Violence in Northern Areas: An Analysis," *Across LOC*, July-September 2005.

Shekhawat, Seema, "The Bhasha Dam Controversy," *Across LOC*, January- March 2006.

Shekhawat, Seema, "The Bhasha Dam," *Daily Excelsior*, March 23, 2006.

Sorbo, A. H., "Paradise Lost," *The Herald*, June 1988.

Subramanian, Nirupama, "What the Elections in PoK Mean," *The Hindu*, August 15, 2006.

"Take Gilgit Violence Seriously!," *Daily Times*, April 29, 2005.

"The plight of the Northern Areas," *Daily Times*, June 4, 2004.

Varadarajan, Siddharth, "Gilgit Leaders Deny they're Indian Agents," *Times of India*, March 28, 2002.

"War within Pakistan," *Daily Times*, February 1, 2007.

Yasin, Muhammad, "N. Areas Representatives to Get Constitutional Powers," *Dawn*, January 17, 2007.

Internet Sources

"A Comprehensive Note on Jammu & Kashmir". *http://www.indianembassy.org/policy/Kashmir/Kashmir_MEA/POK.html.*

"After 21 days of freedom, 60 years of colonization." *http://www.nerve.in/news:25350043769.*

"Azad Kashmir" and "Northern Territories" or Pakistan Occupied Kashmir (POK)?" *http://members.tripod.com/~INDIA_RESOURCE/pok.html.*

Alam, Imtiaz, "Black Saturday Exposed the Rulers, Crowned the People." *www.satribune.com.*

Ali, Syed, "People of Gilgit Baltistan: The Political Orphans." *http://www.chowk.com/show_article.cgi?aid=00006997&channel=civic%20center.*

Choudhry, Shabir, "Musharraf Factor in Azad Kashmir Elections." *http://www.gaash-online.com/articles/90/1/Musharraf-Factor-in-Azad-Kashmir-Elections.html.*

Hussain, Khadim, "Mangla Dam." *http://www.neukol.org.uk/teesblog/index.php/gfac/2006/09/07/mangla_dam.*

Interview of Nawaz Khan Naji. *http://www.hvk.org/articles/0304/116.html.*

Jan McGirk, "Kashmir: The Politics of an Earthquake." *http://www.opendemocracy.net/debates/article.jsp?id=2&debateId=43&articleId=2941*

Khaled, Ahmed, "Islamic Extremism in Pakistan." *http://www.southasianmedia.net/magazine/islamicextremism_Pakistan.htm.*

Khan, Abdul Hamid, "If we had a Choice between India and Pakistan, we would not be Part of Pakistan." *http://www.tehelka.com/channels/currentaffairs/2001/dec/3/ca120301abdul2.htm.*

Khan, Abdul Hamid, "Pakistan's Heart of Darkness." *http://www.atimes.com/atimes/South_Asia/DH22Df03.html.*

Khan, Fakhar Mehmood, "Gilgit-Baltistan's Short Freedom." *http://www.balawaristan.net/GB.html.*

Khan, Hamid Abdul, Interview. *http://www.stratmag.com/page05.htm.*

Khan, Hamid Mandozai, "Free Balawaristan from Pakistani Occupation." *http://india.indymedia.org/en/2003/02/3306.shtml.*

Mehdi, Ghulam, "What a Beautiful Sectarian.Political Arrangements in Northern Areas." *http://www.balawaristan.net/sectwise.html.*

Niazi, Tarique, "Victims of the Deadly Quake should not become Cash Cows for Usurpers," *www.satribune.com.*

Price, Susannah, "Ex-general elected to Kashmir post," BBC News Online, August 1, 2001. *http://news.bbc.co.uk/1/hi/world/south_asia/1468287.stm.*

Rahman, Rashed, "Nothing Left to Lose." *http://www.himalmag.com/99May/lose.htm.*

Raman, B., "Gilgit & Baltistan, China & North Korea." http://www.saag.org/papers3/paper289.html.

Raman, B., "Pakistan: The Shia Anger." *www.saag.org/papers9/paper810.html.*

Raman, B., "Unrest in Gilgit-Baltistan." http://www.saag.org/papers13/paper1241.html.

Rehman, Shams, "Dam extension in Pakistani administrated Kashmir: General Musharraf uses army to crush Kashmiris." *http://kashmir.ahrchk.net/mainfile.php/v2n1/265/.*

Schofield, Victoria, "Pakistan's Northern Areas Dilemma : Resentment is Growing over the Local Population's Lack of Political Status." *http://news.bbc.co.uk/1/hi/world/south_asia/1491179.stm.*

Shaheen, Sultan, "How Azad is Azad Kashmir." *http://www.jammu-kashmir.com/insights/insight990902.html.*

Shahin, Sultan, "Free Balawaristan movement gains momentum." *http://www.jammu-kashmir.com/insights/insight20000206b.html.*

Shehzad, Mohammed, "Textbook Controversy in Gilgit." *http://www.sikhspectrum.com/082003/textbooks.htm.*

Ulph, Stephen, "Jehadists Respond to Earthquake Victims in Pakistan." *http://www.jamestown.org/terrorism/news/article.php?articleid=2369816.*

Zaidi, S. Akbar, "Emergency Relief in a Military State." *http://www.inwent.org/E+Z/content/archive-eng/12-2005/debate_art3.html.*

Newspapers and Magazines

Asia Times
Daily Excelsior
Daily Times
Greater Kashmir
Hindustan Times
India Today
Kashmir Images
Outlook
Pakistan Observer
Public Opinion Trends
State Times
The Daily Excelsior
The Herald
The Kashmir Times
The Nation
The News International
The News
The Pakistan Tribune
The Times of India
The Tribune
The Week
Viewpoint

Index

A

Abdul Hamid Khan,
 120, 122, 146,
 149, 151, 153
Abdul Rahman, 85
Accession, 13, 14,
 Of Kashmir, 15, 80, 96, 97
Actual Ground Positioning Line,
 221
Afghan Terrorists, 151
Afghanistan, 68, 119, 145, 205
 Crisis, 248
 Military, 136
 War, 117, 119
Afridis, 19
Agha Zia-ud-din Rizvi, 125-127,
 138
'AJK', ('Azad Jammu and Kashmir'), 13, 28, 39, 31, 36, 39-49, 50-53, 63-65, 67, 70-74, 79-83, 84-87, 89-98, 101-103, 106, 110, 116, 132, 143-145, 152-158, 176, 193, 185-190, 193, 197-199, 201, 202, 204, 205, 208, 210, 211, 213, 214, 219, 225, 231, 233, 234, 238, 248, 250
Administrative Divisions, 36
 Bagh, 36
 Bhimber, 36
 Kotli, 36
 Mirpur, 36
 Muzaffarabad, 36
 Neelam, 36
 Poonch, 36
 Sudhnati, 36
 Council, 84, 87, 157
 Constitution, 40, 42, 49, 90
 Elections, 91, 97, 100
 Electoral Politics, 82
 High Court, 62, 74, 91
 Judiciary, 96
 Languages Spoken, 36
 Legislative Assembly,74,
 89, 187
 Police, 91
 Population, 36
Akbar Bugti, 149
Al Badr, 208
Al Hude Foundation, 212
Al Qaida, 209
Al-Ikhwan, 122
Al-Khair Trust, 210
All J&K
 Muslim Conference , 15, 66

National Conference, 16
Al-Rasheed Trust, 210, 211, 213
Amanullah Khan, 91
Anti-Bhasha Dam
Campaign, 167
APHC Leaders, 226
APNA, 156, 167, 169, 246, 248
Armed Forces (Special Powers)
Act, 233
Army-Jehadist Nexus, 211
Article 370 of Indian
Constitution, 39, 52
Asian Development Bank, 203
Astor, 116
Attique Ahmad Khan, 231
Ayub Khan, 84, 85
Azad J & K Basic Democracies
Act, 84
Azad Muslim Conference, 88

B

Bagh, 198
Balakot, 198, 201
Balawaristan, 136, 143, 151, 152
Balawaristan Labour Party, 168
Balochistan Provinces, 120
Baltistan, 35, 116, 143
Basic Human Rights, 145, 150, 153
Basohli Paintings, 226
Bhasha Dam, 154, 162-168, 170, 174-177, 248
Bhasha Dam Naam Namanzoor Committee, 172
Bhutto, Benazir, 89
Biradari System, 82
Bisham-Batta Gram Fault Line, 177
Bolor, 174
British
Agency, 33
East India Company, 32
Government, 14, 323
India, 13
Buddhist Monuments, 169

C

Chamba, 14
Chaudhary Mohammad Yasin, 101
Chaudhury Ghulam Abbas, 30, 41, 83
Chilas, 116, 177, 179
China, 18, 54-57, 61, 68, 115, 119, 133, 144, 154, 246
CIA , 123
Confidence Building Measures, 220, 224
Criminal Tribes, 145
Cross Border Routes, 220
Cultural and Political Rights, 171

D

Dams
Akori, 163
Bonji, 173
Kurram Tangi, 163

Munda, 163
Skardu or Katzara, 173
Yogo, 173
Yulbo, 173
Demilitarization, 232
Deobandi Islamist Group, 119
Deobandis, 119
Diamer-Bhasha Dam, 161, 176, 178, 179, 190
Dogra, 13
Dynasty, 28

E

Earthquake, 79, 177, 197-215, 247, 249
Reconstruction and Rehabilitation, 92
Relief Measures, 220
Economic Growth, 230
Economy, 147, 190
Election, 45, 87, 91, 93, 95, 96, 98, 100, 102-104, 106
Election Commission, 101
Electoral Politics, 84, 97, 102
Environmental Impact Assessment, 170
EU Parliament, 155

F

Fanatics, 115
Farhad Burney, 213
Federal Advisory Council of Pakistan, 105
Freedom Struggle, 13
Frontier Crimes Regulations, 145
Fundamental Rights, 48, 90, 108, 115, 146, 179, 250

G

Gayyasuddin, 125
Gilgit, 32, 35, 73, 123, 125, 128, 129, 134, 138, 162, 167, 168
Agency, 33, 34, 55
And Hunza, 133
And Ladakh, 33
And Lahore, 65
Scouts, 34, 35, 243
Wazarat, 32
Gilgit, Skardu and Hunza, 105
Gilgit—Astor, 36
Gilgit—Kohistan, 150
Gilgit-Baltistan, 13, 30, 31, 34-36, 39, 52-55, 62, 72-75, 79, 103-108, 115, 117-122, 126, 128, 134, 137, 138, 143-147, 149, 153-155, 157, 161, 166-170, 173-176, 178, 179, 181-183, 190, 228-230, 244, 246-249
Administration of-, 103
Agencies, 104
Alliance, 168, 169
Bar Association, 73
Jamhoori Mahaz, 110, 150
Legislative Council, 132
Thinkers Forum, 154
United Action Forum for Self-Rule, 150
United Front, 150

General Scott, 34
Ghansara Singh, 35
Ghazi Anwar, 148
Gherib Avaam Quami
Movement, 150
Gross Jehadi Terrorist Product,
120
Globalization, 220
Govt. of India Act, 1935, 15, 20
Gulab Singh, 32

H

Hafeez-ur-Rahman, 118
Hamid Ullah Khan, 40
Harkat-ul-Mujahideen, 122
Hazara District, 19
Hezb-e-Islami, 119
High Court Lahore, 64
Human Rights, 156, 192
Activists, 149
Commission of Pakistan,
123, 145, 146, 149, 155, 212
Violations, 146, 150, 224,
233
Hunza, 54, 56, 123
Hunza-Nagar Movement, 148

I

Idara-Khidmat-e-Khalq, 209
Illegal Occupation, 145
Imamia Council of Gilgit, 134
Independence Act, 1947, 15
India and Pakistan, 14, 15, 18,
24-26, 29, 74, 197, 222, 226,
228, 249
Indus
Basin Project, 182
River System, 58
Water Treaty, 182
Infiltration, 233, 234
of Armed Groups, 17
of Tribesmen, 19
Instrument of Accession, 15, 19,
20, 24, 51
Terms and Conditions, 20-
24
Inter-Ethnic/Inter Tribe
Marraiges, 117
International
Court of Justice, 147
Donor's Conference, 207
Kashmir Alliance, 82
International Union for
Conservation of Nature and
National Reservoirs, 170
Intra-Kashmir Dialogue, 219,
225, 249
Iqra Foundation, 212
Iran
Religious School, 121
Revolution, 117, 248
ISI, 81, 101, 121, 149, 152, 157
Iskandir Mirza, 84
Islamic
Council, 51
Education, 121
Judicial System, 51

J

J&K (Jammu and Kashmir), 17,
18, 20, 21, 28, 31, 39, 41, 47,
56, 62, 79, 81, 90, 92, 93, 96,

107, 119, 144, 150, 153, 156, 174, 177, 178, 191, 197, 199, 207, 208, 219, 222-227, 237, 245, 247
Independence League, 156
Legislative Assembly, 154
Muslim Conference, 41
National Awami Front, 91
People's National Party, 150
Princely State, 13, 14, 28
Telegraph System, 17, 18
Jammu and Kashmir Liberation Front, 91, 96, 102, 156, 168, 171, 173, 182, 190, 192, 246
Jaish-e-Mohammad, 122, 208, 214
Jalabad—Manewar, 123
Jamiat Ulema-e-Islam, 94
Jehadi
Groups, 213
Madrasas, 212
Militias, 137
Organization, 210, 213
Terrorist, 120
Training Camps and Bases, 208
Jehadis in Afghanistan, 121
Jinnah's All India Muslim League, 16
Junagarh and Hyderabad, 14, 15

K

Kalabagh Dam, 161, 163-166, 173, 176, 177, 179, 182, 183, 189, 190
Kaman Bridge, 208
Karachi Agreement, 30, 40, 55, 72, 73, 104, 106, 243
Karakoram, 121
Highway, 121, 122, 126,133, 147, 162, 167-169, 246
National Front, 146, 150
National Movement, 148, 167
Range, 59
Kargil, 121, 152, 153, 228, 230
Crisis, 220
War, 117, 122
Kargil-Skardu, 223, 228, 229
Kashmir
Liberation Front, 171
Muttahida Mahaz, 91
Valley, 16, 24, 28, 79, 225
Kashmiri (s), 24
Militant Groups, 236
Mujahideen, 152
Nationalist, 97
Refugees in Pakistan, 31
Refugees, 93, 98
King Daleep Singh, 32
Kofi Annan, 198

L

Ladakh Wazarat, 32
Lahore State, 14
Lahul, 14
Lashkar-e-Jhangvi, 119, 125, 132
Lashkar-e-Toiba, 117, 122, 208, 209, 214
Lease Treaty Main Provisions, 33-34

Leh and Kargil, 150
Liberal League, 88
Line of Control, 28, 30, 39, 79, 94, 103, 143, 152, 178, 205-208, 220, 221, 222, 226, 227, 228-233, 235, 236-238, 243, 247, 249
Livelihood Support Cash Grant Programme, 204
Lord Birdwood, 15
Lord Curzon, 32
Lord Mountbatten, 17, 18, 25

M

Madrasas, 120
Maharaja
  Gulab Singh, 13, 14
  Hari Singh, 14-17, 20, 24, 29, 33
  Of Patiala, 17
  Partap Singh, 14
  Ranbir Singh, 14
  Ranjit Singh, 32
Malaysia, 210
Malik Miskeen, 144
Mangla Dam, 161, 164, 182, 183, 186, 187, 189-192, 248
  Controversy, 157
  Upraising, 192
Manmohan Singh, 221, 224, 228, 235, 249
Manshera-Muzaffarabab Road, 19
Manzoor Geelani, 91
Map of Kashmir, 54
Martial Law, 87, 145
Menon, VP, 17
Militancy, 221
Military
  Aggression by Pakistan, 24
  Rule, 114
Ministry of
  External Affairs, 178
  Kashmir Affairs (Pakistan), 40, 41, 90, 106
  Water and Power, (Pakistan), 166, 187
Mintaka Pass, 56
Mirwaiz Yusuf Shah, 83
Mirza Hassan, 35, 36
Miskeen Case, 243
Mohammad Ibrahim Khan, 30
Mohammad Javed Mirza, 146
MQM, 94
Mufti Mohammad Sayeed, 223
Multi-Tiered System, 85
Muslim
  Conference, 16, 30, 31, 66, 73, 80, 82, 83, 84, 40, 41, 87-89, 93, 94, 98-102, 106, 245
  League, 108
  Population of Poonch, 17
Muzaffarabad, 17, 48, 52, 62, 67, 81, 198, 199, 201, 209, 210, 213, 222, 223

N

Nagar Valley, 116, 123
National
  Book Foundation, 130
  Conference, 16
  Democratic Alliance, 223

Disaster Management Council, 204
NATO, 200, 213
Nawaz Sharif, 89
Neelam and Jhelam Valley, 210
Non-Aligned Movement Summit, 235
North West Frontier Provinces, 19, 31, 104, 108, 116, 120, 122, 123, 130, 166-168, 172, 173, 175, 179, 193, 211, 212
Textbook Board, 130
Resolutions, 107-108
'Northern Areas', 33, 64-67, 69, 71, 74, 105-107, 129, 143, 144, 146, 168, 171, 181, 233, 243, 244, 246, 248, 250
Advisory Council, 104, 105
Legislative Council, 105-107, 109, 132, 144, 166-169, 174, 176, 179, 246
Northern Light Infantry, 147, 153

O

Operation Datta Khel, 35
Osama-bin-Laden, 124

P

Pakistan, 16-19, 24, 25, 27, 28, 30, 31, 35, 39-43, 46-49, 51-56, 58-60, 62, 79, 80, 82, 87, 90-93, 95-98, 100-106, 109, 115-118, 120, 122, 124, 126, 133, 136-139, 143-145, 147, 148, 150, 151, 155-158, 161, 163, 165-167, 169-179, 182, 186-191, 193, 200, 204-206, 219, 222, 234, 235, 245-250
And China, 56
Armed Forces, 96, 152
Army, 87, 122, 134, 153, 210, 247
Atrocities, 154
Bureaucracy, 93
Military Regime, 189
Military, 81
Occupation, 120, 153
Occupied Kashmir , 101, 152, 191, 227, 229
Minorities and Women-, 149
Parliament, 145
People's Party , 87-89
Policy, 137
Rangers, 132
Security Forces, 208
Troops, 40
Vision-2025, 161, 162
Pakistan's Military Intelligence, 157
Pakistani
Administration, 120
Army, 197, 201, 202, 205, 206, 211
Forces, 24, 26
Islamic Organization, 211
Military Rulers, 154
Nationals, 25, 26
Wahabis, 122
Palandri/Dalai Camps, 84

Partition of India, 13, 14, 16
Pass,
    Karakoram, 60
    Khunjerab, 58
    Parpik, 58
    Zojila, 229
Peak,
    Chogri, 59
    Teramn Kankri, 60
Plebiscite, 27, 31, 35, 54, 55
Policy of Islamization, 248
Political
    and Socio-Economic Rights, 145
Political Parties, 87, 97, 204
    Of Jammu and Kashmir, 94
Poonch, 19, 28, 40, 41, 156
    Rawalakote Route, 156, 207
    Rawalakote Bus Service, 227
    Uprising, 17
Princely States, 13, 15
Proxy War, 81
Public Safety Act, 233

Q

Quit Kashmir Movement, 16

R

Rais Khan, 35
Raja Mumtaz Hussain Rathore of PPP, 88, 89, 245
Rehabilitation, 200, 203
Relief
    and Rescue, 200, 203
    Operation, 200, 201, 211
Research and Analysis Wing, 123
Reservoirs, 164
    Chashma, 164
    Mangla, 164
    Tarbla, 164
River
    Akjelga, 58
    Elechin, 59
    Hunza, 58
    Indus, 13, 161, 168
    Jhelum, 188
    Jhelum, Chenab and Indus River Basins, 182
    Muztagh, 59
    Neelam, 226
    Shingo, 228
    Taghumbash, 58
    Tashkurgan, 58

S

Saeed Durrani, 34
Sahibzada Ishaq Zafar, 98
Sardar
    Anwar Khan, 198
    Attique Khan, 93, 100, 101, 204, 225, 234, 245
    Ibrahim Khan, 83, 87, 243
    Ijaz Afzal Khan, 94
    Mohammad Ibrahim, 106
    Muhammad Anwar Khan, 89

Saudi Arabia, 210
Sectarian Violence, 121, 122
Sectarianism, 143, 247
Sect-Based Violence, 121
Security
  Council, 25, 26, 65, 70
  Forces, 201, 224
Seismic Zone, 177
Self-Determination, 96, 151, 243, 244
Shah Rais Dynasty, 31
Shah Haji Ghandal, 172
Shaksgam—Muztagh Valley, 56
Shamsher, 32
Sharia Law, 51
Shaukat Aziz, 176, 200, 234
Sheikh Abdul Aziz, 62, 67
Sheikh Ghulam Mohiyuddin, 134
Sheikh Mohammad Abdullah, 16, 17, 20, 24, 230
Shias, 116-118, 123-125, 128, 129, 132, 151
  Community, 127, 128
  Extremists, 119
  Majority, 54
  Militant Organization, 122
  Organization, 148
Shais and Sunnis, 136
Shia-Anjuman-I-Islami, 132
Sialkot, 19
Sikander Hayat Khan, 89, 97, 198
Sino-Pakistan Border, 57
Sipah-e-Mohammad, 119
Sirajul Haq, 164
Skardu, 229, 230
Skardu and Gilgit, 120, 126
Slavery, 143
Socialist Revolution of 1917, 32
South Asian Association for Regional Cooperation, 221
South Asian Free Media Association, 97
Soviet
  Intrusion, 13
  Socialist Republic, 18, 68
  Union, 32, 121
Speedy Trial Courts Act, 1992, 146
Standards of Weights and Measures, 44, 45, 50, 53
Standstill Agreement, 18, 24
State of Jammu and Kashmir, 25-30, 51, 55, 62-64, 72, 96, 171
Sunni, 116, 118, 121, 122, 128, 129, 246, 247
  And Shia Sects, 117
  Deobandi Cadres, 129
  Islamists Parties, 119
  Islamization, 119
  Jehadi Training, 124
Syed Jaffar Shah, 53
Syllabus Issue, 129

T

Taj Mughal of Badakhshan, 32
Taliban Regime in Afghanistan, 210
Tanger, 116
Tangir—Skardu, 122
Tanzeem-e-Millat, 150
Tarakhan Dynasty (Gilgit), 32

Tarbela Dam, 161, 164, 193
Tarin River System, 58
Tehrik Ammal, 88
Terrorism, 79, 213, 224
Terrorist
 Attack, 197
 Camps, 211
 Groups, 235
 Organizations, 156, 211
Training Camps, 122
Textbook
 Controversy, 127, 248
 Of Punjab, 127
TNFJ, 124, 125
Treaty of
 Amritsar, 13, 32
 Jammu, 33
 Lahore, 14
Tribal
 Areas, 55
 Forces, 24

U

UJC, 232, 235, 236
United Nations, 13, 26, 47, 55, 147, 148, 154, 171, 175, 182, 188, 199, 206, 222, 243
 Charter, 25
 Commission for India and Pakistan, 25, 27, 30, 31, 40, 43, 47, 49, 55, 56, 65, 143, 171
 Emergency Relief Coordinatioin, 198
 High Commission for Refugees, 199
 Resolution, 25-27, 74, 40, 53, 54, 57, 174
 Security Council, 25, 55, 56, 174
UNICEF, 199
United States of Gilgit, 36
US, 151, 220
US Military Base, 144

W

Wahabis, 132
Wajahat Khan, 154
Wakhan Corridor of Afghanistan, 31
WAPDA, 162, 166, 167, 176, 177, 184, 185, 186, 187, 193
Water Reservoirs, 161
World
 Bank, 203
 Commission on Dams, 170
 Food Program, 205
 Health Organization, 199

X

Xinjiang, 31

Y

Yahya Khan, 85

Z

Zia-Ul-Haq, 52, 87, 105, 118-120, 123, 124, 129, 147, 247